Public Sector Marketing

Visit the *Public Sector Marketing* Companion Website at **www.pearsoned.co.uk/proctor-psm** to find valuable **student** learning material including:

- Links to relevant sites on the web
- Advice on careers in public sector marketing

We work with leading authors to develop the strongest educational materials in marketing, bringing cutting-edge thinking and best learning practice to a global market.

Under a range of well-known imprints, including Financial Times Prentice Hall, we craft high quality print and electronic publications which help readers to understand and apply their content, whether studying or at work.

To find out more about the complete range of our publishing please visit us on the World Wide Web at: **www.pearsoned.co.uk**

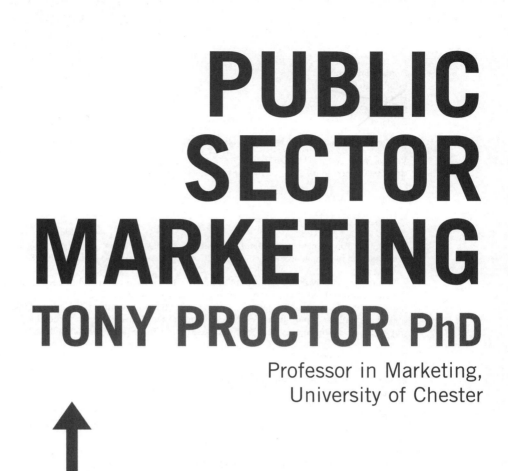

PUBLIC SECTOR MARKETING

TONY PROCTOR PhD

Professor in Marketing,
University of Chester

FT Prentice Hall
FINANCIAL TIMES

An imprint of **Pearson Education**
Harlow, England • London • New York • Boston • San Francisco • Toronto
Sydney • Tokyo • Singapore • Hong Kong • Seoul • Taipei • New Delhi
Cape Town • Madrid • Mexico City • Amsterdam • Munich • Paris • Milan

Pearson Education Limited
Edinburgh Gate
Harlow
Essex CM20 2JE
England

and Associated Companies throughout the world

Visit us on the World Wide Web at:
www.pearsoned.co.uk

First published 2007

ISBN 978-0-273-70809-4

British Library Cataloguing-in-Publication Data
A catalogue record for this book is available from the British Library

10 9 8 7 6 5 4 3 2 1
11 10 09 08 07

Typeset in 10pt Palatino by 3
Printed and bound by Bell & Bain Limited, Glasgow

The publisher's policy is to use paper manufactured from sustainable forests.

Brief contents

Full contents

Preface

This text provides an essential introduction to the ideas and skills of marketing as it can be applied in the public sector. It takes a subject traditionally associated with private sector and profit-making organisations and puts it in the context of the public not-for-profit sector.

Using case studies and case histories, together with extensive diagrams, examples and thought-provoking questions, the book provides the most up-to-date and extensive approach to this important topic.

The book is divided into 14 chapters as follows.

CHAPTER 1 MARKETING IN THE PUBLIC SECTOR

This chapter introduces the book, explaining that there are many different types of organisation, some of which are profit motivated and others that are not. In this book we will pay prime attention to the functioning of municipal authorities in the belief that the varied activities and purposes they serve provide a veritable panacea for a new understanding and appreciation of the concepts that are being put forward. At the same time, it is recognised that more recent changes in local government in particular have led to the establishment of a trend towards managerialism with its accent on targets and accountability, and to the formation of joint venture companies where the profit motive is usually present. However, many of the comments and suggestions here will be relevant both to the large variety of non-profit-making organisations and to profit-making organisations.

CHAPTER 2 THE STAKEHOLDER VALUE APPROACH

This chapter examines the concept of stakeholder value and how it is created, and introduces ideas about how it may be measured. First we will look at what is known as stakeholder theory. It is in the context of this theory that we set marketing and its purpose in the public sector. Next we comment on the importance of delivering stakeholder value since this is how the needs and wants of stakeholders may be satisfied. Finally we introduce ideas relating to the measurement and assessment of value as it may be experienced by different stakeholder groups.

CHAPTER 3 CREATING AND MEASURING STAKEHOLDER VALUE

In order to create and deliver stakeholder value it is necessary to have a stakeholder focus. This is somewhat akin to having a customer focus and we will look specifically at ideas relating to customer focus and customer relationship management in this chapter, drawing similarities with stakeholders where appropriate. First we look at the concept of relationship marketing, pointing out its relevance to the broader context of managing relationships with all stakeholders in an organisation. Central to this notion of marketing is the concept of creating value in relationships and the use of effective communication. Relationship marketing within the organisation is achieved through internal marketing and we discuss its relevance in terms of creating stakeholder value among employees.

Like customers or consumers, stakeholders are influenced by cultural factors so that any value delivery has to take account of these. But, in the same way that customers are influenced by a variety of social, psychological and external environment factors so too are stakeholders. Any communications or actions need to bear this in mind.

Since the aim is to reconcile stakeholder interests, some means of measuring the value attached to the interests of stakeholders is useful. This in turn then makes it possible to ascertain how actions or communications have changed or affected stakeholder perceptions and thinking. The chapter outlines a method for achieving this purpose.

CHAPTER 4 DEVELOPING AND IMPLEMENTING STRATEGIES

This chapter argues that strategic management is about laying down an organisation's objectives, developing policies and plans to achieve these objectives, and allocating resources to implement the plans. It is the highest level of executive activity, usually performed by the organisation's senior management team, and it provides overall direction to the whole enterprise. Strategy has to be formulated in line with the resources available, the circumstances and objectives. It involves matching the organisation's strengths and weaknesses with opportunities and threats in the marketplace taking into account changing environmental forces and how the organisation interfaces with them. A key objective is to put the organisation into a position to carry out its mission statement effectively and efficiently. Good corporate strategy should integrate an organisation's goals, policies and action sequences (tactics) into a cohesive whole.

CHAPTER 5 VALUE DRIVERS, PORTFOLIO ASSESSMENT AND PLANNING AHEAD

In this chapter we will examine the various factors that create value for the organisation and its stakeholders and how these factors might be assessed. We also look at how future scenarios might be constructed that reflect where the organisation may be heading and examine ways and means of discerning the impact this will have on strategies that are adopted to create value for stakeholders. Portions of this chapter were previously published in *Creative Problem Solving for Managers*, Proctor, T. (2005), Routledge. Reproduced by permission of Taylor and Francis Books UK.

CHAPTER 6 MARKETING RESEARCH

Marketing research connects the customer and the public to the organisation through the medium of information. This information is used to distinguish and define marketing opportunities and threats or problems. It is also used to create, improve and assess marketing actions and to monitor marketing performance, helping to improve understanding of marketing as a process. Marketing research identifies the information required to address these issues. It comprises methods for collecting data, analysis of the data collected and its interpretation, and communication of the findings and their implications. It takes account of experience, the present situation and the likely future so that marketing executives can make sound decisions. Marketing research can help in a variety of studies and makes use of both primary and secondary data sources. It can be conducted either in-house by an organisation's own staff or by external specialist marketing research companies. Such external companies or agencies offer a wide range of services, ranging from off-the-peg studies to tailor-made studies to meet the needs of individual clients.

CHAPTER 7 MARKET MEASUREMENT AND FORECASTING DEMAND

Planning ahead for service provision requires both knowledge of the current size of existing markets and informed estimates of how the markets are going to change in size and makeup over time. Getting forecasts reasonably correct can spell the difference between success and failure. The chapter looks at methods of assessing market size and outlines various forecasting methods too. The usefulness of simulation modelling is introduced to show how different assumptions can affect projected developments

Forecasting amounts to estimating some future event outside the control of the organisation and that provides a basis for managerial planning. The estimates produced often form the basis of service creation planning, customer contact staff planning, setting advertising appropriations, estimating cashflow and assessing the need for innovation. Marketing plans are only useful if the size of current and future markets is carefully measured and estimated. Such information is a useful starting point from which to determine how resources should be allocated among markets and/or services.

CHAPTER 8 THE MARKETING PLANNING PROCESS

In this chapter we look at the marketing planning process and how it relates to public services. First we look at the need for systematic marketing planning commenting on the need for the organisation to keep abreast of changes in the environment and exploiting opportunities for creating value for stakeholders. We then look in more detail at the process of marketing planning. Next we examine in detail ideas relating to market segmentation, targeting and positioning, suggesting how these may be interpreted as far as public sector organisations are concerned. We also consider the step-by-step approach to developing and applying these methods. To aid the process of strategy formulation and to evaluate its post facto usefulness we then look at perceptual mapping as a way of enabling us to appreciate stakeholder perceptions of a service or range of services. We review ways in which a service may be evaluated and the final section is concerned with the need to develop creative strategies.

CHAPTER 9 CORPORATE BRAND BUILDING AND DELIVERING THE SERVICE

We look first at the nature and the concept of branding before examining how a brand can create value for stakeholders. We distinguish between service or product branding and corporate branding, noting the shift in recent times in favour of corporate branding as a means of creating value for customers and other stakeholders. The values in building brand extensions are also explored.

Establishing a corporate identity and projecting this to customers and other stakeholders is seen as a key component of marketing management. This is particularly the case in services marketing where the service encounter plays such an important role in expressing the quality of the brand. Internal marketing is seen as an important influence in achieving customer focus and customer brand relationships are seen as a determinant of brand equity.

CHAPTER 10 PRICING SERVICES

First we discuss the relevance of pricing in public sector organisations pointing out than in some instances there is a latitude to charge customers a price but in others there is not. We quickly review some economic aspects of pricing before going on to look at its practical aspects. We then discuss cost-oriented approaches to prices, which in the main reflect the basis on which 'prices' may be set in the public sector, and look specifically at the usefulness of breakeven analysis as a tool in the context of setting prices for new services. We also look at an alternative view of price where opportunity cost is taken into account. Price perceptions and price changes are briefly considered followed by dynamic pricing and price boundaries/price flexibility. Finally, we look briefly at pricing in a social marketing context and at local government pricing practices.

CHAPTER 11 COMMUNICATING VALUES

In this chapter we consider how different forms of communication, which we broadly define as being under the umbrella of external and internal marketing activities, create stakeholder value. An important pre-requisite for this is to understand something about the decision-making processes engaged in by customers and other stakeholders. We therefore turn to what has been written about consumer behaviour and to models that have been developed, in particular those relating to the influence that marketing communications have on consumer behaviour. While our sole interest is not on consumer behaviour many of the ideas and concepts involved have a direct bearing on communicating with stakeholders more generally.

We stress the importance of people, processes and physical evidence as a means of communicating with stakeholders and employees in particular. Preparing employees to be envoys of the organisation is seen as a most important strategy and we consider how employees acquire the values we want them to communicate to other stakeholders.

CHAPTER 12 SOCIAL MARKETING

In this chapter we examine aspects of social marketing and its good practice. First we will explain what is meant my social marketing. Social marketing is often associated with health issues and is integrated with other forms of bringing about changes in habits among the population. Social marketing faces many challenges and we explore some of these. Its prime aim is to change behaviour and basic marketing techniques such as segmentation can be used to aid this process. Based on experience we look at what best practice has to offer in the way of suggesting a strong basis for successful social marketing. Finally, we suggest social marketing should be viewed within the setting of relationship marketing rather than viewed as a transactional process.

CHAPTER 13 INTERNAL MARKETING

Local government exists to serve the community and has to find ways and means of satisfying the wants and needs of its customers and other stakeholders. Internal marketing provides a way of ensuring a customer focus in the way in which employees of an organisation go about their work and in particular how they interact with customers and other stakeholders. It also provides a means of engendering employee trust, commitment and loyalty to the organisation and is a means of creating employee satisfaction through empowerment. Internal marketing can help to project the corporate entity, both internally and externally, and tackle problems of low morale within the organisation. Most public bodies tends to be traditionally bureaucratic in nature but over recent years many have been the object of rationalisation and change, providing an opportunity for internal marketing to be used effectively.

CHAPTER 14 MARKETING VIA THE INTERNET AND INTRANET

Information technology has changed the way in which business is conducted in the public sector. Linked with marketing it creates a 'one-to-one market', providing individuals with vast of amounts of information on whatever interests them. In this chapter we look at ways in which information technology can be used in marketing. We also examine how recent trends in local government have led to an increasing use of information technology in the drive to be more customer focused. E-government has arrived and should continue to grow at a substantial pace over the coming years.

What applies to marketing in terms of service provision applies also to e-government since the electronic service encounter is a central feature of both. Assessing just how satisfactory this encounter is requires some thought and we point to the SERVQAL tool as a mechanism for facilitating this. We conclude the chapter by stating some reservations regarding the likely take-up of e-government and e-marketing by members of the public at large. These reservations are based on the difficulties that some people may encounter in making use of on-line services.

I would like to express my thanks to my recent MBA students for insights and ideas they have afforded me over the past few years into the workings of local government.

Tony Proctor is Professor in Marketing at the University of Chester. His other publications include *Strategic Marketing* (Routledge, 2000), *Essentials of Marketing Research* (Financial Times-Prentice Hall, 2005) and *Creative Problem Solving for Managers* (Routledge, 2005).

Publisher's acknowledgements

We are grateful to the following for permission to reproduce copyright material:

Figure 4.1 reprinted by permission of *Harvard Business Review,* from Exhibit 1, *'Strategies of Diversification',* by Ansoff, H. I., Issue No. 25(5), Sept/Oct. 1957, pp. 113–25. Copyright © 1957 Harvard Business School Publishing Corporation, all rights reserved; Figure 4.3 adapted with the permission of The Free Press, a Division of Simon & Schuster Adult Publishing Group, from *'Diffusion Of Innovations',* 4th Edition by Everett M. Rogers. Copyright © 1995 by Everett M. Rogers. Copyright © 1962, 1971, 1983 by The Free Press. All rights reserved; Figure 5.1 reprinted by permission of *Harvard Business Review,* from Kaplan, R. S., & Norton, D. P., (1996), *'Four Perspectives'.* In the *Harvard Business Review,* Jan/Feb., pp. 75–85, 1996. Copyright © 1996 Harvard Business School Publishing Corporation, all rights reserved; Figure 5.2 © Max Moullin, 2007, reprinted by permission of the author; Figure 5.6 Copyright Market Modelling Limited; Figure 11.3 from *Consumer Behavior* 10th edition by Blackwell, 2006. Reprinted with permission of South-Western, a division of Thomson Learning: **www.thomsonrights.com**. Fax 800 730-2215; Figure 14.1 reprinted by permission of Global Software Publishing from *Clipart,* GSP Pictures 5000.

Taylor & Francis Books UK for extracts from 'Creative Problem Solving for Managers' by Tony Proctor © 2005 Routledge.

In some instances we have been unable to trace the owners of copyright material, and we would appreciate any information that would enable us to do so.

1 Marketing in the public sector

INTRODUCTION

There are many different types of organisation, some of which are profit motivated and others which operate without making a profit in mind. This book is about marketing in the public sector (essentially a non-profit-making sector). There are many non-profit-making organisations ranging from large corporations carrying out public services (i.e. municipal councils) to charitable institutions and other bodies of various sizes and purposes. In this book we will pay prime attention to the functioning of municipal authorities in the belief that the varied activities and purposes they serve provide a veritable panacea for a new understanding and appreciation of the concepts that are being put forward. At the same time, it is recognised that more recent changes in local government in particular have led to the establishment of a trend towards managerialism with its accent on targets and accountability, and to the formation of joint venture companies where the profit motive is usually present. However, many of the comments and suggestions here will be relevant both to the large variety of non-profit-making organisations and to profit-making organisations as well.

THE NATURE OF MARKETING

There are numerous definitions of marketing, but the official definition from the Chartered Institute of Marketing is:

> 'Marketing is the management process responsible for identifying, anticipating and satisfying customer requirements profitably.'

Many people think of marketing as just advertising and/or selling of goods and services despite the argument put forward in the marketing literature that these are just two of the many marketing activities carried out by organisations (MOTI, 2005). Marketing activities are those associated with identifying the particular wants and needs of a target market of customers, and then going about satisfying them at least as well as or better than competitors. This view is consistent with the definition by Boone and Kurtz (1998):

> 'Marketing is the process of planning and executing the conception, pricing, promotion, and distribution of ideas, goods, services, organizations, and events to create and maintain relationships that will satisfy individual and organizational objectives.'

In the public sector much of the marketing related activity is concerned with the satisfaction of customers despite the fact that frequently there is no direct or even indirect form of competition. Having a monopoly in terms of supply does not in itself kill off the need for marketing. In the case of the public sector a poor customer image does not enhance the organisation's image in the eyes of its other stakeholders. Indeed, in the context of such organisations, marketing may have a broader role to play by having to satisfy the needs of different and sometimes conflicting interests.

We might consider replacing the term 'customers' with stakeholders in any definition of the role and scope of marketing since these include customers as well as the many other individuals, groups and organisations that deal with or are even employed by an organisation. A definition of marketing that best suits the purpose here is:

> 'Marketing is the management process responsible for identifying, anticipating and satisfying stakeholder requirements and in so doing serves to facilitate the achievement of the organization's objectives.'

The various means that a public sector organisation employs to bring about satisfaction are used to communicate ideas, benefits and values about products and services that it has to offer the stakeholder. Communication then is central to the effective conduct of marketing operations. Three primary types of corporate communication exist within an organisation – management, marketing and organisational (van Riel 1995). In addition it has been suggested (*Ibid.*) that management communication refers to messages conveyed by management to both internal and external stakeholders. Marketing communications are those directly aimed at the consumer (e.g. advertising, direct mail, personal selling and sponsorship).

Organisational communication covers all other communications based within an organisation, such as public relations (PR), public affairs, environmental communications, investor relations and internal communication. While not disputing these definitions, it could be argued that values communicated to stakeholders occur through a combination of all three forms of communication. Moreover, the view expressed here is that persuasive communications of all forms involve marketing in one form or another.

By and large public sector organisations are concerned with providing services rather than products. There are some differences involved in the marketing of services and we will look at these in the next section.

THE DIFFERENCE BETWEEN MARKETING SERVICES AND PRODUCTS

Marketing a service-based business differs from marketing a product-based business. Cowell (1984) argued that what is significant about services is the relative dominance of intangible attributes in the makeup of the 'service product'. As a consequence, services may require special understanding and special marketing efforts. For example, the personnel providing the service are just as important as the service itself and the interaction between service provider and service receiver is of paramount importance. Service-based organisations are essentially concerned with managing relations because they manage the total 'buyer–seller' interaction process (Reid and Worthington, 2004). This is done as part of attracting, maintaining, and improving customer relationships.

While many services marketed in the public sector are amenable to the same kinds of treatment as one would follow with services in the private sector some services have a different aim. Use of marketing techniques and concepts within some aspects of public service are concerned with promoting ideas and are frequently referred to as social marketing. Kotler and Zaltman (1971) suggest that social marketing is:

> 'The design, implementation and control of programs calculated to influence the acceptability of social ideas and involving considerations of product, planning, pricing, communication, distribution and marketing research.'

Social marketing aims to bring about specific behavioural goals relevant to social good, for example the prevention of anti-social behaviour such as vandalism or alcohol abuse in the community. However, it is only one of a number of possible intervention strategies and its limitations or suitability for particular purposes does have to be well understood. We will look at social marketing in more detail in Chapter 12.

To understand more about marketing and its relevance to public sector organisations let us first review how marketing has developed over the years in the private sector.

MARKETING AND THE ORGANISATION

Marketing was first conceptualised in the context of the profit-making organisation where various economic theories of the firm had influence on its perceived purpose. Most management theories have focused on the firm's responsibility to its shareholders, with some degree of duty owed to employees or customers. Whether economic theories of the firm indicated that firms should maximise sales, profits or simply stay in business, they maintained that it was marketing's role to assist in achieving this purpose.

Market conditions influence how profit-making organisations pursue their primary purpose and aims and this is reflected in their business orientations. At the turn of the 20th century, Henry Ford saw this in terms of finding a way of reducing the unit costs of production through more efficient production methods, driving down prices to the consumer and hence making the motor car available for enjoyment by the masses. At the heart of this business philosophy was the idea of creating consumer satisfaction. Consumer satisfaction, along with the various ways in which it might be achieved, was to become a central theme in what marketing was all about. However, the business philosophies that followed later were somewhat different to that of Henry Ford's.

While all the business orientations shown in Figure 1.1 can be successful, their likelihood of being so depends very much upon the market conditions in which they are employed. If people do not want cheap, mass-produced products then production orientation has no value. Similarly if the market is well served with high-quality products then it may not be possible to produce anything better and market it as such. Where customers are well informed about the product or service on offer then it is unlikely that a sales orientation will be very successful. Only marketing and societal orientations seem likely to succeed in the long run in sophisticated modern day markets in the developed economies of the world. However, the societal approach may only be successful if both consumer and producer believe that adopting the product or service to be strictly in society's best interest is truly worthwhile.

Markets are dynamic and the environments in which they operate are constantly changing. Political, economic, social-cultural, technological, legal and ecological forces all influence the way in which marketers seek to achieve their objectives. Consumer and other stakeholder satisfaction objectives, along with achieving organisational objectives, underpin the strategic direction that marketers prefer, but the manner in which they seek to achieve this end may differ according to market conditions.

The rise of marketing as a force within the business world has been paralleled in the business literature by questions about the main underlying objectives of enterprises. Mere survival of the organisation, often stated as the principal objective, may seem too vaguely stated an objective to bring any poignancy of meaning to what firms are seeking to achieve. In the case of profit-making organisations various alternatives have been suggested. Central to most recent thinking has been the idea of creating value for owners of the business. Profit-making businesses can vary in terms of ownership from sole traders to large multinational organisations with many shareholders who own or have a stake in the organisaton. As the organisation continues to create value for its owners, they will want to continue their investment in terms of time and money spent or invested in the organisation.

Shareholders are only one set of stakeholders in a business: customers, employees, suppliers and many others also have a vested interest in how the organisation fares. A more complex overall objective for a profit-making organisation would be to create value for its stakeholders in order to retain their interest and commitment of time and investment, financial or otherwise, to the organisation.

During the 1980s and 1990s academics and practitioners in the field of strategic management began to focus on creating 'shareholder value' as the overall purpose of any commercial enterprise (Rappaport, 1986). The benefits suggested for this approach to strategic management were considered twofold: first, it put the interests of the owners of the business at the heart of strategy, and, second, it engendered a more long-term approach to business decision making than an emphasis upon profitability. Doyle (2000) argued that the creation of shareholder value should be used as the yardstick against which to measure marketing strategies. The shareholder

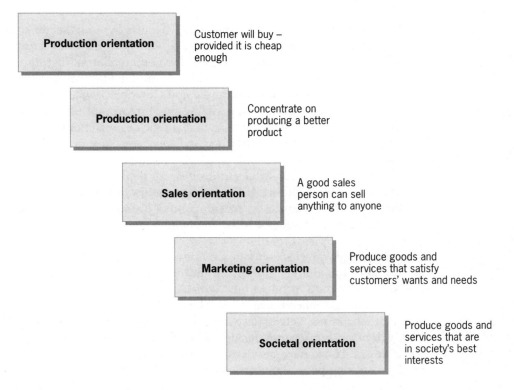

Production orientation — Customer will buy – provided it is cheap enough

Production orientation — Concentrate on producing a better product

Sales orientation — A good sales person can sell anything to anyone

Marketing orientation — Produce goods and services that satisfy customers' wants and needs

Societal orientation — Produce goods and services that are in society's best interests

Figure 1.1 Business orientations

value criterion replaces older notions, for example that the aims of marketing strategy should be to generate increased sales or to build market share. Slater (1997:164) argued that: 'Superior performance is the result of providing superior customer value; it is not an end in itself.' He cited evidence that businesses achieving long-term excellence focus on delivering value to customers, rather than directly on profitability. Here we will argue that at least in the case of the non-profit-making sector the objective is to create value for stakeholders. Such a view is complicated by the possible existence of conflicting stakeholder interests and an implicit hierarchy of preferences that may be built into an organisation when resolving stakeholder interests in the pursuit of attaining objectives. Such is the situation in many public sector organisations.

MARKETING CHALLENGES FACED BY PUBLIC SECTOR MANAGERS

In the 1990s, the public sector in various European countries started to see its clientele as customers and perceived the benefits of applying marketing tools and strategic marketing planning (Cousins, 1990), in order to 'sell' policies to citizens. Public organisations employ four types of marketing, which differ from each other in the objectives underlying them.

- First, 'marketisation' means that certain aspects of public sector activities become akin to commercial marketing in the private sector by subjecting products and services to the competitive forces of the commercial marketplace. The aim is to bring down the price level and to bring the standard of quality more into line with customer demands (Chapman and Cowdell, 1998).
- Second, all organisations use marketing for promoting their self-interest. For instance, Burton (1999) suggests that public organisations use stakeholder marketing to secure their continued existence by support from the market and society.
- Third, in the case of local authorities, marketing is used to promote the area under the responsibility of the public organisation, such as city marketing.
- Finally, marketing may be instrumental in promoting key political objectives, i.e. the realisation of social effects.

Marketing skills developed in the private sector can be employed in the public sector to promote and deliver non-profit-motivated services. A municipal council, for example, can have a 'product mix' which comprises product categories from a plant nursery to refuse collection and a legal department, and can use the same techniques as private sector marketers. Research, graphic design, mail-shots and advertising can all be done in-house and the use of retail marketing skills can be employed in launching various new services. Raising awareness of the services, existing or planned, among potential users of those services is a priority for most public sector organisations.

The possession of a marketing strategy enables public organisations to go about their business in a customer orientated fashion, since setting priorities is helpful in giving the public what they want. It could encompass providing residents with a full range of leisure, education, recreation, economic and social services, and making them aware that their local authority does that efficiently and quickly. Yet another important priority for local authorities is concerned with speaking on behalf of the people they serve. People expect the local authority to speak on their behalf and even protest on their behalf, particularly when there may be a threat such as plans to build a new motorway in the area or some other new development which impinges on their lives.

It has been suggested that the public and non-profit sectors are badly in need of improved marketing practices (Kotler and Zaltman, 2001). However, given the many political and economic complexities of the public sector, marketing within this environment is more problematic than within the private sector. An example of marketing at work is where a local council conducted borough-wide market research on library usage which led to a closer understanding of the nature of its customers and their experience. As a result, residents actually receive the services they required. In another instance, a council commissioned in-depth market research to investigate the views of both its own residents and those in over 400 local authorities towards environmental issues. It found that 83% of the area's residents wanted the council to establish a formal policy explaining its position and aims on green issues. As a result of its findings, the council brought in an environmental audit to be conducted by its environment and leisure department, and a range of other initiatives on recycling and pollution.

In the past, public sector organisations have concentrated more on the way in which services are delivered rather than on putting emphasis on the end user. Arguably this has developed because an organisation has had an idea of what the customer wanted, or considered that it knew what the customer needed from a professional perspective (Bean and Hussey, 1997).

CONSTRAINTS FACED BY PUBLIC SECTOR ORGANISATIONS

The public sector is constrained in terms of the services it is obliged to provide and hence may be unable to implement a customer-led approach even if this is desired.

Constraints may include (Bean and Hussey, 1997):

- legislative restrictions,
- political philosophies,
- lack of physical resources,
- lack of financial resources.

Another problem has been to do with something which is fundamental to the marketing concept – respecting the customer's wishes at all times. Marketers maintain 'the customer is always right', but in the public sector this principle is sometimes compromised. The customer can sometimes be wrong *and* the public sector organisation always has to adopt the best professional practice whether the customer agrees or not. Many public sector organisations provide services for the public good which are often restrictive and controlling in nature. In such cases the user is far from happy with the service. Unlike the private sector, the public sector does not depend on individual users for its survival: many organisations are in place due to legislation, government policies, and so on.

This does not mean that the public sector organisation loses customers, because it may be (Bean and Hussey, *Ibid.*):

- a monopoly provider so the customer has no choice but to accept the service on offer even if it does not fully meet its requirements (e.g. social services);
- offering a free service so the customer has to accept that something is better than nothing – this is especially so if the customer cannot afford to pay for an equivalent service (e.g. basic education services);
- providing a service to customers which they must have even if they do not want it (e.g. Revenue & Customs services).

THE TOOLS OF MARKETING

Marketing has a number of tools at its disposal. The first of these is what is known as the 7Ps of the marketing mix (see Figure 1.2).

The seven Ps and four Cs of the marketing mix

In the pursuit of marketing objectives an organisation requires a strategy that makes use of the *marketing mix*. This term, originally used by Borden (1965), comprised of the 4Ps (Product, Price, Promotion and Place). The original 4Ps of the marketing mix were considered by many to be too restrictive, particularly with the developing service economy. Other academics (e.g. Booms and Bitner (1981), Moorthi (2002) and Gilmore (2003)) extended this framework to include three additional variables – People, Physical evidence and Process – thus making the 7Ps. Each element affects the other and are all dynamic. A successful marketing mix will combine these variables in a way that will facilitate meeting or exceeding organisational objectives.

An alternative view has also been put forward (Baker (2001); Elliott de Sáez (2002)) where the focus is on the 4Cs (developed by Lauterborn, 1990) – see Figure 1.3. He argued that the 4Ps approach was passé and that instead marketers should examine customers' needs and wants, their costs and issues of convenience and communication.

The 4Cs reflect a more client-oriented marketing philosophy, which meets with the principle of a customer-centred approach to marketing (Graham, 1995).

People	Product	Price	Promotion	Physical evidence	Processes	Place
Those involved in service delivery, their behaviour, attitudes and interactions	Quality, features, options, style, brand name, packaging, services	Listed price, discounts, allowances, payment period, credit	Advertising, selling, sales promotion, publicity, public relations	Information in leaflets, components facilitating the performance and communication of the service	Viewed as a system of inputs and outputs (e.g. information, people); mechanisms involved in the delivery of a product or service; policies and procedures	Distribution channels, coverage, location, convenience, availability
Stakeholders	*The service* Features, location, design, branding	*Financial management,* Tendering contracts	*Vision, values, culture* Branding, design of literature, letterheads, leaflets	*Prospectus* Website, newsletters, organisation's facilities and buildings	*Surveys* Evaluation of surveys, complaints procedure, quality management, consultation, Charter Mark, Investors in People, Open Door Policy	*The organisation* Where situated, opening times

Figure 1.2 The 7Ps of the marketing mix

However, as indicated by Elliott de Sáez (2002), the real issue is what constitutes the best way to offer value to the user. Gilmore (2003) describes the services marketing mix as 'the set of tools and activities available to an organisation to shape the nature of its offer to customers'. She also describes it as having distinguishing characteristics and say these are important in the design of an appropriate marketing mix. Here we will keep to the earlier nomenclature (the 7Ps) when referring to the marketing mix while bearing in mind that it can be thought of from the more client-oriented approach.

In order to create stakeholder value the elements of the marketing mix have to be managed effectively. This is achieved by recognising that stakeholders make up different segments of a market and that they will need to be addressed in different ways with different marketing strategies. Individual strategies will require different marketing mixes. Each group of stakeholders will have to be targeted in turn and the

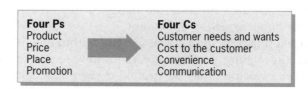

Figure 1.3 The 4Cs

service positioned in stakeholders' minds in such a way that it will be perceived to create value for stakeholders.

MANAGING THE MARKETING PROCESS

The first step involves segmenting the market.

Segmentation

Both Wind (1978) and McDonald and Dunbar (1995) argue that one of the most important aspects of managing the marketing process is market segmentation. Where clear differences can be identified, it is possible to group people together in to market segments. Groups of people who share common characteristics as interested parties (i.e. stakeholders) are identified and services are adapted to fit their needs. It allows the organisation to identify stakeholder groups, target the groups and deploy resources effectively. Segmentation should begin with a clear analysis of stakeholder interests and wants/needs.

Positioning

Positioning services in people's minds and making the services attractive to market segments requires careful formulation of the marketing mix. All the elements have to be put together and interrelated in such a way as to convey the message or image that the service will create the kind of value that stakeholders desire.

THE NEED FOR STAFF TO BE MARKETING ORIENTED

Changes in government legislation in more recent times have produced competitive practices in the public sector that were previously only experienced in the private sector. These have created internal markets and a competitive culture whereby local authorities are expected to respond to the needs of their local communities. As a consequence they are departing from their established role, as providers of social services, towards meeting the needs of local residents, or 'customers', under the banner of a market-led orientation.

Marketing principles can be applied within the public sector but there may be difficulty in relating service delivery entirely to market principles. In suggesting that 'market' principles may be applied in the public sector, there is an assumption that the market is an efficient and appropriate allocating mechanism for distributing public sector goods and services. Mellors (1993) argues that the notion of a 'public good' and the 'public interest' remain problematic in adopting market solutions to service provision. However, whatever the context, marketing principles can apply and staff need to be marketing oriented.

VALUE-BASED MARKETING

The governing objective of an enterprise is to create value for stakeholders. Strong brands, customer awareness, market share and satisfied customers are means to creating stakeholder value. In competitive markets the key to creating value is possessing a *differential advantage* that gives customers superior value through offers that are perceived as either superior in quality or lower in cost. Achieving this differential advantage in turn depends upon the effectiveness of the firm's business processes. In the public sector the competitive element may be absent but stakeholder expectations demand that superior value is created in a similar way.

Core business processes are the drivers of the organisation's ability to create stakeholder value and these processes themselves are founded on the organisation's *core capabilities*, which derive from the *resources* or assets it possesses. An organisation cannot have superior business processes unless it has access to the necessary resources and the ability to coordinate them effectively. Resources can be divided between tangible and intangible assets. Investors increasingly view intangible assets – the organisation's knowledge, skills and reputation – as the key to superior business processes. Maintaining the up-to-date asset base depends upon investment in physical assets, recruitment, training, staff development and even brands, advertising and communications.

HOW MARKETING SHOULD BE SEEN AS RELEVANT TO MANAGEMENT AT ALL LEVELS

Stakeholders interact and participate in the organisation at all levels. Indeed the very functioning of an organisation may be thought of as the outcome of interactions between different stakeholder groups in the organisation. A behavioural theory of organisations would see the decisions and policies that are set as being produced by a coalition of people representing the ideas and wishes that they are pursuing. Outcomes may well be related to the power possessed by individual groups of stakeholders or coalitions between sub-groupings. With any decision that is taken or policy that is set there may be parties that are satisfied or dissatisfied with the outcome of the interaction that has taken place and what it has produced in the way of policies or decisions. Marketing has a dual role: to help promote the view that the most satisfactory outcome has been achieved and to persuade all parties that there interests have been taken into account in achieving the outcome.

Large public sector organisations, such as municipal councils, often have several layers of management coordinating the work of a large number of employees. All levels of management therefore have to take account of employees as stakeholders and take into account employees' interests when setting policies or making decisions. Individuals in such organisations who deal with the organisation's customers or other groups such as government departments have got external stakeholders whose interests must also be taken into account. In all these instances marketing has relevance to the cross-boundary interactions that have to take place.

In the past the public sector may have been lacking in possessing a marketing orientation. Indeed, as indicated in the box below this may still be the case.

A cry for more marketing in the public sector

Des Pearson, Auditor General, Government of Western Australia, said at a conference in 2000:

'Public confidence in public administration can be reduced to three fundamental principles of transparency, accountability and trust. There is a persistent trend across the developed world that public confidence in public institutions is in a state of decline. ... I believe we, the public sector collectively and individually, have sold ourselves short, very short in fact. The best light I believe we can put on our lack of achievement to date is that generally speaking we have tended to be too task orientated and conscientious, to a fault. In consequence I strongly believe our skills inventory and record of achievement is grossly underrated. Marketing oneself, and our function, especially in the public sector is not easy. Nevertheless we cannot continue to ignore the need. Demonstrably we recruit the better educated. We possess tremendous intellectual capital and do a very effective job. Regrettably though we have not capitalised on this as well as we might have. I believe we should more clearly establish our role and purpose in the eyes of our stakeholder and client groups.'

Source: 'Contemporary issues in public sector accountability' conference, Des Pearson, Auditor General, Government of Western Australia, Wednesday 23 February 2000, Mercure Hotel, Perth.

Questions

1   How relevant is marketing to the successful functioning of a public sector organisation. Discuss.

2   It is argued by some that 'marketisation' of public services does not always bring down the price level and often creates an unacceptable standard of quality for recipients of certain services. Marketing is not a universal antidote for bureaucratic inefficiency. Discuss.

3   In setting policies and making decisions it is not always possible to reconcile differences of interest. In trying to reconcile conflicting interests, marketing is bound to fail. What evidence would you advance to support this argument and what evidence might you call upon to gainsay it?

Case study 1.1	Riverside Ambulance Services

The primary functions of the organisation are to deliver an emergency medical service within the pre-hospital environment and to provide transport provision for clients to hospital outpatients and day units. The secondary functions of the service are aimed at income generation and include:

- delivery of health and safety at work first aid training to external bodies,
- provision of medical cover at organised public events,
- collection of clinical waste from GP surgeries and dental practices.

Very limited marketing is conducted by the organisation and is mostly reactive to situations, with a press officer dealing with media issues. The organisation attends careers evenings in schools occasionally, though this area has no clear direction or strategy. Other activities include school visits with the other emergency services to emphasise safety, etc.

The organisation feels that it does not market what it does. The public on the whole is unaware of the level of pre-hospital care that can be delivered by paramedics working for the Riverside Service. Often the service is called out to trivial issues, toothache being a prime example, or a cut finger. It feels that by marketing the skill level of paramedics and technicians, raising public awareness, it could change now the public views its services so that it is not called upon for trivial issues but is viewed as a service for more serious injuries.

The organisation receives both letters of appreciation from the public and also letters of complaints, but does not undertake any customer satisfaction studies. It is exploring alternative care pathways for patients in conjunction with other stakeholders and feels this could be an area to explore for marketing. The objective is to reduce the volume of patients being taken into accident and emergency departments, so there are benefits to the NHS in general.

Among some of the ideas that Riverside has come up with are:

- obtaining greater patient and public involvement;
- putting more emphasis on accident prevention;
- increasing collaboration with other emergency services;
- promoting school-based projects to raise awareness in children;
- improving public awareness of paramedic cover at events;
- developing a dedicated team to deliver first aid at work training to the public.

There is no budgetary allocation specifically for marketing so on that basis it does not have a high priority within the strategic aims of the organisation.

Question

1 Discuss how a role for marketing might be developed within this organisation.

Case study 1.2 | The GP surgery

Woods, Mather, Fotherdew and Oglethorpe provide a GP service under the NHS to patients in Grimsborough. The practice is one of four similar establishments providing such a service in the town. The practice has a fairly modern approach to customer care but it is not without its shortcomings. In the past few years quite a few patients have left the practice indicating their dissatisfaction with the service offered.

Dr Woods, the senior associate and founder of the practice, is keen to maintain the practice's reputation and asked the office manager, Pam, who has been there for many years, to identify the kind of complaints and grumbles that its patients have made known to her in the past and to set up a system whereby complaints/suggestions for improvements can be collected and solicited. In response Pam has done three things:

1 She has written down all the complaints she can remember receiving over the previous six months.
2 Set up a 'complaints/suggestions' box in reception.
3 Produced and circulated a wad of short forms to all staff in the surgery (GPs, nursing staff and administrative/clerical staff) that asks them to record briefly the nature of any complaints/suggestions received and to place the completed forms in the box provided in reception.

Recently, Pam and Dr Woods reviewed the list of complaints/suggestions that had been recorded and sorted them into similar types. The following are typical of the kind of complaints/suggestions received:

- 'Can't stand Fotherdew's manner. One of the rudest people I know!'
- 'Sister Meredith is too bossy!'
- 'Need new carpets in the waiting rooms.'
- 'Can't you get something different to fish tanks in the waiting room? They make me dizzy.'
- 'Why do I have to wait a fortnight to see Oglethorpe? Is he always very busy?'
- 'Never seem to be able to make a telephone appointment at the surgery and have to trudge in two miles to make it in person.'
- 'Why should I have to ring the surgery to find the results of blood tests? Why not just let me know if there is something wrong?'
- 'Fotherdew has B.O.'
- 'Do you really think I can get into the surgery when I am running a temperature of 104 and coughing my heart out!'

Question

1 What action do you think Dr Woods should consider?

Case study 1.3 | Marketing and the NHS

Billion of pounds of taxpayers' money could be saved with the help of social marketing. Preventable ill health caused by smoking, poor diet, alcohol, unsafe sex and obesity costs the taxpayer billions of pounds. While the UK has been very slow to invest in a marketing approach to public health, countries such as Canada and Australia have found that such an approach works well. Preventable ill health every year costs:

- individuals, in extra spending and loss of income;
- British business, in days lost to sickness;
- NHS and other public care services;
- society, from the impact of early death and disability.

Question

1 Discuss how marketing might be developed on a grand scale to counter the problems met above.

References

Baker, S. (2001), *New Marketing: How to achieve a consumer driven transformation process*, Management Focus: Cranfield University School of Management. Volume Winter 2001, Issue 17.

Bean, J. and Hussey, L. (1997), *Marketing Public Sector Services*, London: HB Publications.

Booms, B. H. and Bitner, M.-J. (1981), 'Marketing Strategies and Organisation Structures for Service Firms', in *Marketing of Services*, Donnelly, J. H. and George, W. R. (eds), Chicago: American Marketing Association.

Boone, L. E. and Kurtz, D. L (1998), *Contemporary Marketing*, Cincinnati: Southwestern/Thomson Learning.

Borden, N. H. (1965), 'The concept of the marketing mix', in G. Schwartz, (ed.), *Science in Marketing*, New York: Wiley, pp. 386–397.

Burton, S. (1999) 'Marketing for Public Organisations: new ways, new methods', *Public Management*, Vol. 1. No. 3, pp. 373–385

Chapman, D. and Cowdell, T. (1998), *New Public Sector Marketing*, London: Financial Times/Pitman.

Cousins, L. (1990), 'Marketing planning in the public and non-profit sectors', *European Journal of Marketing*, Vol. 24, No. 7, pp. 15–30.

Cowell, D. W. (1984), *The Marketing of Services*, London: Heinemann.

Doyle, P. (2000) 'Value-Based Marketing: Marketing Strategies for Corporate Growth and Shareholder Value', Chichester: John Wiley.

Elliott de Sáez, E. (2002), *Marketing Concepts for Libraries and Information Services*, London: Facet Publishing.

Gilmore, A. (2003), *Services Marketing and Management*, Gateshead: Sage Publications Ltd.

Graham, P. (1995), 'Are public sector organisations becoming customer centred?', *Marketing Intelligence and Planning*, Vol. 13, No. 1, pp. 35–47.

Kotler P. and Zaltman, G. (1971) 'Social marketing: an approach to planned social change', *Journal of Marketing*, Vol. 35, pp. 3–12.

Lauterborn, B. (1990), 'New marketing litany: four Ps passe: C-words take over', *Advertising Age*, Vol. 61, Issue 41.

McDonald, M. and Dunbar, I. (1995*), Market Segmentation – A step-by-step approach to creating profitable market segments*, London: Macmillan Business.

Mellors, J. (1993), 'The commercialisation of common services provided by the Department of Administrative Services: outcomes and emerging issues'', *Australian Journal of Public Administration*, Vol. 52, No. 3, pp. 329–338.

Moorthi, Y. L. R. (2002), 'An approach to branding services', *Journal of Services Marketing,* Vol. 16, No. 2/3, pp. 259–275.

MOTI (Marketing On The Internet) (2005), *What is Marketing?* Retrieved 2 June 2005 from http://iws.ohiolink.edu/moti/homedefinition.html

Morgan, C. and Murgatroyd, S. (1994), *Total Quality Management in the Public Sector: An International Perspective*, Buckingham: Open University Press.

Moriarty, P. and Kennedy, D. (2002), 'Performance Measurement in Public Sector Services: Problems and Potential', in Neely, A. and Walters, A. (eds), Proceedings of the Performance Measurement Association Annual Conference, Boston, pp. 395–402.

Moullin, M. (2002), *Delivering Excellence in Health and Social Care,* Buckingham: Open University Press.

Neely, A., Adams, C. and Kennerley, M. (2002), *The Performance Prism*, Harlow: Financial Times Prentice Hall.

Niven, P. (2003), *Balanced Scorecard Step-by-Step for Government and Non-Profit Agencies*, New Jersey: John Wiley and Sons.

Radnor, Z. and Lovell, B. (2003), 'Success factors for implementation of the Balanced Scorecard in a NHS multi-agency setting', *International Journal of Health Care Quality Assurance*, Vol. 16, No. 2, pp. 99–108.

Rappaport, A. (1986), *Creating Shareholder Value*, New York: The Free Press.

Reid, M. and Worthington, S. (2004), *Contemporary Marketing Practice in the Professional Services: preliminary report,* Monash University, Business and Economics.

Slater, S. F. (1997), 'Developing a Customer Value-Based Theory of the Firm', *Journal of the Academy of Marketing Science*, 25(2), 162–167.

van Riel, C. B. M. (1995), *Principles of Corporate Communication*, Harlow: Prentice Hall.

Wind, Y. (1978), 'Issues and advances in segmentation research', *Journal of Marketing Research*, 15: 317–337.

Further reading

Baker, F. P. (1995), 'Marketing in a local authority', *Journal of Marketing Practice: Applied Marketing Science*, Vol. 1, No. 4.

Martin, J., Haines J., Bovaird, T. and Wisniewski, M. (2002), 'Developing a Balanced Scorecard in Somerset and Social Services Community', in Neely, A. and Walters, A. (eds) Proceedings of the Performance Measurement Association Annual Conference, Boston, pp. 749–756.

Wisniewski, M. and Dickson, A. (2001), 'Measuring performance in Dumfries and Galloway Constabulary with the Balanced Scorecard', *Journal of the Operational Research Society*, Vol. 52, No. 10, pp. 1057–1066.

2 The stakeholder value approach

INTRODUCTION

In this chapter we will look at the concept of stakeholder value and how it is created. We will also introduce ideas about how it may be measured. Since stakeholders are central the ideas we are advancing about marketing in the public sector first we look briefly at some aspects of stakeholder theory. It is in the context of this theory that we set marketing and its purpose in the public sector. Next we will comment on the importance of delivering stakeholder value since this is how the needs and wants of stakeholders may be satisfied. Finally we introduce ideas relating to the measurement and assessment of value as it may be experienced by different stakeholder groups and how value may be measured and assessed.

STAKEHOLDER THEORY

Stakeholders are held to be those individuals or groups that have a 'stake' in the organisation (see Caroll, 1993:22). Other definitions include: those individuals with explicit or implicit contracts (Donaldson and Preston, 1995); 'any group or individual who can affect or is affected by the achievement of an organisation's purpose' (Freeman, 1984:52); and those with a legitimate claim (Hill and Jones, 1992). Stakeholders often include customers, employees, management, stockholders, creditors, suppliers, the wider community and sometimes even competitors.

Stakeholders may be active or passive (Mahoney, 1994); the former being those that seek to participate in the organisation's activities. However, stakeholders do not necessarily have to be part of an organisation's formal structure. Management and employees are active stakeholders but this group may also be expanded to include groups from outside an organisation (e.g. pressure groups). Passive stakeholders are those that do not normally seek to participate in an organisation's policy making. One should not infer from this that the latter are less interested or less powerful but simply that they are not actively involved in formulating an organisation's strategy. In the public sector, passive stakeholders normally include government and local communities.

Stakeholders can have different perceptions of the importance of their own stake in an organisation's business and how management values or takes note of their stake. They can also have different ideas about the power of influence they have with management (Hill and Jones, 1992). However, we cannot say with certainty that these perceptions imply that different stakeholders should expect different levels of priority when decisions are being made (see Caroll, 1993). Nevertheless, it has been argued that powerful stakeholders possessing legitimate claims can expect preference to be shown to their opinions and wishes (Starik, 1994). On the other hand, there is an argument that 'all persons or groups with legitimate interests participating in an enterprise do so to obtain benefits and that there is no *prima facie* priority of one set of interests and benefits over another' (Donaldson and Preston, 1995:68). Further support for this view is voiced by Evans and Freeman (1988) who argue that stakeholder theory does not give primacy to one stakeholder group over another, though there will be times when one group will benefit at the expense of another.

Despite these differing opinions, common sense would seem to dictate that preferential attention will be given to certain stakeholders over others when making decisions or setting policies where there is a conflict of interest among stakeholders. Indeed it will be argued here that it may be one of the roles of those engaged in marketing in the organisation to show how decisions are made with equanimity and are fair to all parties.

STAKEHOLDER INTERESTS

We argue that the aim of an organisation is to create value for stakeholders and in so doing to satisfy their wants and needs. This in turn requires that we can first identify the various specific interests of different stakeholder groups. Let us by way of example consider the various stakeholder groups that may be associated with a university and the differing interests that they may have (see Table 2.1).

Decisions, projects and plans need to be carried out at the university in such a way that they will satisfy the various *interested* groups of stakeholders. We say *interested* simply because for certain decisions or projects certain stakeholders may not have a specific interest in seeing that they are carried out in a specific way.

Clearly, however, by setting out the different interests of the stakeholders, as in Table 2.1, we are in a position to identify whether or not a group of stakeholders may have an interest in a specific project or decision. We would seek confirmation

Table 2.1 Table of stakeholder interests in a university

Internal		*External*	
Group	*Interests*	*Group*	*Interests*
Staff	• Provision of quality education • Self-development and promotion prospects • Achievement of recognised quality status • Job satisfaction • Work in a safe and good quality environment	**Local community/ groups/ societies**	• Use of facilities • Good quality facilities • Pleasant, safe surroundings • Access to facilities
Students	• Achieve good levels of education • Enhance future career prospects • Self-development through training and opportunities • Access to information • Support from peers/staff/ parents	**Government**	• Quality standards • Legal requirements/health and safety/equal opportunities/pay and conditions • Challenge failure in achievement, set standards, monitor standards • Financial management, ensure resources being used and managed effectively • Reduction in unemployment
Governors	• Assist in development and improvement of university – including physical environment and teaching standards – achievement of recognised quality status • Good working relationship with all staff to achieve objectives • Ensure working practices and business plan targets are upheld • Development and contribution to committees (e.g. special needs, equal opportunities)	**Funding agencies**	• Ensure investment is monitored and resources are managed effectively • Recognition of their involvement • Quality standards

Table 2.1   continued

Internal		External	
Group	*Interests*	*Group*	*Interests*
Unions	• Responsibility to members to ensure fair working practices, safe environment • Support and advise members in all areas of employment rights, e.g. equal opportunities, discrimination, racial incidents • Recruitment of new members	**Investors**	• Protection of their investment • Quality standards • Management of resources • Recognition of their involvement • Publicity
		Accreditation agencies	• Raise standards • Support and assistance in order to achieve quality standards • Set and measure targets • Monitoring
		Press	• Provision of information to local community • Questioning • Praise and publicity for high achievement • Adverse publicity – making the facts known • Challenging use of finances
		Alumni	• Connections with the university, possibly as parents, interest in becoming part of governing body or teaching staff • Potential investors • Loyalty to the university, willing to offer support in their line of expertise
		Government inspectors	• Raise standards • Monitoring and challenging standards • Measurable targets • Financial implications

Table 2.1   continued

Internal		External	
Group	*Interests*	*Group*	*Interests*
		Prospective students	• Good quality education in safe, pleasant surroundings • Access to information – use of new technology to assist in learning • Career prospects • Choices • Self-development • Achievement of recognised qualifications

of this by asking the group to state their specific interest as and when the occasion arises. Of course, within the various stakeholder groups there may be minority interests and these would have to be taken into account and reconciled.

In order to satisfy stakeholder interests it is necessary to create value for them. Let us first explore this concept of value and what it may mean to different stakeholder groups.

THE CONCEPT OF VALUE

Value is a term that can be interpreted in many different ways. Among these the following dictionary definitions of the term are relevant in the context of assessing shareholder value:

- the worth, desirability or utility of a thing, or the qualities on which these depend;
- worth as estimated; valuation;
- the equivalent of a thing; what represents or is represented by or may be substituted for a thing;
- the ability of a thing to serve a purpose or cause an effect.

First let us look at some pointers as to what the operational meaning of value may signify to different stakeholders by examining two in particular.

Customer value and supplier value

Zeithaml (1988) researched the concepts of perceived price, perceived quality and perceived value, and discovered that customers thought of value in four ways:

1   Value is low price.
2   Value is whatever I want in a product.
3   Value is the quality I get for the price I pay.
4   Value is what I get for what I give.

Zeithaml (1988:14) suggested the following definition of customer perceived value:

> 'Perceived value is the consumer's overall assessment of the utility of a product based on perceptions of what is received and what is given ... value represents a trade-off of the salient "give and get" components.'

An exchange requires at least two parties, and for voluntary exchange to take place, both parties must believe that they will be better off as a result (Blaug, 1997). In this context supplier value is 'the perceived trade-off between multiple benefits and sacrifices gained through a customer relationship by key decision makers in the supplier's organization' (Walter *et al.*, 2001:366). This is a simple transference of the give–get concept of customer value to the supplier.

PRINCIPLES OF STAKEHOLDER VALUE

Stakeholder value incorporates the salient features of 'give and get' and may be thought of as (Murman *et al.*, 2002):

> 'How various stakeholders find particular worth, utility, benefit, or reward in exchange for their respective contributions to the enterprise.'

The first stage involves discovering stakeholder values and to do this we need to:

*   identify stakeholders;
*   identify what part of a programme or process adds value for each stakeholder;
*   determine each stakeholder value;
*   establish what kinds of exchanges are required to provide this value;
*   establish stakeholder expectations and contributions.

The second stage of creating value is a dynamic and interactive process requiring:

*   the development of a value proposition, i.e. an approach to providing the required values;
*   the delivery of the promised values.

Referring back to Table 2.1, we have already identified the stakeholders for a university. Let us assume that a decision has to be made about the introduction of a new degree course into the range of courses offered by the university. One could in fact argue that such a new course would create value for most of the stakeholder groups identified. Even in the case of the Press it would be a valuable piece of news that it could announce to the local community and run a feature on. It would thus have value for the Press. Similarly, values could be determined for the other stakeholder groups. Keeping with the Press for the moment, in the remaining two stages the university needs to know how to make the information available to the Press so that the latter can use it to good effect. It needs to know the expectations of the Press in terms of information that the university should supply.

Not all situations may involve a relatively simple exchange of information. Often, developing a value proposition, i.e. an approach to providing the required values, requires a marketing strategy. There may be different strategies available for each value proposition, hence there is a need to value the different strategies that are possible.

STRATEGIES THAT SUSTAIN VALUE

Through maintaining good long-term relations with stakeholders organisations can engender and sustain value. First let us consider a number of ideas about value in a relationship context (Christopher *et al.*, 2002)

- Value is created as an offering and delivered through recurrent transactions within a managed relationship.
- Value is created through mutually interactive processes and shared through negotiated agreement within the life of a relationship.
- Value is created and shared by interactions that emerge from within networks of relationships.

The first of these conditions stresses satisfaction of stakeholder requirements and the adoption of a long-term management perspective. The second assumes that value is created and shared mutually between the parties involved. The third argues that the organisation creates value jointly with stakeholders cutting across normal organisational boundaries.

Action taken with respect to one stakeholder can affect another. For instance, action with respect to customers can affect the supplier and probably the employee and may even have wider environmental impacts. Stakeholder orientation in marketing goes beyond markets, competitors and channel members to understanding and addressing all stakeholder demands.

VALUING DIFFERENT MARKETING STRATEGIES

Marketing entails the development of strategies and plans. The strategies are developed with specific goals in mind and all are carefully planned in such a way that they provide the best opportunity for their successful implementation. Value-based planning looks at marketing plans from the viewpoint of investors and asks if the strategy will generate a return that exceeds the investors' opportunity cost of the time they invest in dealing with the organisation. The strategy valuation process should permit managers to answer questions such as:

- Does the proposed marketing strategy create value for the organisation's stakeholders?
- Would alternative marketing strategies create more value?
- How sensitive is the strategy to the marketing assumptions *and* to unexpected changes in the organisation's environment?

An example of the strategy valuation process

Let us consider an example of the strategy valuation process. A city council is intending to set up a call centre adopting the government policy of implementing e-government. An executive summary of its marketing strategy is as follows:

Strategic objective

To create stakeholder value by establishing market leadership in this new area of opportunity in e-government. The service would provide information to members of the public and also deal with queries.

Strategic focus

The focus would be on volume growth by attracting customers to switch from conventional methods to using a 'call centre'.

Marketing mix

- *Product* The service comprises a call centre that can be accessed by people over the telephone. The aim is to transform the interaction from a reactive face-to-face one, only available at set times during the day in the city centre offices, to a telephone one that can resolve a high percentage of customer requests on first contact.
- *Price* Services will be made available free to all users but users pay for the telephone calls.
- *Promotion* The service will be promoted through listings in *Yellow Pages*, on the city council's website and through posters on display in all public buildings in

the city. In addition a leaflet explaining the service is to be circulated to all premises along with all information and forms circulated in connection with council tax bills.

- *Distribution* Users of the call centre will be able to access the service from any telephone.
- *People* Those who have expert knowledge in the areas to which enquiries may be directed will make up the call centre staff. They will be trained in how to handle customers over the telephone link.
- *Processes* Guidelines will be laid down regarding how calls through the call centre will be handled.
- *Physical evidence* Customers will not be able to see the call centre or its operators but the manner in which staff will interact with callers will be of key importance in place of visual contact. All staff will receive training in this aspect.

Valuation

Key measures will relate to the take-up of the service and consumer satisfaction with the services provided. This will be assessed on an individual service basis. Targets will be set for resolution of queries.

Stakeholder analysis of performance

A multi-step process can be used in the methodology as follows:

1 Desk audit
2 Management workshops to determine key performance areas
3 Determine stakeholder groups and members
4 Face-to-face interviews and telephone
5 Final survey
6 Mail survey
7 Follow up
8 Analysis.

A *desk audit* involves the collection and evaluation of government reports and other documents concerning the project. This may be followed by *workshops* wherein the research team and senior project management liaise for the purpose of establishing potential *stakeholder groups* and potential key performance areas.

A draft of the *survey document* may be developed. An extensive range of *face-to-face interviews* with individuals from all stakeholder groups may then be held to determine whether the constituent attributes accurately and fully reflected all the attributes that the stakeholders perceived to be important. Each new version can be tested with the next stakeholder interview.

The next step involves *surveying* the sample individuals using 'value perception' measures. These highlight key performance areas, subdividing them into basic attributes, which can then be used to produce a value index alongside other useful intermediate data. A primary concern of the survey may be the determination of the relative importance of key performance areas of value and the relative importance of the attributes within each key performance area.

The next step may involve *follow-up* interviews to maximise the response rate. The final step involves *analysis* of the questionnaires.

DIFFICULTIES AND RESTRICTIONS IN IMPLEMENTING STAKEHOLDER VALUE ANALYSIS

Top management's capacity to take into consideration the interests and expectations of multiple stakeholders can create problems when formulating and implementing strategies. Measurement systems may help deal with the complex uncertainty that exists with respect to stakeholder and public expectations. However, while financial measures are well developed, non-financial measures such as those of assessing and balancing stakeholder expectations are less refined.

Not taking note of stakeholder interests and/or information stakeholders provide can easily lead to disaster (Nutt, 2002). However, there has been little research conducted on performance management using multiple stakeholder approaches (viz. Mitchell *et al.*, 1997; Bendheim and Graves, 1998; Wisniewski and Stewart, 2004). Nor has there been much research that indicates how to identify and analyse stakeholders (Bryson, 2004) or how to manage the various complex and often competing stakeholder relationships. Performance management approaches that are grounded in the underlying assumptions of public sector policy and practice (Moullin, 2002) and that address the complexity and multiplicity of stakeholders (Fletcher *et al.*, 2003; Leitch and Davenport, 2002) are essential.

Thus while it would seem that stakeholder value analysis is a critical factor in the whole process, monitoring to ensure that stakeholder value has been created and delivered is beset by measurement problems.

THE IMPORTANCE OF DELIVERING STAKEHOLDER VALUE

Stakeholder value increases when organisations concentrate on effectiveness rather than efficiency. Efficiency is reflected in controlling costs and resources and it has always been the concern of many organisations. Effectiveness, on the other hand, requires that right decisions are made with respect to how and where resources are deployed. Decisions have to be made with the future in mind and effectiveness is about making the right decisions for the future.

Performance management specifically tries to assess the business of managing effectively. It facilitates organisational decision making by trying to identify operations and activities that give rise to value or prevent it from being created. Performance management advocates appropriate action to be taken and as a consequence should lead to the creation of stakeholder value and improved stakeholder satisfaction provided the problems of measurement can be tackled satisfactorily. These kinds of demands on managers require a new approach to decision making supported by a new set of applications.

Let us consider two developments that may be useful in the context of what we have discussed above.

PERFORMANCE EVALUATION AND MANAGEMENT

Performance management, defined by the Treasury, as 'managing the performance of an organisation or individual' (HM Treasury, 2001), is a form of results-based management, measuring performance against goals, and has been around in the private sector for some time (Try and Radnor, 2004; Pollet and Bouckhaert, 2000). One of the most well-known results-based, management approaches – the 'balanced scorecard' (Kaplan and Norton, 1996) – has been adopted widely across the private sector. There has been a growth in the use of multi-dimensional performance frameworks, such as the balanced scorecard, within the public sector, which may be seen as an expansion of the purpose of results-based management to include managerial accountability (Wilcox and Bourne, 2002). However, it has been argued that the public sector requires a modified approach (see for example Bourn, 2000), particularly as Radnor and McGuire (2004) argue its primary purpose is accountability to central government rather than the management of the drivers that delivers outcomes for all stakeholders.

A value driver is a measure of the strategies, processes, activities, or assets that create value and whether they are being utilised in a manner that creates sustainable value. In the case of a public organisation the focus is placed on increasing stakeholder value. Typical stakeholder value drivers include increasing service growth and lowering the cost structure of providing services.

In Chapter 5 we will look at the 'balanced scorecard' and a more recent addition, 'the public sector scorecard', in detail.

BEST VALUE POLICY CONCEPT

The *best value policy* initiative was one of several features of planned local government reform that arose as a response to perceived problems of variable quality, lack of clarity in direction and a lack of coherence and cohesion in service delivery. The reform measures were intended to give responsibility for service provision back to local government and to ensure local government's responsiveness to the local community. It provided encouragement for authorities to employ a more strategic view of service provision. The policy called for the systematic review of service activities, to encourage performance planning and to facilitate continuous improvement.

Questions

1   Stakeholder theory does not prescribe answers to problems so in what ways might it be useful to marketers in public sector organisations?

2   How can an organisation create value for its stakeholders?

3   Assuming that an organisation is trying to create value for its stakeholders then how might this be assessed in performance management terms?

Case study 2.1	The day centre

East Kirkby Day Centre provides up to 30 places per day to enable older people to remain in the community and maintain or improve their quality of life or that of their carer through social contact and therapeutic activities. The centre provides support in times of personal stress and helps to reduce the likelihood of admission to hospital, avoiding or delaying the need for permanent residential or nursing care. The aim of the centre is to enhance the independence and social acceptance of service users and provide a breather for carers through day support, respite care and carers groups. The service is for older people who are experiencing mental health ill health (such as depression, schizophrenia, anxiety) and is open Monday to Friday, 9.00am to 5.00pm.

Service users are encouraged to form self-supportive social networks outside opening hours and are expected to take an active role in their own and each other's treatment in the groups and reviews. There is an ethos of challenge within a supportive environment. The centre is well accepted within the local community and regular interaction with the latter takes place. It provides opportunities for people to meet and talk with other people whose circumstances may be similar to their own. The centre encourages its users to take part in a variety of social and leisure activities and also tries to help with personal care where appropriate.

The centre prides itself on the friendliness of its staff who go to considerable effort to make service users' days as enjoyable as possible. There are opportunities to join in the daily activities which include: table games, music, arts and crafts, quizzes, indoor sports, cookery, reminiscence and exercises. Some activities can be arranged to meet individual needs and service users are encouraged to talk about these with staff. There is also a TV, plus video and hi-fi equipment for service users' enjoyment. In addition to all this the centre provides the following other services:

- chiropody,
- a library,
- personal care,
- an optician,
- hairdressing,
- a garden,
- a laundry service,
- hearing aid advice,

- welfare benefits advice,
- support for carers.

Question

1 Identify the various stakeholders and their interests in the organisation. What potential sources of conflict of interest can you identify?

Case study 2.2   Alcohol abuse

Alcohol abuse among young people is becoming an increasing problem but comparatively little research has been undertaken to delve into why young people abuse alcohol. Parents, peers and other reference groups have an impact on young people generally and this is also bound to affect youth drinking. The influence of alcohol marketing on young people is a hotly debated topic and evidence seems to be emerging that alcohol marketing may play a significant role in a young person's attitude to drinking alcohol. In this latter context, much of the research carried out is related to advertising in particular. There is no doubt that the drinks industry is among the foremost in terms of sponsoring creative, sophisticated advertising both in magazines and on TV.

While many public services advocate that advertising plays an important role in adolescent drinking, the alcoholic beverage industry has argued against any connection. It contends that advertising is aimed at adults and is intended to influence brand choice, not the decision whether or not to drink. Unfortunatley, there is little objective data to support or refute the link between advertising and underage drinking.

Question

1 Discuss what marketing actions a municipal council might take to discourage alcohol abuse among teenagers. What would comprise the makeup of the various stakeholder groups associated with this problem? How might the council try to influence the various stakeholder groups that have an interest in the problem.

References

Bendheim, C. and Graves, S. (1998), 'Determining best practice in corporate-stakeholder relations using data envelopment: an industry level study', *Business and Society*, Vol. 37, No. 3, pp. 306–339.

Blaug, M. (1997), *Economic Theory in Retrospect*, Cambridge: Cambridge University Press.

Bourn, J. (2000), 'Improving Public Services', *International Journal of Government Auditing*. Vol. 27, 1–2, p. 4.

Bryson, J. M. (2004), 'What to do when stakeholders matter. Stakeholder identification and analysis techniques', *Public Management Review*, Vol. 6, No. 1, pp. 21–53.

Carroll A. S. (1993), *Business and Society*, Ohio: South Western Publishing Company, p. 22.

Christopher, M., Payne, A. and Ballantyne, D. (2002), *Relationship Marketing: Creating Stakeholder Value*, Oxford: Butterworth Heinemann.

Donaldson T. and Preston L. E. (1995), 'The stakeholder theory of the corporation: concepts, evidence and implications', *Academy of Management Review*, Vol. 20, No. 1, pp. 65–91.

Evans, W. and Freeman, R. (1988), 'A stakeholder theory of the modem corporation: Kantian capitalism', in Beauchamp, T. and Bowie, N. (eds), *Ethical Theory and Business*, 3rd edn, Vol. 97, Englewood Cliffs, NJ: Prentice-Hall, pp. 101–105

Fletcher, A., Guthrie, J., Steane, P., Roos, G. and Pike, S. (2003), 'Mapping stakeholder perceptions for a third sector organisation', *Journal of Intellectual Capital*, Vol. 4, No. 4, pp. 505–527.

Freeman, R. E. (1984), *Strategic management – A stakeholder approach*, Stanford: Stanford University Press.

Fry, M. and Polonsky, M. J. (2004), 'Examining the unintended consequences of marketing', *Journal of Business Research*, Vol. 57, pp. 1303–1306.

Greenley, G. E., Hooley, G. J., Broderick, A. J. and Rudd, J. M. (2004), 'Strategic planning differences among different multiple stakeholder orientation profiles', *Journal of Strategic Marketing*, Vol. 12, pp. 163–182.

Hill, C. and Jones, T. (1992), 'Stakeholder Agency Theory', *Journal of Management Studies*, Vol. 9, No. 2, pp. 131–154.

HM Treasury (2001), *Choosing the Right Fabric*, accessed via www.hm-treasury.gov.uk

Kaplan, R. S. and Norton, D. P. (1996), 'Using the Balanced Scorecard as a Strategic Management System', *Harvard Business Review*, January–February, pp. 75–85.

Leitch, S. and Davenport, S. (2002), 'Strategic ambiguity in communicating public sector change', *Journal of Communication Management*, Vol. 7, No. 2, pp. 283–300.

Mahoney, J. (1994), 'Stakeholder responsibilities: turning the ethical tables', *Business Ethics – A European Review*, Vol. 3, No. 4, pp. 212–218.

Mitchell, R., Agle, B. and Wood, D. (1997), 'Toward a stakeholder identification and salience: defining the principle of what really counts', *Academy of Management Review*, Vol. 22, No. 4, pp. 853–887.

Moullin, M. (2002), *Delivering Excellence in Health and Social Care*, Buckingham: Open University Press.

Murman, E., Allen, T., Cutcher-Gershenfeld, J., McManus, H., Nightingale, D., Rebentisch, E., Shields, T., Stahl, F., Walton, M., Warmkessel, J., Weiss, S., Widnallet, S. (2002), *Lean Enterprise Value*, Basingstoke: Palgrave.

Nutt, P. (2002), 'Why Decisions Fail: Avoiding the Blunders and Traps that Lead to Debacles', San Francisco, CA: Jossey-Bass.

Pollet, C. and Bouckhaert, G. (2000), *Public Management Reform: a comparative analysis*, Oxford: Oxford University Press.

Radnor, Z. and McGuire, M. (2004), 'Performance management in the public sector: fact or fiction?', *International Journal of Productivity and Performance Management*, Vol. 53, No. 3, pp. 245–260.

Starik, M. (1994), 'Should trees have managerial standing?', *Journal of Business Ethics*, Vol. 14, No. 3, pp. 207–218.

Try, D. and Radnor, Z. (2004), 'An evaluation of how the public sector has responded to changing accountability requirements', Papers from the fourth International Conference on Performance Measurement and Management, PMA 2004, Cranfield: Cranfield School of Management.

Walter, A., Ritter, T. and Gemunden, H.-G. (2001), 'Value Creation in Buyer-Seller Relationships', *Industrial Marketing Management*, Vol. 30, pp. 365–377.

Wilcox, M. and Bourne, M. (2002), 'Performance Measurement Research and Action, Paper for the Performance Management Association Conference, Boston MA: Centre for Business Performance.

Wisniewski, M. and Stewart, D. (2004), 'Performance measurement for stakeholders: the case of Scottish local authorities', *International Journal of Public Sector Management*, Vol. 17, No. 3, pp. 222–233.

Zeithaml, V. A. (1988), 'Consumer Perceptions of Price, Quality, and Value: A Means-End Model and Synthesis of Evidence', *Journal of Marketing*, Vol. 52, pp. 2–22.

Further reading

Kimery, K. M. and Rinehart, S. M. (1998), 'Markets and constituencies: an alternative view of the marketing concept', *Journal of Business Research*, Vol. 43, pp. 117–124.

3 Creating and measuring stakeholder value

INTRODUCTION

In order to create and deliver stakeholder value it is necessary to have a stakeholder focus. This is somewhat akin to having a customer focus and we will look specifically at ideas relating to customer focus and customer relationship management in this chapter, drawing similarities with stakeholders where appropriate.

First we look at the concept of relationship marketing, pointing out its relevance to the broader context of managing relationships with all stakeholders in an organisation. Central to this notion of marketing is the concept of creating value in relationships and the use of effective communication. Relationship marketing within the organisation is achieved through internal marketing and we discuss the relevance in terms of creating stakeholder value among employees.

Like customers or consumers, stakeholders are influenced by cultural factors so that any value delivery has to take account of these. But, in the same way that customers are influenced by a variety of social, psychological and external environment factors, so too are stakeholders. Any communications or actions need to bear this in mind.

Since the aim is to reconcile stakeholder interests, some means of measuring the value attached to the interests of stakeholders is useful. This in turn then makes it possible to ascertain how actions or communications have changed or affected stakeholder perceptions and thinking. This chapter outlines a method for achieving this purpose.

DEVELOPING A STAKEHOLDER FOCUS

A view of marketing that has received a considerable amount of attention over the years is that of 'relationship marketing'. This view argues that all marketing activities need to be directed towards establishing, developing and retaining customer relationships. One can argue that there are a number of approaches to formulating marketing strategy. At one extreme, there is the *transactional* exchange whereby there is a single, short-term exchange with a distinct beginning and ending. This occurs often in the case of consumer goods firms with mass markets and little contact with their ultimate customers. In contrast, *relational* exchange involves continuous or regular transactions taking place over an extended or indeterminate time frame (see Grönroos, 1994). The relationships are complex, long-term in nature, and mutually beneficial. They are characterised by trust, commitment, mutual benefit, adaptation, respect, and regard for privacy. Effective application of relationship marketing within consumer markets requires that 'relationships' should incorporate these integral elements (O'Malley *et al.*, 1999).

Many organisations practise relationship marketing and acknowledge the need to build and sustain long-term relationships with customers through the creation of superior customer value and satisfaction. The success of marketing performance depends also on the creation and retention of long-term relationships with other parties, for example, suppliers, retailers and distributors. Kotler and Armstrong (1996:550) define relationship marketing as:

> 'The process of creating, maintaining, and enhancing strong, value-laden relationships with customers.'

Taken together, these various other bodies may constitute stakeholders in the organisation and thus relationship marketing is applicable to serving the interests of stakeholders.

Traditionally, marketing concepts focused on creating transactions rather than relationships. Relationship marketing shifts the focus from merely selling to customers to serving them effectively. As competition intensifies and markets mature, organisations recognise the importance of retaining their customers by emphasising customer satisfaction and value, and hence creating customer loyalty. Relationship marketing seeks the accomplishment of long-term customer retention and stresses the provision of superior customer service as a prerequisite for this. In relationship marketing there is a shift from transactions to relationships: 'Customers become partners and the firm must make long-term commitments to maintaining those relationships with quality, service and innovation' (Webster, 1992).

THE BROADER CONTEXT

There is also increasing recognition of the importance, not just of customer relationships, but also of relationships with all relevant parties involved in the marketing process, including consumer groups and end users. Relationship marketing extends the single-minded emphasis on customers to embrace relationships with all customers and publics. There are several ways of developing such relationships and these reflect financial, social and structural strategic perspectives.

The *value-building approach* searches for ways of *adding financial benefits to customer relationship*. For example, some retailers reward loyal customers with free or reduced-priced goods. However, such reward programmes are the first step in the process of building a close customer relationship but are not a sustainable long-term strategy (Wulf, 1998).

Adding social benefits as well as financial benefits constitutes another approach. Here personnel personalise their customer relationships. That is, they gain knowledge of an individual customer's needs and wants and then personalise the company's products and services to satisfy the individual.

Adding structural ties in addition to financial and social benefits is yet another approach. For example an organisation may supply customers with special equipment, such as software programs and/or computer links to enable them to manage their orders and inventories.

In the case of service organisations it is easier to *customise* the customer relationship in the pursuit of long-term customer relationships. Service providers can acquire knowledge of the specific characteristics and requirements of individual customers and hence tailor the service to the situation at hand.

Grönroos (2004) argues that relationship marketing is not for marketing specialists but for market-oriented managers. By placing marketing in the hands of the service deliverers the importance of communications, interactions, quality and value for the customer is stressed. Relationship marketing applies equally to the not-for-profit sector

To facilitate relationship marketing an organisation should:

- *Engage its customers in an ongoing dialogue* – it should determine what services its customers actually want, i.e. engage in market research.
- *Manage the interaction processes* – it should use its existing internal marketing techniques more aggressively to improve service standards.
- *Focus on the value elements of its business* – it should examine how its activities could be used to add value to its customers' operations.

The above suggestions are made in the context of customers rather than stakeholders but one can apply these suggestions to developing relationships with stakeholders too. Central to the notion of relationship marketing and the creation of stakeholder satisfaction is the notion of trust. Trust means a belief that those on whom we depend will meet our expectations of them. This kind of trust can be established and maintained by making and keeping simple agreements. It could also be reflected in a willingness to engage in reciprocal sharing and openness, to share relevant information when it is needed.

An individual exhibits trust if they understand and agree with another's intentions. This means:

- understanding the other's motives;
- believing that the other is forthright and honest with them and is not withholding information for their own interests or to manipulate anyone;
- believing that the other is really interested in them as a person and has their best interests at heart.

THE NEED FOR EFFECTIVE COMMUNICATION

Communication requires individuals to share meaning. It provides the means of creating and implementing behavioural changes both within and without an organisation (see, for example, Dibb *et al.*, 1991; Cheney, 1991). In the context of the external world, the role of the marketing communicator includes the facilitation of a sense of shared understanding with external customers about the organisation itself, its values, the identity of its brands and the specific benefits of its products/services. Within the organisation, however, the communication process has been shown to have a variety of additional roles including:

- encouraging the motivation and commitment of employees by ensuring an understanding of the company's objectives and goals (McDonald, 1995; Foreman, 1997);
- enhancing overall levels of service quality by ensuring that an understanding of the needs of the customer are fostered at every level within the organisation (Acito and Ford, 1980; Piercy and Morgan, 1994; Reukert and Walker, 1987; Wolfinbarger and Gilly, 1991).

The above highlights the need for effective communication with specific stakeholder groups but it is argued here that this needs to be extended to include all stakeholders in the organisation.

INTERNAL MARKETING

Internal marketing first appeared on the scene in the mid 1970s as a way of achieving consistent service quality (Ahmed and Rafiq, 2003). The underlying premise was that to satisfy external customers, it was desirable, if not a necessity, to have satisfied internal customers, namely employees (Sergeant, 1999). The logic of this is that by satisfying the needs of internal customers, an organisation should be in a better position to deliver the quality desired to satisfy external customers.

Organisations that have adopted internal marketing may have done so in order to achieve a 'people' orientation that helps to produce good service quality and customer satisfaction. Many of the activities that are an integral part of the internal marketing practice are geared towards the achievement of:

- high quality in the internal and external service interactions;
- internal and external customer satisfaction.

Internal communication is an important integral part of internal marketing practice and is one of the core elements of implementing internal marketing. It is important to develop a formal, coordinated and organisation-wide internal communication system that facilitates the implementation and practice of internal marketing. Internal marketing can be used to change the attitudes and behaviour of staff towards being more service- and customer-oriented, and it is necessary to create awareness and understanding about internal marketing in a structured and consistent way. A lack of an internal communication system regarding internal marketing suggests that internal marketing information is not properly communicated to staff, which could hamper its effective implementation.

The services marketing literature clearly identifies one of the key drivers of growth and profit as customer loyalty which, in turn, is a direct result of customer satisfaction (Heskett *et al.*, 1995). Thus developing a 'service culture' among customer-service personnel with a view to improving employee–customer interactions and, as a consequence, customer satisfaction is a key issue (Deshpande and Webster, 1993). The practice of internal marketing can assist in the development of a customer-conscious organisational culture (Cahill, 1995). The need for effective internal marketing strategies goes beyond 'front-line' customer service staff alone. Even those employees who do not interact directly with customers may affect perceived service quality because they directly influence the service providers (George, 1990). The importance of internal marketing is a key issue for all organisations in the non-profit and government sectors (Cahill, 1995).

In the above sections we have looked at how an organisation can take steps to create stakeholder value. In the next section we will turn to examining how one can assess the extent towards which service quality and stakeholder value has been achieved.

DELIVERING VALUE

To understand the value people put upon things, we a need to explore the factors affecting their process of valuation. These processes are influenced by psychological, cultural and social factors. Decisions will depend on the motivations of those involved and this will influence how they perceive things, how they receive and interpret information, how they form and change their attitudes, how much they remember and how they retrieve information that may affect their future decisions. It is a complex process because it involves a mixture of psychological, social and cultural elements. These elements interact and integrate with one another to influence behaviours. They have to be dealt with effectively because such knowledge can provide useful inputs to marketing strategies and guide marketing decisions.

Let us examine the case where the stakeholder is in fact the customer or the consumer of the service. The first step in the process is the customer recognising that there is a need that has to be satisfied or that requires a solution. This leads the customer to seek information. Such an information search may lead the customer to consulting many information sources. They may talk to friends, read magazines, newspapers or books, consult expert advisors, or even watch TV or listen to the radio. Based on the information that has been gathered, the customer will then judge the value on offer. The process of deciding may take a short period of time or it may take longer. This will depend on what is on offer and on other external and internal factors that may influence the situation. The customer's psychological state, which reflects their attitudes and perceptions, will also influence the decision that is taken. In addition, external factors such as cultural influences (e.g. ethnicity and religious values) will also affect decision making. All of these factors combine to affect the decision.

Once a decision has been made, the customer will evaluate whether the outcome has met their expectations and has led to satisfaction or whether the decision was a wrong one. This evaluation will influence future decisions.

Decision making involves the process of evaluating, assessing and deciding and this process is influenced by marketing strategies developed by the those seeking to offer value. One can adapt the process outlined above for the case where the stakeholder is the consumer to other stakeholders who may have a vested interest in the evaluation.

CULTURAL FACTORS

Behaviour is greatly influenced by the set of cultural factors that characterise the society in which the individual grows up. Culture includes those values, ideas and perceptions that are nourished by various institutions such as family and schools and embedded in people's beliefs, preferences and behaviours. Cultural beliefs that are evident in all societies have a direct impact on behaviour and therefore marketers need to have knowledge and understanding in order to incorporate these beliefs in their marketing products and strategies

Subculture

All cultures are divided into smaller subcultures on the basis of nationalities, religions, racial groups and geographical regions that provide more specific identification for their members. These nationalities nourish their inherited values and ideas, which in turn influence people's behaviours.

GROUP INFLUENCES

Reference groups

A reference group is a set of people to whom individuals look for guidance in terms of developing their attitudes, knowledge, behaviours and norms. Individuals often compare themselves to these reference groups and look to them in guiding their behaviours. Reference groups may be formal or informal in nature. Family, friends and colleagues are informal groups whilst groups that are set up formally such as church groups, schools or clubs, are formal reference groups.

Marketers need to identify the different reference groups because the latter have a direct or indirect impact on people's behaviour. Marketers need to understand the aspirational reference groups (those to which a person would like to belong) of the target market in order to associate their brands with these reference groups. Thus, planning the right marketing strategies in line with these reference groups is vital. On the other hand, identifying and understanding dissociative reference groups (those whose values or behaviour an individual rejects) is also crucial to prevent any marketing efforts that may not be well accepted by some.

Roles and statuses

A person is a member of many groups such as families, clubs and organisations. In each group, the individual has a certain role and status, which determine their position. Individuals' decisions will be influenced by their different roles. People often seek value satisfaction that reflects their status in society. Each role carries a status reflecting the general esteem given to it by society. Self-esteem and that conveyed on people by others is often greatly valued and does much to bolster self-confidence and, often, happiness as well.

PERSONAL FACTORS

Behaviour is not only influenced by cultural characteristics and social factors but is influenced by age and stage in the life cycle, occupation, economic status, lifestyle and personality.

Personality

People have a unique personality that influences their behaviour and certain psychological characteristics that influence their behaviour in society. Personality is usually described in terms of traits such as self-confidence, dominance, defensiveness, aggressiveness, autonomy, sociability and adaptability. Personality types can be classified accurately and strong correlations exist between certain value-satisfying choices.

Demanding and vocal

In the case of demanding and vocal people we have to be clear, specific and direct. It is important to be prepared and organised, and to stick to the business in hand. We need to present facts logically, ask specific questions and take issue only with facts. We also need to provide win/win solutions and a choice of options. We should not ramble on and waste their time or engage in idle gossip. It is also important not to be vague or leave loopholes or to ask useless questions. Finally, we should avoid personalising issues or make a decision for such people.

Expressive and animated

Some people may claim they have power and influence with senior officials and these people tend to be expressive and animated in their interactions. It is important to allow them to discuss their dreams and spend time in socialising with them, attempting to understand their goals and relationships with others. We should also seek out their opinions, supply ideas and provide testimonials for their inspection. On the other hand, we should avoid quoting facts/figures to support an argument. We should also be avoid being too impersonal or businesslike. Firm outcomes, decisions and undertaking are needed to keep these personalities satisfied.

Ultra-sociable

A third type of person is the one who likes to stop and talk to everyone. In this process they are actually reflecting and trying to come to decisions as they interact. They have to justify everything to themselves as they go along and so it is important to show sincere interest in them and their problems/uncertainties during any interaction. Being a good listener is important as is being sensitive to their concerns. We should allow them time to reflect and try to give personal assurances and guarantees. Avoid rushing right into business, sticking rigidly to the facts or demanding quick responses. Such people do not respond positively to threats or demands. It is also important to bear in mind that their acceptance of your solution for a problem may not satisfy them despite their assurances that it will. They must make up their minds about something for themselves.

Impassive

With some people it is hard to judge what is in their minds at the time of an encounter since they always have the same look on their face. With such people it is important to be straightforward and direct and consider all the dimensions of an issue, giving them time to think and reach decisions. We should not be casual, informal, or personal, or be vague and not follow through. We should also not promise too much or use emotions or feelings in discussions.

Clearly these are just a few personality types from the many different ones that may be encountered. Getting a feel for the personality type of the other person in an encounter may be critical to the eventual outcome of the interaction.

Psychological processes

Psychological processes refer to the internal processes individuals use to interact with the world and to understand themselves and their relationship to it. The level of motivation, perception, attitude formation and the learning process are all psychological factors that will influence behaviours. The psychological processes reflect thoughts, feelings and attitudes towards a value-giving object. They also stress the importance of personality and personal experiences, and assess the level of understanding that an individual has towards the object.

STAKEHOLDER VALUE METRICS

In managing enterprises, managers must continuously strive to strike a balance between the competing priorities of all stakeholders. Donovan *et al.* (1998) propose an 'Enterprise Value Scoreboard' that attempts to guide an organisation to decisions which achieve an 'optimal' balance among three stakeholders: customers, shareholders, and employees. The purpose of this approach (Mize and Hallam, 2002) is to balance tradeoffs company-wide, such that cross-organisational impacts are considered. Various other graphical approaches have been developed and these are considered below.

Systematic stakeholder mapping consists of identifying those groups or individuals likely to have an interest or stake in a proposed development or project, and the mapping of these to create a diagram that shows their relationships with the development or project (Nwankwo and Richardson, 1996). The representation in such a diagram is intended to aid understanding of the extent to which the identified stakeholders are likely to support or obstruct a proposed strategic development.

A useful model for demonstrating how stakeholders exert influence on an organisation's objectives is that proposed by Mendelow (1991). In the model, stakeholders can be ranked on two factors: their interest and their power (see Figure 3.1). Power refers to ability to influence the organisation and interest refers to the willingness to exert the influence. It is argued that stakeholder influence = power × interest.

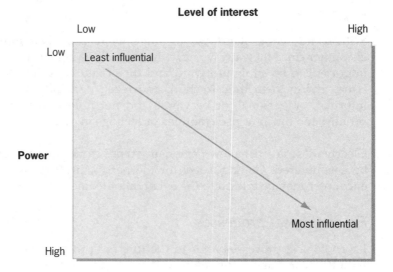

Figure 3.1   The power/interest matrix

However, the actual influence that a stakeholder has will depend upon where they are positioned with respect to ability to influence and willingness to influence. A stakeholder with both high power and high interest will be more influential than one with low power and low interest.

The matrix provides a picture of which stakeholder is likely to exert the most influence and where potential stakeholder conflict is most likely to occur. For example, in the case of a new housing development on reclaimed urban land the picture shown in Figure 3.2 might arise.

The matrix indicates the type of relationship that organisations might seek to establish with stakeholder groups in the different quadrants. In the example shown in Figure 3.2, when viewed from the site developer's point of view it becomes clear that the main stakeholders having an interest in the development are in segments B and D and that while the prime interest may be in satisfying local authority wants and needs the views of local residents need to be considered too. Failure to offer a proposed project that at least satisfies both these parties' wishes may result in its rejection.

Stakeholder mapping in this way can assist in promoting a better understanding of the following issues (Johnson and Scholes, 2002):

- whether the levels of interest and power of stakeholders adequately reflect the corporate governance framework within which the strategy is being developed;
- who the main supporters and opponents of a strategy are likely to be and how their requirements could be addressed;
- whether organisations should consider trying to reposition certain stakeholders, for example to ensure that there are more key players who will support a particular strategy;
- the extent to which stakeholders may need assistance in maintaining their levels of interest or power.

Power	Level of interest: Low	Level of interest: High
Low	A	Housing site developers Local residents B
High	C	Local authority D

Figure 3.2 Power/interest example

LIMITATIONS ON THE USEFULNESS OF ASSESSING STAKEHOLDER POWER AND INTEREST

It can be argued that the stakeholder model cannot explain how managers are able to treat each stakeholder in an equitable manner since it fails to prescribe how to prioritise or choose between expressed or latent interests. Sternberg (1997) argues that stakeholder theory is incompatible with business because the definitive stakeholder aim of balancing benefits for all stakeholders precludes all objectives that favour particular groups. In her opinion balancing stakeholder benefits is an unachievable objective since the number of people who can affect or are affected by an organisation is infinite, and that for a balance to be struck their numbers would somehow have to be limited. She also points to various other limitations among which is the question of how individuals who belong to more than one stakeholder group should be dealt with.

While Sternberg is critical of the value of stakeholder theory in explaining business behaviour, she does acknowledge that there is some meaningful use in the concept of a stakeholder. It does act as a convenient label for the various groups and individuals that organisations should take into account when pursuing their objectives. It can also serve to illuminate the proper meaning of 'social responsibility', i.e. if individuals have views as to how organisations should be conducted, they should ensure that their individual choices accurately reflect those views.

Such an argument is not without merit but it is possible to think of many situations in public sector organisations where policies and decisions may be of prime interest to certain stakeholders, of only secondary interest to others and even of no interest to certain groups. While not providing a perfect framework for policy making and decision making, giving primacy in terms of weighting to those who have the greatest interest may produce a pragmatic application for stakeholder theory.

Social marketing along with public policy, are often employed in government action to produce enhanced social outcomes (Kotler and Roberto, 1989). Public policy possesses a social marketing spotlight despite not being usually viewed as a social marketing activity. Some consider public policy to be marketing and that it veers to the social marketing perspective. In this guise it aims to produce voluntary changes in stakeholders' behaviour so that effective public policy is developed and implemented (Buurma, 2001; Altman and Petkus, 1994).

Social marketing campaigns require a comprehension of stakeholders' attitudes and motivations with regard to the issue of concern, in addition to the sought after modified behaviour (e.g. desisting from anti-social behaviour). The factors that need to be considered in social marketing relate to targeted stakeholders' motivation, opportunity and ability to undertake the desired actions (Rothschild, 1999). Understanding these factors allow government and others to put together strategies that may produce changes in stakeholders' behaviour. One might conclude that it is important for those creating regulations to comprehend stakeholders' motivation, opportunity and ability in relation to dealing with the issue of concern. As a consequence, policy makers might then identify areas where existing activities are ineffective or where more effective marketing of policy needs to be put into action (Polonsky *et al.*, 2001).

Questions

1   What role might 'relationship marketing' play in creating stakeholder value?

2   Discuss how cultural and other factors might influence stakeholder thoughts and opinions about the development of a new inner city shop precinct that has been given the go ahead for development by a city council.

3   An NHS hospital trust is considering outsourcing up to 50% of its routine operations to the private sector. How might it assess whether the levels of interest and power of stakeholders adequately reflect the corporate governance framework within which the strategy is being developed. Who are likely to be the main supporters and opponents of the strategy and how this could their needs be addressed.

Case study 3.1	# The city council – getting a government-sponsored initiative off the ground

The Best Start Initiative is a government grant-funded project aimed at children from birth to age four living in the most deprived areas of the country. Each city council is responsible for ensuring that the grant is spent appropriately and submitting grant claims. Decisions are made by local management boards composed of various statutory agencies (including the city Council), community groups and parents. The Department for Education and Skills (DfES) is responsible for delivering the programme as part of an agenda to reshape children's services. However the DfES has identified that the Best Start Initiative has some specific communications challenges relating to:

- extremely diverse stakeholders and delivery partners,
- diverse group of services,
- low public awareness of the Best Start Initiative offer.

In order for the project to be effective and ensure that every child gets the best start in life its message has to be communicated to a wide range of audiences including parents, providers, delivery partners, MPs and the media. Families have to know what is on offer and what to expect in terms of quality so they will take up services and ultimately benefit from them.

However, while the DfES offers a variety of advice and information regarding marketing, there is evidence to suggest that marketing of the project by the city council has not been as effective as it could have been. Various factors have hindered the effectiveness of the programme. One of these has been the lack of an effective, coordinated and pro-active publicity and promotion strategy that had led to a lower take up of some services and activities than that which might have been achieved, particularly amongst hard to reach groups.

The implications are ultimately that the grant may be underspent unless contingency action is taken. Ultimately, if the grant is not spent within the financial year it is lost income to the city. It is therefore important that the grant is maximised and meets central government objectives.

Marketing of the project has concentrated on promotion using local advertising, newsletters and leaflet drops to publicise events or services. This is fairly typical of local authorities as many local authority managers associate marketing primarily with publicity and promotion, and there is a lack of understanding about what marketing actually entails.

In order for the project to be effective and meet its objectives it must become 'customer centred' in its marketing approach and to do this it is imperative that there is an effective marketing plan in place and that this is managed correctly. This will include analysis, planning, organisation, implementation and control of marketing activities.

Questions

1 How might relationship marketing help in such a case?

2 What factors might affect interested stakeholder values and perceptions and how might these be ascertained/measured?

Case study 3.2   Monitoring customer performance in the public sector

Most public services have performance standards and report to Parliament and the public on how well they have met these. Most public service providers measure levels of customer satisfaction though this is often perceived as not particularly rigorous and comparisons even within sectors are difficult to make. The fundamental drivers of customer satisfaction within public services are considered to be:

- delivery of promised outcomes and handling problems effectively;
- timeliness of service provision;
- accurate and comprehensive information, and progress reports provided;
- professionalism and competence of staff and treating customers fairly;
- staff attitudes – friendly, polite and sympathetic to customers' needs.

Question

1 How would you set about assessing levels of customer satisfaction in your organisation?

References

Acito, F. and Ford, J. D. (1980), 'How advertising affects employees', *Business Horizons*, Vol. 23, February, pp. 53–59.

Ahmed, P. and Rafiq, M. (2003), 'Internal Marketing issues and challenges', *European Journal of Marketing*, Vol. 37, Issue 9, pp. 1117–1186.

Altman, J. A. and Petkus, E. (1994), 'Toward a Stakeholder-Based Policy Process: An Application of the Social Marketing Perspective to Environmental Policy Development', *Policy Sciences*, Vol. 27, pp. 37–51.

Bansal, M. K. (2004), 'Optimising Value and Quality in General Practice within the Primary Health Care Sector through Relationship Marketing: A Conceptual Framework', *International Journal of Health Care Quality Assurance*, Vol. 7, No. 4, pp. 180–188.

Bee, C. and Bott, V. (1991), 'Customer treatment as a mirror of employee treatment', *Advanced Management Journal*, Vol. 5, No. 1, p. 27

Barry, T. (1993), 'Empowerment: the US experience', *Empowerment in Organisations*, Vol. 1, No. 1.

Buurma, H. (2001), Public Policy Marketing: Marketing Exchange in the Public Sector. *European Journal of Marketing*, Vol. 35, Issues 11 and 12, pp. 1287–1302.

Cahill, D. (1995), 'The managerial implications of the new learning organization: a new tool for internal marketing', *Journal of Services Marketing*, Vol. 9, No. 4, pp. 43–51.

Cheney, G. (1991), *Rhetoric in an Organizational Society*, Columbia, University of South Carolina Press.

Cook, S. (1994), 'The cultural implications of empowerment', *Empowerment in Organisations*, Vol. 2, No. 1, pp. 9–13.

Deshpande, R. and Webster, F. E. (1993), 'Corporate Culture, customer orientation and innovativeness in Japanese firms: a quadrad analysis', *Journal of Marketing*, Vol. 57, No. 1, pp. 23–27.

Dibb, S., Simkin, L., Pride, W. and Ferrel, O. (1991), *Marketing Concepts and Strategies*, New York, NY: Houghton-Mifflin.

Donovan, J., Tully R. and Wortman B. (1998), *The Value Enterprise: Strategies for Building a Value-Based Organization*, Toronto: McGraw-Hill/Ryerson.

Foreman, S. (1997), 'IC and the healthy organisation', in Scholes, E. (ed.), *Handbook of Internal Communication*, Aldershot: Gower.

George, W. R. (1990), 'Internal marketing and organizational behavior: a partnership in developing customer-conscious employees at every level', *Journal of Business Research*, Vol. 20, No. 1, January, pp. 63–70.

Grönroos, C. (1994), 'From Marketing Mix to Relationship Marketing towards a Paradigm Shift in Marketing', *Management Decision*, Vol. 32, No. 2, pp 4–20.

Grönroos, C., (2004), 'The Relationship Marketing Process: Communication, Interaction and Dialogue', *Journal of Business and Industrial Marketing*, Vol. 19, No. 2, pp. 99–113

Heskett, J., Jones, T., Loveman, G., Sasser, E. and Schlesinger, L. (1995), 'Putting the service-profit chain to work', in *Managing Services Marketing*, Bateson, J. (ed.), Fort Worth: Dryden Press, pp. 419–428.

Johnson, G. and Scholes, K. (2002), *Exploring Corporate Strategy*, Harlow: FT Prentice Hall.

Kotler, P. and Armstrong, G. (1996), *Principles of Marketing*, Prentice-Hall International Editions pp. 12, 16, 663–665, 667.

Kotler, P. and Roberto, E. (1989), *Social Marketing Strategies for Changing Public Behavior*, New York: The Free Press.

McDonald, M. (1995), *Marketing Plans*, Oxford: Butterworth-Heinemann.

Mendelow, A. (1991), Proceedings of Second International Conference on Information Systems, Cambridge, MA.

Mize, J. and Hallam, C. (2002), 'Stakeholder value metrics', Module to Support Team Assignment in Course 16.852J/ESD.61.J – Fall 2002 'Integrating the Lean Enterprise'.

Nwankwo, S. and Richardson, B. (1996), Organizational leaders as political Strategists: a stakeholder management perspective, *Management Decision*, Vol. 34, No. 10, pp. 43–49, MCB University Press.

O'Malley, L., Patterson, M. and Evans, M. (1999), *Exploring Direct Marketing*, London: Thomson Learning, Chapter 7.

Piercy, N. and Morgan, N. A. (1994), 'The marketing planning process: behavioral problems compared to analytical techniques in explaining marketing plan credibility', *Journal of Business Research*, Vol. 29, No. 3, pp. 167–178.

Polonsky, M. J., Carlson, L. and Fry, M. L. (2001), 'The Harm Chain: A Stakeholder and Public Policy Development Perspective', 2001 Marketing & Public Policy Conference, pp. 3–4.

Reukert, R. W. and Walker, O. C. (1987), 'Marketing's interaction with other functional units: a conceptual framework and empirical evidence', *Journal of Marketing*, Vol. 51, January, pp. 1–9.

Rothschild, M. (1999), 'Carrots, Sticks, and Promises: A Conceptual Framework for the Management of Public Health and Social Issues Behavior', *Journal of Marketing*, Vol. 63 (October), pp. 24–37.

Sargeant, A. (1999), *Marketing Management for Nonprofit Organizations*, Oxford: Oxford University Press.

Sternberg, E. (1997), 'The Defects of Stakeholder Theory', *Scholarly Research and Theory Papers*, Vol. 5, No. 1 (Jan.).

Webster, F. E. (1992), 'The changing role of marketing in the corporation', *Journal of Marketing*, October, pp. 1–17.

Wolfinbarger, M. F. and Gilly, M. C. (1991), 'A conceptual model of the impact of advertising on service employees', *Psychology and Marketing*, Vol. 8, Fall, pp. 215–37.

Wulf, K. D. (1998), 'Relationship Marketing', in Loovy, B. V., Dierdonck, R. V. and Gemmel, P. (eds), *Services Management: An Integrated Approach*, Harlow: Financial Times/Pitman Publishing, pp. 61–78.

Further reading

Caruana, A. and Celleya, P. (1998), 'The effect of internal marketing on organisational commitment among retail bank managers', *International Journal of Bank Marketing*, Vol. 16, No. 3, pp. 108–116.

George, W. R. and Grönroos, C. (1989), 'Developing customer conscious employees at every level – internal marketing', in Congram, C. A. and Friedman, M. L. (eds), *Handbook of Services Marketing*, New York, NY: AMACOM.

Greene, W. E., Walls, G. D. and Schrest, L. J. (1994), 'Internal marketing: key to external marketing success', *Journal of Services Marketing*, Vol. 8, No. 4, pp. 5–13.

Parasuraman, A., Zeithaml, V. A. and Berry, L. L. (1988), 'SERVQUAL: a multiple item scale for measuring consumer perceptions of service quality', *Journal of Retailing*, Vol. 64, No. 1, Spring, pp. 12–37.

Parasuraman, A., Berry, L. L., Zeithaml, V. A. (1991), 'Understanding customer expectations of service', *Sloan Management Review*, Spring, pp. 39–48.

Parasuraman, A., Zeithaml, V. A. and Berry, L. L. (1985), 'A conceptual model of service quality and its implications for future research', *Journal of Marketing*, Vol. 49, Fall, pp. 41–50.

Sargeant, A. and Asif, S. (1998), 'The strategic application of internal marketing – an investigation of UK banking', *International Journal of Bank Marketing*, Vol. 16, No. 2, pp. 66–79.

Zeithaml, V. A. (1996), 'The behavioral consequences of service quality', *Journal of Marketing*, Vol. 60, April, pp. 31–46.

4 Developing and implementing strategies

INTRODUCTION

Strategic management is about laying down an organisation's objectives, developing policies and plans to achieve these objectives, and allocating resources to implement the plans. It is the highest level of executive activity, usually performed by the organisation's senior management team, and it provides overall direction to the whole enterprise. Strategy has to be formulated in line with the resources available, the circumstances and objectives. It involves matching the organisation's strengths and weaknesses with opportunities and threats in the marketplace taking into account changing environmental forces and how the organisation interfaces with them. A key objective is to put the organisation in a position to carry out its mission statement effectively and efficiently. Good corporate strategy should integrate an organisation's goals, policies and action sequences (tactics) into a cohesive whole.

STRATEGY FORMULATION AND IMPLEMENTATION

Strategy formulation involves analysing both the internal and external situation from both micro- and macro-environmental perspectives. It involves fitting together vision statements (a long-term view of a possible future), mission statements (the role that the organisation gives itself in society), overall corporate objectives (both financial and strategic), strategic business unit objectives (both financial and strategic) and tactical objectives. The objectives should be set bearing in mind the situation analysis and the plan should provide the details of how to achieve these objectives. This three-step strategy formation process is often thought of as determining where you are now, determining where you want to be, and then determining how to get there. These three steps are the essence of strategic planning

DEVELOPING STRATEGIES

Strategies are produced in order to find ways of filling gaps between how or what the organisation provides in the way of service provision now and what it would like to achieve in the way of service provision in the future. This means that it has to be well aware of its current provision and changes occurring in its environment that will affect how future service provision should develop. Strategy facilitates the achievement of the desired end result. Choice of strategy will be affected by what is possible and practical to achieve, and also by what it will cost in terms of time, money and available skills to carry through a particular strategy.

The steps in the process are as follows:

1   Assess the current situation – find answers to the question 'where are we now?'
2   Identify all the relevant factors that are likely to affect what is done currently.
3   Assess the likely impact that these factors will have on how provisions should be made.
4   Decide how to develop in view of the envisaged potential developments.
5   Come up with specific objectives to be achieved so as to move towards the desired end result.
6   Develop appropriate strategies that facilitate movement towards the goal.

SITUATIONAL ANALYSIS

It is necessary to conduct a situation analysis in order to ensure that well thought out procedures are set up for assessing the environment and the performance of the marketing effort. A situation analysis evaluates the internal strengths and weaknesses of the organisation, and involves the continuous gathering and analysing of both external and internal information.

Organisations should look for threats and opportunities that exist within the marketing environment taking into account in particular the competitive situation. Trends that affect demands should be studied in order to enable marketing strategies to be carefully planned. Collecting data in this way provides relevant information that will help detect problems and opportunities. At the internal level, information on resource availability and service performance data and indicators should be assessed and matched with information relating to issues external to the organisation.

DEMAND FOR GROWTH OR CHANGE

Demand for growth in services provided can come from different sources. In essence the manifestation of the source will be pressure exerted by a stakeholder group but may reflect changes taking place in the more general business environment. These changes may be political, economic, socio-cultural, technological, legal or ecological. For example, an ageing population has ramifications for the provision of care for the elderly. The onus on care provision may be felt more by local councils rather than by the families involved. Pressure may be exerted by councillors or other stakeholders to increase the facilities available for care of the elderly. Local authority management may feel that this provision is best achieved through outsourcing and forming partnerships with private organisations that can provide the service in a cost-effective manner.

As a result of these pressures exerted by influential stakeholders there will be a gap between what is currently being provided and what is needed. It is essential to find a cost-effective way of filling the gap. The search for a solution will involve finding one that most satisfies stakeholder interests, bearing in mind that the influence of the different stakeholders on the process may vary.

CONSTRAINTS ON GROWTH OR CHANGE

Constraints on growth or change may be imposed by what is considered a feasible solution to plugging the gap, bearing in mind the nature of stakeholder interests. For example, in order to provide a more user-friendly service it may be necessary to install a new computerised information system. Both central government and users of such a system may be in favour of it and actively support its installation. However, both groups may be unwilling to pay for the cost of a highly developed system and technology may act as a constraint upon what kind of system can be made available. The result may be a compromise which is found satisfactory to both central government and users who help to pay for the service through council tax. Even then a third element – employees as a stakeholder group – may enter into the equation. The implementation of the system may be delayed and associated costs escalate because employees may require retraining in order to get the system up and running.

The above represents a very simplified view of what may be involved in bringing about growth in provision or effecting change in services provided. Not only are there different stakeholder interests to satisfy but the stakeholders themselves may have multiple interests that require serving. Employees, for example, may require retraining and guarantees about job security as well. The latter would require negotiations, too.

WAYS OF ACHIEVING GROWTH

Traditionally growth in strategic marketing terms has been thought of in terms of the Ansoff product–market expansion grid (see Figure 4.1). Product is a generic term which also refers to services.

Essentially, the grid suggests that growth is achieved either by serving new market segments or by introducing new products or services into the marketing mix. The strategies themselves can be varied and complex. For example, the market penetration strategy could be:

- to increase purchase use by existing customers, and
- to win customers from competitors.

Similarly for the market development strategy (e.g. to explore new distribution channels), the product development strategy (e.g. to implement new features) and the diversification strategy (e.g. to diversify through joint ventures).

All of the above strategies are available to all non-profit-making organisations, public sector or otherwise.

Market penetration strategy

A municipal council or local authority offers a wide range of services and users (as a stakeholder group) will already make use of some of the existing services. They may be encouraged either to seek more specific advice and information about services or even to make use of services that they currently do not access.

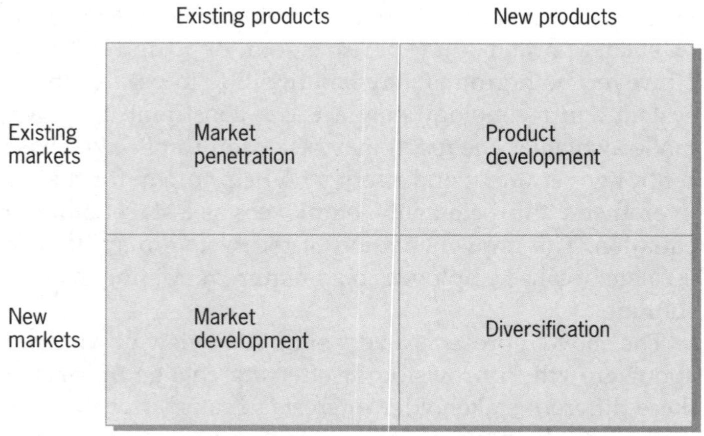

	Existing products	New products
Existing markets	Market penetration	Product development
New markets	Market development	Diversification

Figure 4.1   Ansoff product–market expansion grid
Source: Exhibit 1, p. 114 from *Strategies of Diversification* by Ansoff, H. I. Harvard Business Review, Issue No. 25(5), Sept/Oct 1957, pp. 113–25. Reprinted with permission.

Market development strategy

Councils can identify new market segments for their services. Often older people who are entitled to benefits may not understand how they can take advantage of these (e.g. subsidised travel passes). By targeting younger people and making them aware that this service is available and how it may be accessed, information may then be passed on to older relatives to enable them to benefit from such schemes.

There are various roles involved when making use of a service. The initiator, decider, acquirer and user roles may all be resident in one person – the person making use of the service – and the influencer may simply be an impersonal source such as a flyer in a local library. However, for one reason or another, this need not necessarily be the case. The roles may be taken up by several different individuals and whilst only the user will benefit directly from the service it may be necessary to target one or more of the roleholders with information about the service that is available. Each of the roleholders might represent a *market segment for information projection.*

An example of how *innovation in distribution channels* can bring about growth in service usage is provided by the introduction of one-stop shops into various urban neighbourhoods. People who otherwise would have difficulty in accessing services can find it easier to do so because the one-stop shops are closer to where they live and are staffed by people who can readily serve their wants and needs.

Product development strategy

New features and new services are the predominant way in which growth can be achieved in this instance. Call centres and collection of garden waste are examples of new services that councils have introduced in the past few years. Looking at the internal market of a local authority, the introduction of sophisticated ITC systems has enabled staff to obtain information much more quickly and efficiently than previously. This represents an instance of internal service development.

Diversification strategy

There are many reasons why organisations may seek to diversify their product/market portfolio of offerings. In profit-making organisations these are usually related to the long-term survival of the organisation and the creation of shareholder value. In the case of public sector organisations where the profit-making motive is essentially absent, motivation is in terms of producing better services and/or lowering cost to users of the services – the general public.

Joint ventures seem to be the main mechanism used by municipal councils to achieve diversification. For example, in the pursuit of providing a better service across the board, a council may decide to operate a call centre service. Such a call centre requires considerable investment in terms of expertise, know-how and capital and can best be achieved by a joint venture with telecommunications expertise. This usually requires a venture with a profit-making organisation and the establishment of a joint venture company to develop and provide the service required. The joint venture company is usually set up as a separate legal entity – a public limited company – and may offer its services to users other than those of the council who may have originated its foundations. As a separate entity its business is a diversified one with a specific purpose of offering services to clients via telecommunications technology.

SETTING OBJECTIVES

Objectives and targets stated in strategies and plans should be realistic and achievable, and should be matched to financial and other resources. They should also be explicitly translated into clear responsibilities for implementation. This is very important when working in the public sector since it is characterised by having a variety of stakeholders with potentially diverging and often vague objectives (Boyne, 2002; Bretschneider, 1990; Traunmüller and Wimmer, 2003).

Among the useful strategic analysis models for this stage in the process are the Ansoff matrix and the Directional Policy Matrix (McDonald, 1992). We have already looked at the Ansoff matrix in this chapter and we will look in some detail at the use of the Directional Policy Matrix in Chapter 5. Here, however, we will make some general, relevant comments.

Some products or services generate considerable revenue for the operations of the enterprise while others do not. Where considerable cash is generated, it is often more than is required for essential operational expenditure and for additional investment in facilities and staff. In other cases, however, the cash generated may be insufficient to cover these kinds of expenditure. A profit-making firm might benefit if products or services that are not satisfactorily contributing to profits and overheads of the firm are dropped from the product mix. However, there may well be good reasons why the products are such poor cash generators at a particular time. Indeed it may well be that some of these products will go on to being the future big cash earners for a company. In the case of the public sector the profit motive is usually absent and services may have to be provided irrespective of cost but it is still useful to be able to see how services are using up the various financial resources that are available.

Product portfolio models provide a means of rating products and/or services in order to assess the future, probable cash contributions and future cash demands of each product or service. In the case of the public sector the assessment will be regarding how they use up expenditure. They provide an indicator of the kind of objectives that need to be set for identified services or products (see Chapter 5).

The next stage in the process involves uncovering and specifying objectives. These may or may not be related to specific problems that have been identified.

PROBLEM IDENTIFICATION AND OBJECTIVE FINDING

One possible approach involves using SWOT analysis to identify various Strengths, Weaknesses, Opportunities and Threats. We then consider various combinations of strengths–opportunities, strengths–threats, weaknesses–opportunities and weaknesses–threats to identify potential objectives.

In Figure 4.2 a service provider is reviewing its marketing position and strategies.

	Strengths (S) 1 Well-informed team delivering service 2 Well-established organisational image	Weaknesses (W) 1 High service provision costs 2 Seasonal demand for service
Opportunities (O) 1 Private sector interest in being a joint or sole service provider	How to make use of private sector interest combined with own well-established organisational image (O1, S2)	How to make use of private sector interest in the light of seasonal demand (O1, W2)
Threats (T) 1 Cuts in council financial support given for the service	How to establish organisational image firmly to counteract cuts in financial support given to the service (T1, S2)	How to reduce costs to cope with costs in financial support (W1, T1)

Figure 4.2   Identifying objectives

A more general approach to objective finding involves asking the group to defer judgement and list some major concerns in the company or business.

GETTING IDEAS

There are many ways in which organisations can get new ideas for services that they can offer. In the main these revolve around undertaking research with users/stakeholders to identify unsatisfied gaps in the service or provision. Research can take the form of focus group discussions where people with an interest in the service are interviewed as a group and encouraged to discuss the shortfalls of the service and suggest how improvements can be made. There are several useful structuring techniques that can be used either by one person or by groups of people to aid the process. We will look briefly at some of these below.

Checklists

This involves the use of questions as spurs to generate ideas. The following questions might also be usefully applied to problems in general:

- Adapt?
- Modify?
- Substitute?
- Magnify/maximise?
- Minimise/eliminate?
- Rearrange?
- Reverse?
- Combine?

For example, if we take a service:

- *Adapt?*: make it more convenient for people to access.
- *Modify?*: make it portable.
- *Substitute?*: use internet capabilities instead of face-to-face personal service.
- *Magnify/maximise?*: opening hours/access to the service.
- *Minimise/eliminate?*: excessive form filling.
- *Rearrange?*: rearrange the location of the drawers and integrated trays.
- *Reverse?*: approach customers with potential solutions to service problems instead of have them approach the council with problems.
- *Combine?*: combine services.

The following might also be applied:

- add or subtract something,
- change something,
- vary how the service is provided,
- modify design or style.

The technique facilitates idea generation if we prepare a list of items relating to a problem and check them against certain aspects of the problem. It can be used both as a problem delineation list and as a solution finding list. The purpose of the former is to provide a direction for the idea search, to make sure that no ideas have been overlooked and to evaluate the applicability of ideas borrowed from a previous problem. Checklists used for possible solutions are concerned with developing new ideas. The most common use of checklists involves identifying new service ideas by making alterations to existing services.

Attribute listing

Attribute listing is a good technique for ensuring that all possible aspects of a problem have been examined. Attribute listing involves breaking the problem down into smaller and smaller bits and seeing what can be discovered as a result.

Suppose, for example, you want to improve the quality of a museum service. By breaking the service down into its component parts – target group, features and presentation – you can develop a list of ideas and improve each one (see Table 4.1).

Table 4.1 Attribute listing: improving museum quality

Target group	Feature	Presentation
Young single	Local history	Exhibition
Single parents	Clothes and costumes	Activity
Young married (small children)	Science and technology	Display
Married (teenage children)	Pre-history	Video/film show
Old married	Transport	Shops

Attribute listing is a very useful technique for improving the quality of complicated products and procedures or services. It is a good technique to use in conjunction with other creative techniques, especially idea-generating ones like brainstorming. This allows you to focus on one specific part of a product or process before generating a whole lot of ideas.

Morphological analysis

Morphological analysis is a tool that can help generate a vast number of ideas. It works best as a visual aid but this can prove difficult in circumstances where the problem is complex. Ideally, the problem should have two or three dimensions to permit the construction of two- or three-dimensional grids.

First, possible dimensions are listed describing the problem or system being studied. No more than three dimensions can be represented diagrammatically, and they must be relevant and have a logical interrelationship. For example, if an organisation decides to alter its service in response to changing requirements it should consider what the most important dimensions of the service are. The dimensions would be represented on a two-dimensional grid (or cube for three dimensions) and a list of attributes is then generated under each dimension. Free-wheeling and offbeat ideas are encouraged.

The next step is to examine combinations of attributes across the dimensions, however unusual or impractical they may seem. For example, a cross may be put in a box if the combination is used at present and a nought if it is a potential idea worth pursuing. Promising ideas are then subsequently evaluated for their suitability.

The technique can be used by an individual or a group. If it is used by a group then, ideally, the group should consist of six to eight experienced people who each record their own ideas. There should be a leader who collects the ideas and who must be able to communicate enthusiastically while keeping a steady momentum going. A warm-up session is customary prior to problem solving and this provides an opportunity to select and discuss the dimensions of the problem. It is helpful to express the problem in generic terms, to make much use of imagination, and to ensure that the dimensions and attributes are independent.

Suppose a museum, for example, wants to generate ideas for a new service. The first stage is to identify suitable categories of ideas to use as axes of a matrix, bearing in mind that we are seeking to discover opportunities rather than come up with an immediate solution. The chosen dimensions must be relevant to the problem and have some logical interrelationship. However, the items listed under each dimension can be as off-beat as required. The morphology identifies the dimensions that describe the service and then identifies lists of attributes under each dimension (see Table 4.2 for example).

Table 4.2 Morphological analysis

Target group (families)	Feature	Type of presentation
Young single	Local history	Exhibition
Single parents	Egyptology	Activity
Young married (small children)	Science and technology	Display
Married (teenage children)	Pre-history	Video/film show
Old married	Transport	Theatre
Older single	Clothes and costumes	Shops

In the example given in Table 4.2, the attributes of each dimension can be combined with each other, thus giving $6 \times 6 \times 6$ (216) possibilities. Sometimes it may be necessary to consider three or even four dimensions, but this makes the task of evaluating ideas laborious and so the two or three most important dimensions are usually chosen.

HIGH FAILURE RATE

Many new products or services fail to meet the expectations of the people whose idea it is to create them. In the profit-making sector success or failure is often measured by a yardstick such as sales volume, profit or return on investment. In the non-profit-making sector it is more appropriate to measure relative success in terms of the extent to which a product or service meets with stakeholder expectations. For some stakeholders (those who make financial investments, for example) the revenues and costs of the project may be the main criteria used to effect judgement. For other stakeholders or service users, for example, how well the service operates and whether it provides an answer to their problems and queries will be more important. Thus in the context of providing local authority services judging the success or failure of a new venture may be much more difficult.

SCREENING IDEAS

Usually ideas for new products arise sequentially, one at a time, and cannot be compared and evaluated along with a large set of alternative ideas for new products unless benchmarking against important criteria takes place. The likely financial performance and implications of developing and/or adopting a new product/service idea are key factors that need to be taken into account. The initial screening stage is characterised by a checklist of benchmarks that new products must satisfy. The list includes, for example:

- Can the product/service be priced competitively alongside products of a similar quality?
- Will promotion of the product/service be easy?
- Will there always be users of the new product/service?

This is followed by a more thorough business analysis exercise. At this stage, costs and profit projections have to be made in order to determine whether adoption of the new product into the product mix will satisfy company objectives. Approaches include:

- examining take-up histories of similar products/services,
- surveying market opinion,
- using expert opinions.

CUSTOMER ADOPTION

Consumers can be grouped according to how quickly they adopt a new product. At the one extreme, some consumers adopt the product as soon as it becomes available; at the other extreme, some consumers are among the last to purchase a new product. As a whole, the new product adoption process can be modelled in the form of a bell-shaped diffusion curve.

New product diffusion curve

The diffusion of innovation refers to the tendency of new products, practices or ideas to spread among people. Usually, when new products or ideas come about, they are initially only adopted by a small group of people; later, many innovations spread to other people. The bell-shaped curve frequently illustrates the rate of adoption of a new product. Cumulative adoptions are reflected by the S-shaped curve. The *saturation point* is the maximum proportion of customers likely to adopt a product.

Several forces often work against innovation. One is risk, which can be either social or financial, including the initial effort needed to learn to use new products or services (e.g. it takes time to learn to meditate) and concerns about compatibility with the existing culture or technology. For example, birth control is incompatible with strong religious influences in countries heavily influenced by Islam or Catholicism, and a computer database is incompatible with a large, established card file.

Innovations come in different forms. A *continuous* innovation comprises slight improvements over time. A *dynamically continuous* innovation involves some change in technology, although the service may be used in much the same way that its predecessors were used, for example telephone departments in the council office versus the call centre approach. A *discontinuous* innovation involves a product or service that fundamentally changes the way that things are done, for example the fax and photocopiers. In general, discontinuous innovations are more difficult to market since greater changes are required in the way things are done, but the rewards are also often significant.

Several factors account for the speed with which an innovation is adopted. One issue is relative advantage (i.e. the ratio of risk or cost to benefits). Some products or services, such as cellular phones, have a strong relative advantage which speeds up the adoption process. Other products/services, such as automobile satellite navigation systems, have some advantages, but the cost ratio is high so the adoption process is much slower. The extent to which the product is *trialable* can also speed up the process of adoption. Finally, the extent of switching difficulties influences speed – many offices were slow to adopt computers because users had to learn how to use them. Moreover, sometimes innovations are *dis*adopted: for example, many individuals disadopt cellular phones on finding out that they do not use them much.

Figure 4.3 shows the bell-shaped diffusion of innovation curve. Defining areas one standard deviation wide about the mean, five different product adoption groups can be defined:

- Innovators – well-informed risk takers who are willing to try an unproven product. Innovators represent the first 2.5% of customers.

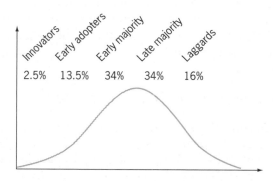

Figure 4.3   The diffusion of innovation curve
Source: Everett M. Rogers, *Diffusion of Innovations*, 4th Edition, 1962. Figure 7.2, p. 262. Reprinted with permission.

- Early adopters – based on the positive response of innovators, early adopters then begin to purchase the product. Early adopters tend to be educated opinion leaders and represent about 13.5% of customers.
- Early majority – careful customers who tend to avoid risk, the early majority adopts the product once it has been proven by the early adopters. They rely on recommendations from others who have experience with the product. The early majority represents 34% of customers.
- Late majority – somewhat sceptical consumers who acquire a product only after it has become commonplace. The late majority represents about 34% of customers.
- Laggards – those who avoid change and may not adopt a new product until traditional alternatives are no longer available. Laggards represent about 16% of customers.

(For this discussion, the term 'customers' represents both individuals and organisations.)

Even if a product or service offers high value to the customer, the organisation nonetheless faces the challenge of convincing potential customers to try the product and eventually to adopt it.

HOW MARKETING HELPS

New products and services have to be marketed and stakeholders, particularly users/customers and employees administering the service have to be persuaded about their merits. The process involves influencing people's attitudes and opinions and in this context it may be seen that the strategy involves exerting influence on the cognitive and affective components of people's attitudes. The *cognitive* component reflects what we know about a product and the *affective* component reflects how we feel about it. In order to get people to use a service it can be argue that it is necessary for them to have a positive attitude towards it. (For more details see Chapter 9.)

IMPLEMENTING STRATEGIES

Strategy implementation involves:

- allocation of sufficient resources (financial, personnel, time, ICT support);
- establishing a chain of command or some alternative structure (such as cross-functional teams);
- assigning responsibility of specific tasks or processes to specific individuals or groups;

- managing the process – monitoring results, making comparisons with bench-marks and best practices, evaluating the efficacy and efficiency of the process, controlling for variances and making adjustments to the process as necessary;
- in the case of specific programmes it can involve acquiring the requisite resources, developing the process, training, process testing, documentation, and integration with (and/or conversion from) previous systems used to perform tasks.

Strategic management operates on several time scales. Short-term strategies involve planning and managing for the present. Long-term strategies involve preparing for and pre-empting the future.

STRATEGIES ADOPTED: PAST AND PRESENT

Until the end of the l970s, hierarchy was the dominant route to the delivery of public services along with the distinctive features of bureaucracy – vertical integration, clearly defined spheres of authority, command-and-control leadership, and an emphasis on rules, routines and standard operating procedures. Communication and coordination between agencies, as well as between functions and departments tended to be problematic, producing rather compartmentalised approaches to dealing with problems. In addition, large bureaucracies were seen by some to be inflexible in adapting to change and inefficient and sometimes ineffective at pro-ducing satisfactory results.

More recently there has been a renewed emphasis on markets and competition in the delivery of public services. In the UK, Conservative governments privatised large parts of the public sector, and exposed what was left to market disciplines through quasi-markets, compulsory competitive tendering (CCT) and market testing. Large multi-functional bureaucracies were accordingly broken up into a network of specialised agencies contracting for services with a variety of public, private and voluntary providers.

The development of a partnership approach to the delivery of public services is, in part, a response to a growing belief that national economies increasingly face an in-built incapacity to finance the provision of public services.

NEW VENTURES, OUTSOURCING AND DIVERSIFICATION AS STRATEGIC APPROACHES

Strategic alliances/joint venture partnerships

Alliances are inter-organisational cooperative structures formed to achieve the stra-tegic objectives of the partnering firms. The purpose of forming strategic alliances includes (Varadarajan and Cunningham, 1995):

- to gain market entry,
- to respond to changes in market structure,
- to improve resource efficiency,
- to facilitate resource acquisition,
- to enable risk reduction, and
- to enhance skills.

Outsourcing

Outsourcing is a contractual agreement between the customer and one or more suppliers to provide services or processes that the customer is currently providing internally. The fundamental difference between outsourcing and any other purchasing agreement is that the customer contracts-out a part of its existing internal activity. There are many reasons why a company may choose to outsource and rarely will it be for one single reason. While they are normally specific to the particular situation, some commonly cited reasons are:

- to reduce cost,
- to improve quality, service and delivery,
- to improve organisational focus,
- to increase flexibility, and
- to facilitate change.

Integrative strategies

Integrative strategies can be horizontal across departmental boundaries or vertically between supply production, distribution and consumption. For example, processing a benefit claim involves claimants inputting data about themselves. This is usually done with the help of an advisor at a reception point in the benefits office. The data form is then passed on to a back office where it is then reviewed and checked before authorisation is confirmed. Re-engineering and help from joined-up electronic services can vertically integrate the whole process so that the data input is controlled by the customers. Integration leads to faster and cheaper services for customers. If data entered by customers are then shared across departments – horizontally integrated – instead of being collected by individual departments, further time and money is saved.

Questions

1   What kinds of initiatives can a public sector organisation such as a city or local council seek to develop in order to expand the scope of its operations? How would you decide which were the best ways of pursuing these new initiatives in terms of the Ansoff matrix?

2   Illustrate how the strengths–opportunities–weaknesses–threats matrix might be put to good effect in terms of identifying general areas for development in a public sector organisation of your own knowledge and choosing.

3   People *en masse* rarely take up new products or services very quickly yet the provider has to set up a system of service that can be very expensive in terms of initial investment and running costs. How might public sector organisations set about trying to reduce the risk associated with such new ventures?

Case study 4.1	One-stop shops

Early in 2006 the borough authority set up a number of one-stop shops in an effort to improve its customer focus in dealing with complaints, enquiries and routine matters that required face-to-face contact with members of the public in the borough. In all, four new one-stop shops were sited at strategic points around the borough. One was sited close to the airport, the second close to the bus station in the city centre, the third on the nearby campus university site and the fourth close to the municipal park, which was about a mile away from the main shopping centre in the city and a half mile away from a leisure complex.

Existing employees in the council were asked if they would like to volunteer to staff the four one-stop shops and managers were advertised for externally in the press as well as internally in the council. Two of the managers eventually appointed came from outside the council and had been working recently as retail store managers in the district.

Take-up of the service facilities by members of the public in the first six months was extremely slow and staff employed at the one-stop shops found they had little business to transact. Often when queries were raised by people coming into the one-stop shops the staff would find that they had insufficient knowledge to help the enquirers and had to go to considerable lengths to locate people in the councils's main offices who could help either over the telephone or in person.

The problem was exacerbated during the holiday season when permanent personnel had to be replaced with temporary staff who knew far less in dealing with queries.

Question

1 Suggest how the council might resolve the current problem. Do you think it should just simply shut down all the one-stop shops and redeploy the staff to other work? Give reasons for your views.

Case study 4.2	New ideas

The council is looking for new ways of attracting potential users of its day centres. It recognises that carers can be relieved of a great deal of stress at home if they can bring their relatives or friends into a centre for a day and have their responsibilities shared or taken off them for a few valuable hours. However, examination of the day centre records has shown that there is a fairly high turnover in terms of people attending the centre and further research has shown that either the carers or the people being cared for have not wanted to continue attendance.

A study carried out with lapsed users suggests that that the carers have found it too much of a hassle to get the cared person ready for collection to be taken to the care centre either using their own transport or the regular bus service that calls to pick them up. As one elderly man caring for his wife who suffered from pre-senile dementia explained:

'I just can't put up with complaints and carry on any longer. She refuses to get out of bed in a morning, shouts at me and even physically attacks me on occasion when I say we are going to start going to the day centre again. I am at my wits end. Every time there is a knock at the door she thinks that it is the people at the day centre who have come for her and barracades herself into her room. I wouldn't mind but when I have taken her in the past she has always said how much she enjoyed the experience. The staff are very good with her and try to get her to engage in all kinds of activities. I think all the trouble started when one of the other people attending started to ask her about her family. Ever since then she imagines people are spying on her.'

Questions

1 What do you think the council might do to make its day centres more attractive to carers and those being cared for? Could any of the creative, thought-provoking techniques identified in the chapter be of any use? How?

2 What might the council do to alleviate the strains and stresses being experienced by the elderly man whose wife has mental health problems?

References

Boyne, G. A. (2002), 'Public and private management: What is the difference?', *Journal of Management Studies*, Vol. 39, Issue 1.

Bretschneider, S. (1990), 'Management Information Systems in Public and Private Organizations: An Empirical Test', *Public Administrations Review*, Vol. 50, No. 5, pp. 536–545.

McDonald, M. (1992), 'Strategic marketing planning: A state-of-the-art review', *Marketing Intelligence & Planning*, Vol. 10, No. 4, pp. 4–22.

Traunmüller, R. and Wimmer, M. (2003), 'E-Government at a Decisive Moment: Sketching a Roadmap to Excellence', in R. Traunmüller (ed.), *Proceedings of the 2nd International Conference, EGOV 2003*, pp. 1–14.

Varadarajan, P. R. and Cunningham, M. H. (1995), 'Strategic Alliances: A Synthesis of Conceptual Foundations', *Journal of Academy of Marketing Science*, Vol. 23, No. 4, p. 282.

Further reading

Ansoff, H. I. (1988), *The New Corporate Strategy*, New York: Wiley & Sons, p. 83.

Brauner, S. (2000), 'Crazy schemes and broken dreams in a city where pigs and pies vie for air space', in *Liverpool Daily Post*, 27 April, pp. 14–15.

De Kare-Silver, A. (1997), *Strategy in Crisis: why business urgently need a new approach*, Basingstoke: Macmillan.

Jaworski, B. J., Stathakopoulos, V. and Krishnan, H. S. (1993), 'Control Combinations in Marketing: Conceptual Framework and Empirical Evidence', *Journal of Marketing*, Vol. 57, No. 1, January, pp. 57–69.

McDonald, M. H. B. (1999) *Marketing Plans: how to prepare them, how to use them*, Oxford: Butterworth-Heinemann.

Proctor, T. (2005), *Creative Problem Solving for Managers*, London: Routledge.

Rao, V. R. and Steckel, J. H. (1998), *Analysis for Strategic Marketing*, Harlow: Prentice Hall.

Saunders, H. (1998), *Marketing Strategy and Competitive Advantage*, Harlow: Prentice Hall.

Senn, L. (1999), *Leaders on leading: insights from the field*, Houston: Gulf Publishing.

Wilson, R. M. S. and Gilligan, C. T. (1997), *Strategic Marketing Management: Planning, Implementation and Control*, Oxford: Butterworth-Heinemann.

5

Value drivers, portfolio assessment and planning ahead

INTRODUCTION

In this chapter we examine the various factors that create value for the organisation and its stakeholders and how these factors might be assessed. We also look at how future scenarios might be constructed that reflect where the organisation may be heading and examine ways and means of discerning the impact this will have on strategies that are adopted to create value for stakeholders.

MONITORING VALUE DRIVERS

Innovation, quality, customer relations, management capabilities, alliances, technology, brand value, employee relations, environmental and community issues taken together are important value creation drivers in an organisation (Low, 2000). Monitoring and assessing these activities shows how well an organisation is performing and gives it important signals indicating where it needs to give attention to the manner in which it conducts business. Interest has developed in recent years, in both the public and private sectors, in how performance and can best be measured and reported to management for corrective action to be taken. This has led to the development of interest in *performance management*, which is a form of results-based management, measuring performance against goals.

The 'balanced scorecard' (Kaplan and Norton, 1996) has been adopted widely across the private sector and used for this purpose. There has also been a growth in the use of the balanced scorecard within the public sector. However, the public sector requires a somewhat modified approach (see, for example, Bourn, 2000) particularly, as Radnor and McGuire (2004) argue, its primary purpose is accountability to central government rather than the management of the drivers that deliver outcomes for all stakeholders. Below we will introduce the *balanced scorecard* and a more recent addition, the *public sector scorecard*. In addition we will review the potential use of portfolio models in the context of creating value for stakeholders.

The balanced scorecard

A balanced scorecard (see Figure 5.1) is a performance measurement technique that strikes a balance between financial and non-financial/operating measures, relating performance to rewards, and taking into account the multiplicity of stakeholder interests. The balanced scorecard examines the organisation from four perspectives:

- the learning and growth perspective,
- the business process perspective,

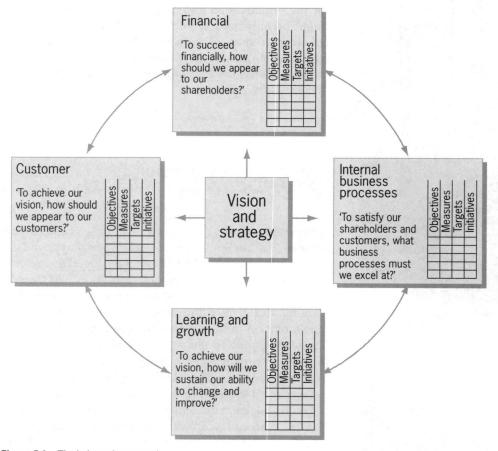

Figure 5.1   The balanced scorecard
Source: Kaplan, R. S., & Norton, D. P. (1996). Using the balanced scorecard as a strategic management system. Harvard Business Review, Jan–Feb, pp. 75–85, *Translating Vision & Strategy – Four Perspectives*. Reprinted with permission.

- the customer perspective, and
- the financial perspective.

Metrics need to be developed and data collected and analysed relative to each of these perspectives.

The balanced scorecard and measurement-based management

In taking measurements executives can get a clear picture of an organisation from different angles and hence make well-considered long-term decisions. Performance measures or indicators enable improvements to be identified. The indicators used are measurable characteristics of products, services, processes and operations that an organisation can observe and should reflect the factors that lead to improved customer, operational and financial performance.

The public sector scorecard

There is some evidence that the balanced scorecard has been used successfully in the public and voluntary sectors (e.g. Wisniewski and Dickson, 2001; Radnor and Lovell, 2003; Niven, 2003). However, problems associated with its use in the public sector have been identified. The financial perspective covers the prime performance criteria for commercial organisations well, but it does not apply satisfactorily to the public sector where performing well on the financial perspective is not the overriding purpose of the organisation.

An alternative approach for use in the public sector is reported in Moullin (2002, 2007) and its structure is illustrated in Figure 5.2.

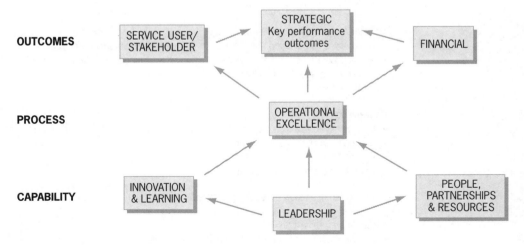

Figure 5.2 The public sector scorecard

Source: Moullin, M. (2007). *'The Public Sector Scorecard'*, Excellence One. European Foundation for Quality Management. Reprinted with permission.

This approach includes taking a strategic perspective, whereby the organisation's performance is examined against its main objectives and key performance targets. It also replaces the term 'customer' with the term 'service user/stakeholder'. In addition, the 'internal' perspective is renamed 'operational excellence' and the term 'growth' is omitted in the innovation and learning perspective. In this last respect, while the meaning of growth in the balanced scorecard is more than just growth in physical or monetary terms, it can be misleading since growth in terms of more service users may be something the organisation wishes to avoid.

SERVICE EXCELLENCE

Some measure or assessment of service quality needs to be incorporated into a public sector scorecard. Service excellence reflects providing services quickly, conveniently and without error. It also means doing so courteously through well-informed staff at an acceptable cost. In setting service quality standards attention should be given to customers' perceptions of the organisation's performance against these criteria and using objective measures of both technical effectiveness and personal interaction (see Figure 5.3).

Features of good service quality	Measure might include
Excellent staff • Speed and efficiency of the service • Expert knowledge of services and processing procedures • Politeness and friendliness of staff • Confidentiality of staff service	• Time queuing for service at counter • Counter transaction service time • Standard of employee behaviour
Efficient operations • Accuracy of information given out • Availability of full range of services • Efficient and effective handling of complaints	• Level of customer satisfaction • Number of customer complaints • Number of errors
Convenience • Convenience of branch location and parking • Minimum waiting time for service • Comfortable, tidy branch environment • Reliable and effective remote access service • Convenient methods of resolving problems	• Quality of the branch environment
Excellent image • Excellent overall corporate image and reputation	

Figure 5.3   Features and measures of good service quality

Customer Satisfaction Survey

Please tick the box to the left of the term that best describes your feelings about dealing with (your department):

1. All things considered, the experience of dealing with our department was:
❏ Delightful   ❏ Positive   ❏ Somewhat positive   ❏ Less than positive   ❏ Unpleasant   ❏ Terrible

2. Overall, was the service you receive from our department:
❏ Better than you expected   ❏ About what you expected
❏ Not quite what you expected   ❏ Not at all what you expected

Please comment: _____

How satisfied were you with

3. the speed and efficiency of the service?
❏ It was great   ❏ Good and solid   ❏ So so   ❏ Something of a let down   ❏ Very disappointing

4. the advice you received?
❏ It was great   ❏ Good and solid   ❏ So so   ❏ Something of a let down   ❏ Very disappointing

5. the processing procedures you experienced?
❏ It was great   ❏ Good and solid   ❏ So so   ❏ Something of a let down   ❏ Very disappointing

6. the politeness and friendliness of staff?
❏ It was great   ❏ Good and solid   ❏ So so   ❏ Something of a let down   ❏ Very disappointing

7. the confidentiality of the service?
❏ It was great   ❏ Good and solid   ❏ So so   ❏ Something of a let down   ❏ Very disappointing

8. the accuracy of the information received?
❏ It was great   ❏ Good and solid   ❏ So so   ❏ Something of a let down   ❏ Very disappointing

9. how we deal with complaints?
❏ It was great   ❏ Good and solid   ❏ So so   ❏ Something of a let down   ❏ Very disappointing

10. where we are located?
❏ It was great   ❏ Good and solid   ❏ So so   ❏ Something of a let down   ❏ Very disappointing

11. the time you have to wait for service?
❏ It was great   ❏ Good and solid   ❏ So so   ❏ Something of a let down   ❏ Very disappointing

12. the surroundings in which you are served?
❏ It was great   ❏ Good and solid   ❏ So so   ❏ Something of a let down   ❏ Very disappointing

13. the service over the telephone or internet?
❏ It was great   ❏ Good and solid   ❏ So so   ❏ Something of a let down   ❏ Very disappointing

14. how we resolve problems?
❏ It was great   ❏ Good and solid   ❏ So so   ❏ Something of a let down   ❏ Very disappointing

15. our corporate image/reputation?
❏ It was great   ❏ Good and solid   ❏ So so   ❏ Something of a let down   ❏ Very disappointing

16. the overall service your received from our department?
❏ I love it!   ❏ I'm pleased   ❏ So so   ❏ I'm disappointed   ❏ I thought it was awful

17. Compared to all other organisations with which you have dealings, our department is:
❏ Very much better to deal with   ❏ Somewhat better to deal with
❏ Somewhat worse to deal with   ❏ Much worse to deal with

Please comment: _____

How could our department improve its services to provide you with greater value?
_____
_____
_____

Figure 5.4 Customer satisfaction survey

A customer satisfaction survey might be conducted on a regular basis to assess customer perceptions of the level of service provided. This could amount to say 10 interviews per month being conducted at various customer contact points via face-to-face interviews using a structured questionnaire in order to elicit the desired information. One might also use a 'mystery' shopper who would visit a sample of locations on a regular basis and who would self-complete the questionnaire to provide an alternative viewpoint.

Times relating to queuing and service counter transaction time, etc. could be measured or monitored on a continual basis with weekly reports issued. Errors and complaints could be logged and monthly trends monitored. An example of a customer satisfaction survey questionnaire is shown in Figure 5.4.

SERVICE QUALITY MEASUREMENT

The SERVQUAL instrument

Parasuraman, *et al*. (1991) devised a 'SERVQUAL' instrument that measured the quality of service provision. In effect it identified a number of gaps that could result in ineffectual service provision:

- *The gap between management perception and customer expectations,* which means that management does not appreciate the needs of customers.
- *The gap between service quality specifications and management perception,* which means that management does not set standards of performance.
- *The gap between service quality specifications and the delivery of service,* which means that operational personnel may be inadequately trained to meet the standards expected.
- *The gap between service delivery and external communications* where the expectations from promotional activity are not matched in practice.
- *The gap between perceived service and expected service* where customers envisage a better service than the one that has been provided.

There seems little doubt that in the past decade SERVQUAL has proved to be the most popular instrument for measuring service quality. It aims to measure perceptions of service across the five service quality dimensions identified by Parasuraman *et al*. (1991):

- tangibles,
- reliability,
- responsiveness,
- assurance, and
- empathy.

The instrument consists of two sets of 22 statements. The first set aims to determine a customer's expectations of a service firm: for example, 'they should have up-to-date equipment'. The second set seeks to ascertain the customer's perceptions of the organisation's performance: for example, 'XYZ has up-to-date equipment'. The respondent is asked to rate their expectations and perceptions of performance on a seven-point Likert scale ranging from 1 (strongly disagree) to 7 (strongly agree). The results of the survey are then used to identify positive and negative gaps in the organisation's performance on the five service quality dimensions. The gap between expectations and performance perceptions (perceived service quality) is measured by the difference between the two scores (performance minus expectations). A more recent version of the instrument includes a third section that measures the relative importance of the five dimensions to the customer. These scores are then used to weight the perceived service quality measure for each dimension, the main purpose being to give a more accurate overall perceived service quality score.

Other approaches

There are also a number of marketing research techniques that can be used to measure comparative performance including 'mystery shopping' whereby purchases are made anonymously in chosen service outlets to ascertain whether or not what happens in practice matches up to that which is planned and expected. A number of criteria are investigated by 'mystery shoppers' including the way the customer is met and greeted, how long they were kept waiting before they were seated and how the ordering process is conducted. It even investigates matters such as the number of staff on duty and the condition of toilet facilities.

Yet another method is to employ regular customer feedback measures whereby service provision is measured anonymously against those of competitors through an independent marketing research agency. This method measures criteria such as how complaints are dealt with, how responsive the company is to the needs of customers and how the company's service matches up to those of competitors.

PORTFOLIO MODELS

Another useful way of assessing the value of the organisation in terms of the services it offers to its stakeholders is to be found in the use of portfolio models. Here we will look at two such models, the Boston Consultancy Matrix and the Directional Policy Matrix. The former is more useful where partnerships or ventures with profit-making organisations are concerned and the profit motive is present.

Portfolio analysis considers the attractiveness of the market and the ability of the business to operate competitively within the market.

The Boston Consultancy Matrix

The Boston approach maps products or services onto a two-dimensional matrix (Henderson, 1970). The method apples equally well to services or any form of strategic business unit. According to the Boston Consulting Group, the two most significant factors which govern the long-term profitability of a product are the rate of growth of its market and the share of the market that the product has relative to its largest competitor. The Boston Consulting Group presented the model in the form of a simple two-dimensional matrix. The two axes of the matrix are relative market share and market growth rate.

The relative market share of a product is assessed with respect to the market share of its largest competitor. The cut off between the high and low market share was originally judged to be equality with the leading competitor, and in the case of market growth rate was originally put at 10% per annum. Both these dividing points were subsequently revised and the matrix was defined less mechanistically.

The strength or limitations of a product are interpreted by its position in the matrix (see Figure 5.5). Products falling into the high growth, high market share quadrant are termed 'stars': they are tomorrow's cash earners. Being high market share businesses, they will be highly profitable and generate a lot of cash, but at the same time their high growth will also mean that they will require a lot of cash both to finance working capital and to build capacity. Thus, though profitable, stars might have either positive or negative net cash flow.

Products positioned in the low growth, high market share quadrant are designated 'cash cows'. These are the real cash generators, being profitable as a result of

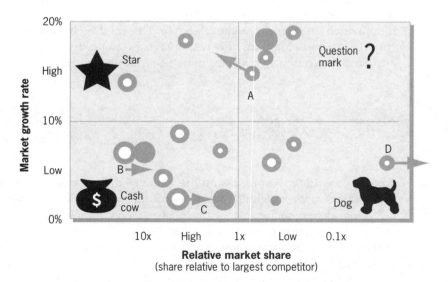

Figure 5.5   Boston Consulting Group growth-share matrix
Source: Boston Consulting Group. From '*The Product Portfolio*' (1970). The Star, the Dog, the Cow and the Question Mark – The Growth Share Matrix.

their high relative market share. It is quite likely that they will also create surplus cash not required to finance growth.

Products falling into low growth, low relative market share quadrant are designated 'dogs'. These are inherently unprofitable and seem to possess no future, though their cash requirements are low.

Products in the high growth, low market share segment have been referred to as 'wild cats', 'problem children' or simply '?'. They are unprofitable as a result of their low market share and consume a lot of cash merely to maintain their market position because of the high growth rate of the market.

The overall strategy is defined simply with regard to the management of cash flows in order to achieve a balanced portfolio over time. Cash is obtained from cash cows and invested in stars to convert them into tomorrow's cash cows. Dogs are divested and problem children (or ?s) are either converted into stars or liquidated. In this way a balanced portfolio should be achieved with an adequate succession of stars ready to take over from today's cash generators, the cash cows.

When drawing growth-share analyses a number of matrices should be drawn. In the first place growth-share matrices should be shown for the various stages of the planning cycle, for example now, in one year's time, two years' time, five years' time, etc. In this way an organisation can track the projected progress over the planning horizon. It is also customary to circle the points on the matrix, as shown in Figure 5.5. The size of circles should reflect the size of sales or profits for a particular product, product line or business unit. In addition to showing information about a specific organisation on the matrix it is also beneficial to show those of competitors on the same matrix.

Matrices should not be too overcrowded with information or else they will be difficult to read. Business units, products or product lines shown on a matrix should also be comparable with one another. For example a vehicle manufacturer might have three types of matrix – cars, vans and buses. One matrix might show a range of cars, another a range of buses, while the third might show a range of vans. It would also be permissible to have a matrix showing the three broad categories of buses, cars and vans in aggregate form.

While the matrix is intuitively appealing, it has important shortcomings which limit its value as an analytical tool.

The Boston Consulting Group's original work from which the matrix resulted was founded on an analysis of 24 different commodities. While this work has been replicated many times with other commodities it has not been replicated with differentiated or branded products. Its empirical foundations depend entirely on an analysis of commodity products selling at market prices, while the substance of marketing is concerned with differentiating products for customers prepared to pay higher than base prices to satisfy their particular needs and wants.

The model is based on an implicit assumption that costs fall with experience and that the business that gains the most experience will have the lowest costs. In a young and rapidly growing market, experience is rapidly acquired, thus increasing the benefits of cost reduction and making it attractive to have a large market share. However, in low growth, mature markets the cost benefits accruing from experience are low and the benefits from increasing market share in order to gain cost advantages are small. The experience curve should not therefore suggest continuous cost reductions but reductions during the growth phase, with cost increases occurring during the maturity stage.

A firm's relative market share was measured as share relative to its largest competitor and the division between high and low relative shares was therefore set at unity. Thus in any industry there could only be one business with a high relative market share. Where industries are experiencing low growth, all but one competitor would fall into the low growth–low share dog quadrant for which Boston's prescription was simply to divest the business.

The Boston model has, of course, been widely criticised by strategists and marketers alike. Strategists have objected to the fundamental proposition that the strategic success of a business could be determined by just two quantifiable factors – market growth rate and market share. This seems too simplistic and could only be true if it was assumed that management itself could not make a difference.

The Directional Policy Matrix

Rather than using single measures of success, i.e. market growth rate and relative market share, the Directional Policy Matrix (DPM) uses a multivariate approach where market growth rate is replaced by market attractiveness and relative market share by competitive strength. Market attractiveness and competitive strength are critical success factors (CSFs). The content of each of these sets of CSFs depends entirely upon the organisaton and the competitive environment.

Market attractiveness

Market attractiveness should be measured in terms of the few key elements you must get right in order to succeed. Some possible factors are:

- market – market size, market growth rate, cyclicality, seasonality, power of sellers and buyers, distributors, price sensitivity;
- competition – number of competitors, type and power of competitors, ease of market entry, risk of product substitution, market share, image in market, possibility of new technology, volatility;
- technological – sophistication of technology, patents, copyrights, maturity;
- economic – financial strength and barriers, economies of scale, capacity utilisation;
- socio-political – social values, attitudes and trends, laws, etc.

Competitive strength

Competitive strength should also be measured in terms of the few key elements you must get right in order to succeed and should enable a comparison to be made of your company relative to your major competitors. Some possible factors are:

- market – market share, company and market image, distribution channels;
- product – pricing policy, product range, reputation for product reliability and quality standards, breadth of product line;

- capability – managerial competence, design capability, ability to respond to changing circumstances, manufacturing strength, R&D, capital strength and finances;
- customer relations – service levels, sales force coverage.

Selecting the competitive critical success factors involves collective effort from key managers and executives in group meetings. Each factor is assigned a range and given a score, from 0 to 10, relative to a firm's major competitors. Weightings are assigned to factors to measure their relative importance, and the total combined score results in the market attractiveness or competitive strength score, which provides the two coordinates for the matrix plot – see Figure 5.6.

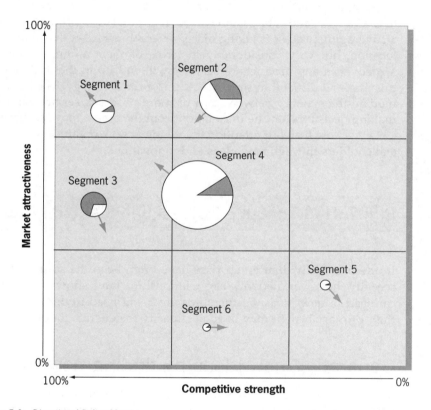

Figure 5.6 Directional Policy Matrix
Source: Market Modelling Limited. **www.market-modelling.co.uk**. Reprinted with permission.

Interpreting the plotted scores on the matrix depends on which of the nine boxes a product or service falls into on the grid.

Ideally we would like products or services that score highly with regard to competitive strength and are strong in terms of market attractiveness. Where market attractiveness is high but competitive strength is weak it may be the best strategy to have someone else offer the service altogether since the organisation cannot take full advantage of the situation.

Comments on portfolio model usage

The directional policy model seems to offer more to public sector organisations than the Boston Matrix. This is because it does not rely on income-related measures for assessing the health of the various services on offer. Indeed there is sufficient flexibility in the approach to use whatever measures appear to be most appropriate.

Portfolio models are easy to use and the benefit of using such models is to gain some idea of the profile of strong/weak products or services in the mix. They may, however, cause an organisation to put too much stress on market-share growth and entry into high-growth businesses. They may also cause firms to pay insufficient attention to managing the current business.

Another problem is that the results produced by using the models are responsive to the weights and ratings and can be manipulated to produce desired results. Since an averaging process is taking place, several businesses may end up in the same cell location, but vary considerably in terms of their ratings against specific factors. Moreover, many products or services will end up in the middle of the matrix and this makes it difficult to suggest an appropriate strategy. The models do not accommodate the synergy between two or more products/services and this suggest that making decisions for one in isolation from the others may be short-sighted.

Let us now turn our attention to looking at how organisations can create value for stakeholders through new ideas and innovation.

INNOVATING THROUGH PARTNERSHIPS AND NETWORKS

In the past individual enterprises have often been the source of innovation. More recently, however, network-like relationships have shown that knowledge sharing can lead to new ideas. Partnerships are being used to deliver services yet perhaps their primary benefit may be their capacity to generate innovation.

Generating new ideas by finding new market spaces

Some successful innovations in the private sector are concerned with establishing a new 'market space' for which there are no direct competitors. For the public sector, the interest in identifying new market spaces is, first, in providing new ways of securing up-take of services, especially to 'hard to reach groups'. Second, identification provides a way of considering whether some aspects of public provision should be improved, reduced, changed or abandoned. Such a process could lead to radical innovation in services if pursued systematically. Nevertheless, there could well be disincentives for doing this since meeting new market spaces may disrupt existing comfortable relationships and cultures. It would be useful to consider how this problem might be tackled.

The essence of such an approach might be that, by understanding customer needs better, a new product or service can be developed which is not simply better or cheaper than existing products or services but is radically different (a 'new value curve'). Marketing research tools can be used to find such ideas.

Focus groups can give the client firm ideas for new services. A gap in the market may be identified and further research can then seek to identify the true size or potential gap in the market. If several focus groups should come up with the same idea it may well be worth serious consideration, even though it may have been considered before and rejected. Focus groups can indicate the likelihood of success with a new service. It would be possible, for example, to test the concept of a new service for the current market by seeking answers to questions such as:

- What would be its advantages?
  - How does the idea compare with other alternatives?
  - What is the reaction of the group to various service features?
  - What does the group think about the service's performance capabilities?

However, novel ideas may not come from market research. Customers can only give retrospective responses about their experiences with services. Research cannot design a new service, but it can act as a catalyst and indicate the direction the innovation should take. However, one of the biggest problems in using discussion group feedback is interpreting exactly what customers mean. Consumers can provide ideas for service improvements and even occasionally identify a new service opportunity in the marketplace. Focus group research may be used to generate service ideas, as it reflects the nature of unsatisfied consumer wants. Through focus group discussion, shortcomings of existing services can be identified as well as desirable new service features.

DIFFUSION OF INNOVATION MANAGEMENT

In recent years, the primary formal model of diffusion in the public sector has been authoritative and process-based (e.g. Best Value, Beacon Councils). In the past, informal processes of diffusion in the public sector have worked well. However, the pace of technological and organisational change is now so great that even the early adopters find it hard to keep up with innovation. In addition, although innovation is encouraged in the public sector, risks are also capped and this shapes the patterns of diffusion. Barriers to diffusion may often exist where services are delivered through partnerships involving public, private and voluntary organisations. These involve the lack of a shared language, few shared timeframes, problems of managing and sharing risk, and overcoming conflicts of interest.

LOOKING INTO THE FUTURE

As a result of innovative thinking new services will have to be evaluated and resources made available or altered to ensure their success if they are implemented. To do this one has to look at the effect of various factors that impinge on the ability to offer both new services and present ones. A starting point for this is PESTLE analysis.

PESTLE analysis is a way of examining how different *external* factors affect an organisation. These factors are:

- P – Political: The current and potential influences from political pressures.
- E – Economic: the local, national and world economy impact.
- S – Sociological: the ways in which changes in society affect us.
- T – Technological: how new and emerging technology affects our business.
- L – Legal: how local, national and world legislation affects us.
- E – Environmental: the local, national and world environmental issues.

These factors are continuously changing so the analysis should include a thorough exploration of what is affecting the organisation at present and what is likely to affect it in future. Such an analysis usually produces a list of positive and negative factors that are likely to affect an organisation. In order to contemplate the likely effects of these six factors they need to be *applied* to the whole of the organisation, or to specific areas, or to specific parts of areas. Such areas could include:

- customers
- technology
- the industry/marketplace
- intermediaries
- competitors
- other stakeholders.

Following PESTLE analysis, an organisation is unlikely to make any clear decision on action until it has also analysed its internal strengths and weaknesses. Internal areas for analysis would typically include:

- resources (assets),
- size and structure,
- culture and style,
- relationship with employees,
- corporate image,
- skills,
- track record,
- rewards,
- leadership.

But we cannot stop here because we need to focus on the impact that these environments can have on the enterprise in the future. A simple tool that can aid this process is cross impact analysis.

CROSS IMPACT ANALYSIS

Cross impact analysis is a technique that helps in examining the impact that a mixture of external threats and opportunities can have on the undertakings of an organisation. The procedure involves assessing the impact that changes or trends in

| | Customers/stakeholders | | |
	Existing	New	Total
Pestle			
Political	+2	−3	−1
Economic	+1	−1	0
Sociological	−2	0	−2
Technological	+1	−1	0
Legal	+1	−2	−1
Environmental	+1	+1	+2
Internal factors			
Resources (assets)	−1	+2	+1
Size and structure	−2	+1	−1
Culture and style	0	−1	−1
Relationship with employees	−1	+1	0
Corporate image	+1	−1	0
Skills	+1	+3	+4
Track record	−1	+4	+3
Rewards	+1	+2	+3
Leadership	0	−1	−1
Total	+2	+4	+6

Figure 5.7 Cross impact matrix

these factors are likely to have on present and proposed undertakings of the organisation. Anything that threatens the prosperity of the organisation is viewed as having a negative effect on the establishment while opportunities are reasoned to have positive effects.

The various impacts are recorded on a grid and on a scale ranging from +4 to −4, where 0 specifies a lack of impact (see Figure 5.7). The sum of various extraneous threats and opportunities on each one of the identified business/organisational activities is then noted. In addition the total scores of opportunities and threats facing each activity of the organisation are recorded. All ratings are a matter of the subjective opinions of executives.

Armed with this analysis we are then in a position to do a more in-depth analysis that explores where the organisation is heading in the future and how it can best develop to create value for its stakeholders. The cross impact analysis will provide signposting for the next part of the analysis.

PREDICTING WHERE THE ORGANISATION IS HEADING

The techniques of scenario writing and scenario day dreaming can be used to provide data that is a useful indicator of where the organisation is heading. The techniques are similar to those of the Delphi method. So, first let us look at this method. The key characteristics of Delphi are anonymity, iteration, controlled feedback and aggregation of group responses. The objective is to obtain the most reliable consensus of opinion via a series of intensive questionnaires, interspersed with controlled opinion feedback usually in the form of scenarios (Hoghton and Streatfeild, 1971). Scenarios are hypothetical sequences of events constructed for the purpose of focusing attention on causal processes and decision points (Kahn and Wiener, 1967).

Scenario writing

Scenario writing is a method of looking ahead and forces an organisation to be receptive to the need for change and creative thinking. It is an experience which involves considering new possibilities and opening up one's mind to consider what might happen.

The method involves all members of a team of co-workers and requires a leader or facilitator who introduces and coordinates sessions and who has the responsibility for producing a final report. Members of the team are referred to as scenario writers and each member is usually an expert in their field. It is important to ensure that there are experts in the group whose expertise is relevant to the problem under study. At the start of the exercise the scenario writers are briefed with the task of considering the developments in their area of expertise over the next 5–10 years. When they have done this individually they are brought together under the guidance of a leader to examine the situation collectively. Participants need to be reminded that they should be tolerant of the views of others because a consensus of informed opinion has to be reached.

The procedure adopted is as follows:

- Briefing – here the scenario writers are requested to consider what developments will take place in their area of specialisation over the next 5–10 years. They are also asked to provide supporting evidence for this and to assess the likely impact of these developments on the organisation (see the cross-impact matrix on p. 81).
- Individual scenario writing – scenario writers spend up to two weeks preparing their individual scenarios independently.
- Collective scenario writing – here the scenario writers meet up to present their individual papers and viewpoints and to reach a consensus viewpoint on possible developments. The output of the meeting is usually the report.

Scenario writing can be extremely useful and productive where the situation under review is a very complex one; it is, however, extremely time consuming. An alternative approach is scenario day dreaming.

Scenario day dreaming

Like scenario writing this method also looks into the future and tries to assess the impact that trends will have on the organisation. It is, however, less formal in its approach and it is not the custom and practice to produce a report. It is usual for the entire process to take up only a couple of days and is an ideal activity for an 'away day' venue, provided there are at least two away days available.

Scenario day dreamers are not expected to substantiate their contributions. The purpose is to stimulate people's imaginations to think in the broader context and to consider more unusual ideas. A good group size is 8–10 people, but of course much depends on the size of the organisation and the complexity of its business. Again there is a leader or facilitator whose role it is to plan the sessions in detail, advise on the selection of participants, brief the participants about the sessions, lead the sessions and help summarise the conclusions that are reached. Minutes of the session also need to be taken by someone.

Questions

1   Evaluate the usefulness of the public sector scorecard to a public sector organisation of which you have knowledge.

2   Compare and contrast the Directional Policy Matrix with the Boston Consultancy Matrix. Do you believe that there are opportunities for applying either of these matrices in a public sector organisation of which you have first-hand knowledge. Explain.

3   Forecasting and planning are key activities in examining how an organisation will develop. Suggest how scenario writing might be used to good effect in developing plans for a new city centre leisure complex to be developed in partnership between a city council and a number of private partnership organisations.

Case study 5.1   Intermediate care in the Shire

In 1997, the Audit Commission produced *The Coming of Age* report, which identified that pressures on hospital beds were increasing and people were being discharged earlier than in the past. However, limited rehabilitation services existed to which older people might be discharged earlier and consequently many of them were unable to return home. These people were being admitted to residential or nursing home care. Many of these people improved after a few weeks in care, but had to accept that they would remain in long-term care. In many cases they had given up their homes which meant that large proportions of Social Services budgets were tied up in residential provision to the detriment of developing preventative services. When a health crisis occurred the only option in the case of older people was to admit them to hospital and this in turn increased the pressure on hospital beds.

Intermediate care was developed to promote independence for older people by developing a range of integrated health and social care services that are intended to: promote faster recovery from illness; prevent unnecessary admission to an acute hospital bed; support timely discharge; reduce avoidable use of long-term residential or nursing home care; and support carers in their caring role, enabling them to promote the independence of their relatives.

Intermediate care, unlike traditional rehabilitation, is time-limited and it is not delivered in an acute hospital bed but where the person's needs are best met. This could include the person's own home, dedicated care homes, housing schemes, day centres and non-acute hospitals. It is not condition specific, and the outcome is pre-defined, with the expectation of a return home.

Intermediate care services in the Shire include a team comprising social workers, occupational therapists and physiotherapists who provide an assessment and treatment service to everyone admitted to the residential and nursing home units. There are also two residential units that mainly admit people from hospital who are not able to return home and do not require nursing care on site. These units also take people from the community who require assessment and re-enablement, including therapy treatment, in order to remain in their own home in the longer term. In addition, there is a day centre attached to one of the residential units that admits people for up to 12 weeks, and provides assessment and rehabilitation. It caters for people discharged from the residential units who require further rehabilitation, and for people who are having severe difficulty in coping in their own homes.

Contracts are in place with three separate nursing homes to provide intermediate care beds. People admitted to these establishments have less significant needs than those admitted to the ward-based services. However, they do require on-site nursing care, which cannot be met by the residential units.

A Rapid Response Team made up of home care staff is also in place. This provides a home care service with a rehabilitative focus to people who are discharged from hospital or who may be identified from an emergency situation in the community.

Intermediate care services are hesitant to offer their expertise to older people with dementia or a mental illness. Such people are often delayed longer in hospital because acute hospital staff do not necessarily have the expertise to provide appropriate mental health care. In addition they are also unaware of the resources available to eliminate risk factors in the person's home environment.

Question

1 One big question faced by the organisation at present relates to forward planning and assessing future demands for the service and what provisions will be required. Evaluate the situation and recommend what steps you think are necessary to set up a logical and efficient method of dealing with this problem.

Case study 5.2	The counselling service

Sidchester counselling service is a joint venture financed by the university and the university hospital. It provides counselling services to a wide variety of people ranging from university students, university staff, hospital staff of all grades, people working for the fire service, ambulance service and police, who may require counselling following traumatic incidents involving fatalities and horrific injuries.

The counselling service recognises the need to keep abreast of all new developments in its field and since it based within a university environment it acknowledges that developing an academic profile to its work would certainly be beneficial both to the service itself and to the university as a whole.

Traditionally staff work a 9–5 day and spend their time at work in counselling activities with clients rather than undertaking any academic research activity which is now perceived as a main objective.

Questions

1 What would be the best way forward in this instance in order to achieve the stated objective?
2 What demands and requests might be made of senior management in order to achieve the objective?
3 How should the service state its case to management?

References

Bourn, J. (2000), 'Improving Public Services', *International Journal of Government Auditing*, Vol. 27, pp. 1–2, 4.

Henderson, B. D. (1970), 'The product portfolio', The Boston Consulting Group, Perspectives No. 66, Boston, Massachusetts.

Hoghton, C., Page, W. and Streatfeild, G. (1971), '. . . and now the future: A PEP Survey of Futures Studies', Volume XXXVII, Broadsheet 529, August.

Kahn, H. and Wiener, A. J. (1967), *The Year 2000,* London: Macmillan.

Kaplan, R. S. and Norton, D. P. (1996), 'Using the Balanced Scorecard as a Strategic Management System', *Harvard Business Review*, January–February, pp. 75–85.

Low, J. (2000), 'The value creation index', *Journal of Intellectual Capital*, Vol. 1, No. 3, pp. 252–262.

Moullin, M. (2002), *Delivering Excellence in Health and Social Care*, Buckingham: Open University Press.

Moullin, M. (2007), *The Public Sector Scorecard – an integrated service improvement and performance measurement framework based on the balanced scorecard*. Excellence One; European Foundation for Quality Management. www.efqm.org, April 2007.

Niven, P. (2003), 'Balanced Scorecard Step-by-Step for Government and Non-Profit Agencies', Hoboken, New Jersey: John Wiley and Sons.

Parasuraman, A., Berry, L. L. and Zeithaml, V. A. (1991), 'Understanding customer expectations of service', *Sloan Management Review*, Spring, pp. 39–48.

Radnor, Z. and Lovell, B. (2003), 'Success factors for implementation of the Balanced Scorecard in a NHS multi-agency setting', *International Journal of Health Care Quality Assurance*, Vol. 16, No.2, pp. 99–108.

Radnor, Z. and McGuire, M. (2004), 'Performance management in the public sector: fact or fiction?', *International Journal of Productivity and Performance Management*, Vol. 53, No. 3, pp 245–260.

Wisniewski, M. and Dickson, A. (2001), 'Measuring performance in Dumfries and Galloway Constabulary with the Balanced Scorecard', *Journal of the Operational Research Society,* Vol. 52, No. 10, pp. 1057–1066.

Further reading

Berry, L. and Parasuraman, A. (1991), *Marketing Services,* New York: The Free Press.

Niven, P. (2003), 'Balanced Scorecard Step-by-Step for Government and Non-Profit Agencies', Hoboken, New Jersey: John Wiley and Sons.

Proctor, T. (2000), *Strategic Marketing*, London: Routledge.

Ward, P., Davies, B. J. and Wright, H. (1999), 'The Diffusion of Interactive Technology at the Customer Interface', *International Journal of Technology Management*, Vol. 17, Nos 1/2, 84–108.

6 Marketing research

INTRODUCTION

Marketing research connects the customer, other stakeholders and the public to the organisation through the medium of information. This information is used to distinguish and define marketing opportunities and threats or problems. It is also used to create, improve and assess marketing actions and to monitor marketing performance, helping to improve understanding of marketing as a process. Marketing research identifies the information required to address these issues. It comprises methods for collecting data, analysis of the data collected and its interpretation, and communication of the findings and their implications. It takes account of experience, the present situation and the likely future so that marketing executives can make sound decisions. Marketing research can help in a variety of studies and makes use of both primary and secondary data sources. It can be conducted either in-house by an organisation's own staff or by external specialist marketing research companies. Such exernal companies or agencies offer a wide range of services, ranging from off-the-peg studies to tailor-made studies to meet the needs of individual clients.

TYPES OF DATA THAT CAN BE COLLECTED

Those involved in marketing need to become familiar with people's perceptions, values, attitudes, beliefs, the way they learn and their needs and wants. With this information, they can influence customers' behaviour as service users or as members of society. They must also know how social, personal and psychological factors can influence behaviour so that they can make use of this information to good effect in the marketing of services and other societal messages.

DECIDING WHO SHOULD DO THE RESEARCH

It is possible that an organisation's own research staff alone may undertake research or it may be given to an outside agency to perform, or some combination of both of these options. Where both an outside agency and internal personnel undertake research on the same problem, consultation between the two parties is essential. Handing over a complex study completely to an outside organisation can be fraught with problems. On the other hand, allowing internal personnel to have too much of an input may prevent new and useful insights emerging. The research proposal should identify who should do what.

RESEARCH SOURCES

Outside research organisations specialise in one or more forms of research assistance and relatively few organisations can offer all methods with equal expertise. The specialised research assistance that can be given is as follows:

- mail surveys,
- personal interview studies,
- telephone studies,
- panels,
- omnibus studies,
- focus groups.

Specialisation in overall marketing measurements might include the following:

- test marketing,
- controlled test marketing,
- simulated test marketing.

There are also research organisations that specialise in the problems of market segmentation, customer/prospect databases, advertising media studies and audience studies.

USING THE INTERNET FOR MARKETING RESEARCH

The Internet has considerable potential as a tool for marketing research. Primary marketing research becomes much less expensive to conduct via the Internet than by using traditional media. Such research can, however, only really be exploratory. In using the Internet for collecting data and information the scope of the sampling frame is restricted to those members of the internet community who agree to respond. It has to be borne in mind that the demographics of users of the Internet are different from the general population. Results from internet marketing research should not usually be generalised to the entire population. However, as more and more households gain Internet access this is a problem which may resolve itself in due course.

Web page self-completion forms facilitate the assessing of attitudes, wants and values of an organisation's customers and stakeholders. For example, an organisation might use a self-completion form to learn about its customers' demographics and service preferences. Such data might then be employed as a basis for segmenting its market.

The Internet might be used during service development. A company can quickly assess globally customers' thoughts about service changes or new services before any research and development investments are made. In the same way, organisations can gain much information through monitoring discussion groups made up of members of the organisation's customer/stakeholder base. Executives can use this information not only to learn about the perceived strengths and weaknesses of their own services, but those of their competitors as well.

DATA COLLECTION

When conducting research we have to decide from whom to collect data and what is the most appropriate way of collecting data. The first of these decisions usually involves drawing a sample of potential respondents, though if the population of interest is sufficiently small then everyone in the population may be included. Choosing an appropriate data collection method depends on the nature of the problem being researched. Where the data required is quantitative in nature the surveys making use of questionnaires that are administered on large samples will tend to be most appropriate. Where essentially qualitative data is required then in-depth interviews and focus group interviews are more appropriate. In either case, however, sampling is important and we will examine this aspect but first, however, we will consider the population from which the sample is drawn.

DEFINITION OF THE POPULATION

The population is the total group to be studied, the target population (sometimes referred to as the universe). It is the grand total of what is being measured: people, stores, homes or whatever. But since most samples in marketing research are of people, homes or stores, the term population, as we use it here, typically refers to one of these. If the purpose of the study has been well-defined, the population is also well-delineated. This is crucial if the study is to be significant and practical for the guidance of marketing management.

SAMPLING

Unless a sample is chosen by a random mechanism, the results that are obtained from a study are likely to be biased in some direction. It is for this reason that methods of *random sampling* have been devised. A random sample can be chosen, for example, by throwing dice. Most commonly, however, when a list of names exists from which a sample can be chosen, the actual technique is to use random numbers generated by a computer. The list is numbered and the computer provides a string of numbers from this list in such a way that various batches of entries in the list have an equal chance of being drawn.

Suppose that a market survey is being taken. A sample group is chosen from the population in the above manner, and the individuals who make up the sample are then interviewed. For example, an individual may be asked about washing powder brand choice. The arithmetic mean of the total answers provided by the individuals yields the proportion preferring one brand or the other. Any statistical population asked this question will also have an average response to it. The responses of the individuals in the population vary about this average response. The variability of the response is described by a quantity called the *population variance*. The arithmetic mean varies from one sample to the next, but it varies about the average response. In addition, the bigger the sample relative to the population size, the more accurate is the estimate determined by sampling.

Some situations permit the population to be split into a few very homogenous groups or strata. The sample may then consist of a random sample taken within each stratum. Such a sample is called a *stratified random sample*.

Thus far we have assumed that a list, or sampling frame, is available. This is not true, however, in all cases. For example, no list exists of the pony population of Dartmoor. Thus the important topic of estimating the size of some populations must be handled differently. Areas are usually chosen at random.

KEY ELEMENTS INVOLVED IN DEVISING A SAMPLING PLAN

Usually, large populations are encountered in marketing research and it is impractical or too expensive to contact all the members. In such cases we have to take a sample from the population – but we must ensure that the sample we choose represents the population as a whole.

There are three decisions to be taken in drawing up a sampling plan:

- Who is to be surveyed? This defines the target population. Once this has been done the next step is to develop a sampling frame: that is a way of giving everyone in the target population a known chance of inclusion in the sample.
- How many people/companies should be surveyed? Large samples give better results than smaller ones. However, samples of less than 1% of a population can often provide good, reliable information provided that the sampling procedure is creditable.
- How should the respondents be chosen? Probability samples allow the calculation of confidence limits for sampling error. Thus in taking probability samples we can attach probabilities to any point estimates that are made. Cost and time often make it impractical to collect data through probability samples. Researchers often use non-probability samples – particularly quota samples. Strictly speaking, sampling errors cannot be measured in such cases.

IMPORTANCE OF PROPERLY DEFINING THE TARGET POPULATION OF INTEREST

A sample should reflect the characteristics of the population of interest to the study – that is, the target population. It is essential to define the target population precisely since failure to do so is likely to lead to the ineffective solving of a research problem.

THE SAMPLING FRAME

Obtaining a sample involves selecting some elements from the target population. In order to do this, it is assumed that it is possible to identify the target population of interest. A *sampling frame* is simply a list that identifies the target population. It can be a list of names and telephone numbers, as in telephone surveys, an area map of housing or a list of addresses purchased from a mailing list supplier. It could also be a database. The frame defines the *sampling unit*, the unit used in the design of the sample. The frame, and therefore the sampling unit, may take the form of households, students, retail stores of a particular defined type (nature and size, for instance), businesses or transactions.

Although lists or other geographic breakdowns can be found, the list rarely matches the target population exactly. For instance, a list of residents of a given district naturally does not include new arrivals or households living in dwellings built since the list was compiled. Lists are rarely up-to-date and often contain duplication, such as households with more than one telephone number or individuals whose names appear on two or more lists (Semon, 1994).

No sampling frame is perfect. For example, the listing in a telephone book omits unlisted numbers and is outdated on the day of publication because of moves in and out of the area it covers (for implications, see McKenzie, 1988). Good research planning requires knowledge of the shortcomings of the sampling frame in order to make adjustments in the sampling design. The sampling frame or list that is used defines what may be termed the *operational* or *working population*.

The difference between the operational population and the target population is usually referred to as the *sampling gap*. This gap appears in most marketing research studies and efforts should be applied to try to minimise the gap since its presence increases the potential for misleading results. This can sometimes be done by combining two or more lists, taking care to remove one set of names that appear on both lists.

Sometimes no sampling frame is available. As a rather extreme example, suppose that for some reason it is desirable to conduct a study of those who are overweight. No such list exists. But it is possible to use screening as a method of locating such people. A general frame of individuals can be used, and filter questions (with standards of overweight set up in advance) can be asked regarding age, height and weight to determine those who qualify.

SAMPLING METHODS

There are two major types of sampling methods: probability sampling and non-probability sampling.

Probability samples comprise samples in which the elements being included have a known chance of being selected. A probability sample enables sampling error to be estimated. This, in simple terms, is the difference between the sample value and the true value of the population being surveyed. A sampling error can be stated in mathematical terms: usually plus or minus a certain percentage. A larger sample usually implies a smaller sampling error.

Non-probability samples are ones in which participants are selected in a purposeful way. The selection may require certain percentages of the sample to be women or men, housewives under 30 or a similar criterion. This type of selection is an effort to reach a cross-section of the elements being sampled. However, because the sample is not rigorously chosen it is statistically impossible to state a true sampling error.

Today, most samples chosen for applied research are non-probability samples. If carefully done – with quotas, for example, of persons to be studied – the findings are usually valid. A true probability sample, because of the stringent requirements, is likely to be far too expensive and too time-consuming for most uses.

The major problem with the quota method of sampling is that the interviewers are allowed discretion in choosing the individual respondents within the quota categories. This discretion introduces a possible source of bias, because the resulting sample can largely omit some types of people, such as those who are difficult to contact.

A much better approach is the probability method of sampling, in which specific respondents are chosen by random selection methods. The result of this method is that no type of individual is systematically omitted from the sample, and the likely amount of error in the resulting data can be calculated.

Statistical laws have established that no matter how large the population being studied (from a small city to a whole country), the size of the sample is the main factor that determines the expected range of error in a probability sample. Most current polls use samples ranging in size from 1,000 to 2,000 individuals. Many polling organisations have adopted probability methods in selecting their samples, but the less-reputable polls still use quota methods or even non-scientific haphazard methods of sample selection – and the quality of their findings suffers accordingly.

FORMS OF PROBABILITY SAMPLING

There are five forms of probability sampling:

- simple random,
- random walk,
- stratified random,
- cluster,
- systematic.

The following are illustrative of the kind of sampling approach that might be taken.

Simple random sample

In this case all members of the population have a known and equal chance of being included in the sample. For example, the names of every stakeholder in a given population could be written on to slips of paper and the slips deposited in a box. The box could then be shaken so that all the slips of paper become thoroughly mixed up. A blindfolded person drawing successive slips of paper from the box would be taking a random sample of the population.

Random walk sampling

This form of sampling is used extensively in market research as a cheap approximation to true random sampling. The sample involves conducting random walks in small areas. These areas are usually wards within constituencies. First, a random sample of constituencies is drawn from a list of constituencies and then within each of the randomly selected constituencies a random selection of wards is chosen. Next, selected random starting points within these areas (wards) are chosen and interviewers are given fixed routes to follow and instructions to obey. The instructions specify the interval of households to contact (e.g. every seventh house) and the action to take at each street junction (e.g. turn alternatively left or right). Special instructions are given about blocks of flats and what to do when non-residential buildings are encountered. Although the resulting sample is not truly random it is usually treated as if it were.

Stratified random sample

This approach is more suitable for sampling large consumer populations. It entails dividing the population into mutually exclusive groups and drawing random samples from each group. Random samples are then drawn from each of these groups. Again, however, there still remains the problem of obtaining suitable lists of people who make up the population and the various groups within it. Stratified sampling may be used in industrial marketing research where it is possible to identify a population of firms. A stratified sample is usually adopted to make sure that minority groups are adequately represented.

Cluster sample

In this case the universe and the frame are defined and classified into homogeneous segments. Random samples are then chosen from each segment. The method offers a sharpening of sampling, virtually guaranteeing that the use of these cells of units – done in two dimensions or more – will provide a cross-section of each.

Cluster sampling is a suitable approach to sampling large consumer populations. Here the population is divided into mutually exclusive groups and the researcher draws a sample of the groups to interview. This time we are not interested in a person's social class but in where they live or some other characteristic. Assuming that residence is the key factor and that the objective is to interview household heads, then the first step is to divide up the locality under study into individual areas of housing. A random or stratified sample of the areas identified is then taken and interviews are held with every household head within each sampled area.

This is a 'single stage' cluster sample since only a sample of the blocks or areas of housing is taken. A 'two stage' cluster sample might involve undertaking the same number of interviews, making sure that a large number of blocks are covered, but that only a sample of households in each block is interviewed. For example, if an area comprises three high-rise tower blocks of flats, we might randomly select one of the three blocks and interview all household heads within that block.

Systematic sampling

In the systematic sampling method, the sampling units are chosen from the sampling frame at a uniform interval at a specified rate. For example, we might use the residential telephone directory. Perhaps the book has 400 pages in it, with an average, after a check of perhaps ten widely dispersed pages, of 400 listings per page, for an estimated total of 160,000 listings (400 × 400). The particular study requires a list of 2,000 for sampling purposes. (For simplicity at this point, we forget the number of completions required.) This means that every 80th listing (160,000/2,000) should be drawn.

So that the method is a true probability method, where every sampling unit has an equal chance of coming into the sample, there also must be a random starting point. So if we are using every 80th listing, we must select a random starting number of between 1 and 79.

FORMS OF NON-PROBABILITY SAMPLING

There are three forms of non-probability sampling:

- quota sampling,
- convenience sampling,
- judgement sampling.

Quota sampling

In the case of quota sampling the researcher starts with the knowledge of how the universe is divided by strata. The investigators are instructed simply to fill the cells, so that the sample obtained is indeed representative in terms of the cells. The procedures used in quota sampling make the choice of respondents the responsibility of the interviewers. Unfortunately, this can lead to substantial bias which cannot be objectively measured. Wide use of quota sampling has been made in marketing research since it is relatively cost effective compared with other methods. However, with the development of random sampling techniques, researchers have become more critical of the drawbacks of this method. Properly applied the method can be successful because it is possible to introduce representativeness by stratifying the quota sample by objective and known population characteristics such as age, sex, family status and socioeconomic group.

Convenience sampling

In convenience sampling, there is no sample design. It is similar to an interviewer questioning people as they meet them on the street or in shopping precincts. Choice of the respondent is left entirely to the interviewer. Some methods, such as this, allow potential respondents to decide for themselves whether or not to respond.

The researcher takes the most accessible population members from which to obtain information. This happens, for example, when a firm producing a prototype new domestic appliance gets some of its employees to test out the product in their own homes. Such a sample provides useful information to the researcher as long as the sample seems to be reasonably representative of the population being studied. However, asking a convenience sample of students about their reading habits might not be appropriate if you are interested in the reading habits of the population as a whole, i.e. all ages and occupations.

Judgement sampling

This type of sampling relies on sound judgement or expertise. It depends on selecting elements that are believed to be typical or representative of the population in such a way that errors of judgement in the selection will cancel each other out. Judgement samples tend to be used more often in business market research than in consumer market research. In business market research a firm may get 50% of its business from 10 large purchasers and the remaining 50% from 300 smaller firms. A judgement sample might therefore comprise five of the large purchasers (50%) and 150 of the remainder (50%). Judgement would be exercised to ensure that the firms chosen in the sample represented the sub-grouping.

SAMPLING AND NON-SAMPLING ERROR

The quality of the data in a particular survey is a function of what is termed the *total survey error*. Total survey error reflects the difference between the overall population's true mean value of the characteristic of interest and its mean observed value obtained from the particular sample of respondents. What is of interest is what causes the information obtained from a sample of respondents to differ from that of the entire population. Total survey error is composed of random sampling error and non-sampling error.

Random sampling error occurs because the selected sample is not a perfect representation of the overall population. It represents how accurately the chosen sample's true mean value reflects that of the population. Random sampling error can be controlled by employing an appropriate statistical design and by increasing the sample size.

Non-sampling error represents the extent to which the mean observed value (on the characteristic of interest) for the respondents of a particular sample disagrees with the mean true value for the particular sample of respondents. The size of the non-sampling error depends on two factors: non-response errors and response errors. Non-response errors occur because not all those included in the sample do in fact respond. Moreover, the true mean value of those respondents who do not respond may be different from the entire sample's true mean value. Response error, on the other hand, occurs when respondents give inaccurate answers.

NON-RESPONSE ERRORS

Very few studies ever achieve a 100% response success rate. The problem of non-response error occurs because those who agree to participate in the study are in some respects different from those who decline to participate. Usually, the higher the response rate the lower the probability of non-response error effects. Nevertheless, response rates are not always a good indicator of non-response error. First, response rates do not reflect whether the respondents are good representatives of the target sample. Second, an increase in response does not always lead to a reduction in the non-response error. Third, the notion of response rate is ambiguous since the number of eligible respondents used in the calculation of response rates frequently differs across studies. Unfortunately, the extent of the difference between respondents and non-respondents can seldom be directly determined (see Hahlo (1992), for a discussion of non-response errors).

RESPONSE ERRORS

People may give an inaccurate response either intentionally or unintentionally simply because they are being interviewed. For example, respondents may deliberately not report their duly considered answer because they want to help or please the researcher. This is often encountered in new product tests. In another instance, even though the respondent intends to respond accurately, response error arises because of faulty memory, fatigue, question format or even question content. It also arises when people have little or no experience with the survey topic, for example, asking a low-income respondent about comparatively expensive goods.

Interviewers can influence respondents' answers, incorrectly record respondents' answers and even falsify respondents' answers. People may also be influenced by their attitude to the organisation conducting the study. Finally, the wish to give socially acceptable answers to sensitive or potentially embarrassing questions can also lead to response errors.

A variety of factors can cause errors in survey results. The onus is on the researcher to:

- determine whether respondents have enough information about the topic on which to base their opinions;
- word and/or pose the questions carefully;

- avoid biases in wording that suggest a socially desirable answer or lead respondents to agree with one side of an issue;
- pretest questions in pilot studies to ensure their clarity and impartiality;
- train interviewers to avoid influencing respondents' answers.

SAMPLING IN PRACTICE

So far we have examined some of the methods of applying sampling in a study. We now consider the choice of a sampling method.

Required precision is a factor in influencing the choice of sampling method. Getting a clear-cut answer about the most likely effect of a proposed price reduction on market share demands a sampling design where precision of results can be measured – some kind of probability sample.

However, an exploratory study that is trying to obtain a rough idea about something can use a non-probability sample. It would not be cost effective to spend additional money on a more precise sample. The availability of an appropriate sampling frame is another factor. Drawing a sample without a frame can be difficult and expensive.

FOCUS GROUPS

A focus group comprises 8–12 people who are led by a moderator in an in-depth discussion on a particular topic or concept. The aim of focus group research is to learn and understand what people have to say about a topic and understand their arguments. The moderator has to get people to talk about a topic at length and in detail. The purpose is to discover how they feel about a product, concept, idea or organisation and how it forms part of their lives. The moderator wants to discover the amount of emotional involvement people possess with the topic under discussion.

QUESTIONNAIRES

A questionnaire is a data-collection instrument. It formally sets out the way in which the research questions of interest should be asked. Even simple questions need proper wording and organisation to produce accurate information. Consideration needs to be given to how questions should be worded, in the light of the objectives of the research, and the target group of respondents who are to be questioned.

Attention also needs to be given to the organisation of the questionnaire and to its pretesting. The procedures recommended here apply to mail, telephone, personal and computer-assisted telephone interviews.

The three major parts of the questionnaire are the introduction, the body of the questionnaire and its basic data.

The introduction

To be successful, the introduction to the questionnaire must achieve two things:

- It must be persuasive.
- It must introduce the researcher and the purpose of the research.

The body or content

The body or content consists of questions that cover information needed to solve the marketing problem. The range of topics covers facts, knowledge, opinions and attitudes, motives and possible future behaviour. Factual questions include such things as ownership, shopping/buying behaviour and media exposure, as well as knowledge possessed by respondents. Questions also attempt to measure opinions and attitudes – feelings about products, firms and advertising. There is also the measurement of motives – still more difficult and uncertain to assess in terms of dependability of results. Finally, there is possible future behaviour. Questioning in this last area must bear in mind that results are an expression of attitude and not an accurate prediction of behaviour. People are often willing to describe their plans, but these are often not carried out.

Basic data

The last section of the questionnaire is mainly information about the household and the individual. It almost always includes demographics about the household, aspects such as family size, nature and income. Typically, it also covers demographics about the respondent and it may include questions about lifestyle and psychographics.

This section of the questionnaire has three purposes. First, where there are known and dependable statistics about the population from which the sample has been selected, such data provide a rough check on the representativeness of the sampling. Second, through analysis of subgroups, it provides a method for identifying differences of key results in response by subgroups such as gender and age. Third, there is identification material such as the respondent's name, address and telephone number.

IMPACT OF SURVEY METHOD ON QUESTIONNAIRE DESIGN

Whether survey data is collected through personal interview, telephone, mail, self-administration customer response time will have an impact on questionnaire design. In a shopping centre interview, for example, there are time limitations that are not encountered in other situations. In the case of a self-administered questionnaire the questions have to be very explicit and short. In the case of a telephone interview a rich verbal description of a concept may be necessary to ensure that the respondent understands what is being discussed.

QUESTION CONTENT

When looking at the content of questions you should ask:

1   *Is the question necessary?* If the answer provided by a question does not contribute to satisfying the research objectives, the question itself should be omitted.
2   *Does the respondent understand the question?* The language of the question should be at the level of the respondent being interviewed.
3   *Will the question be enough to elicit the required data?* Questions may be badly phrased or too ambiguous to produce specific information, for example, 'When do you shop?' Asking the same question, but with the words in a different order, may also produce different answers. For example, asking whether it is right to 'drink and drive' may elicit a different answer to asking whether it is right to 'drive and drink'. You should also avoid questions that pose more than one question, for example, 'When and where do you shop?'
4   *Does the respondent have the necessary information to answer the question?* The ability of a respondent to provide a meaningful answer will reflect:
    (a) *The extent to which the respondent is informed.* Some respondents may not wish to disclose ignorance and may try to bluff their way through certain questions. In constructing and asking questions it is therefore important to ensure that there is no suggestion that the respondent should know the answer.
    (b) *How good is the respondent's memory?* People forget and need something to jog their memories. It is better to ask people if they recognise something rather than to ask them to recall it.
    (c) *How articulate is the respondent?* People vary considerably in this respect. Where open-ended questions are being asked it is inevitable that some people will be better than others at getting over the point they wish to make. Closed-ended questions, where an individual has to indicate a predetermined answer, help to alleviate this particular problem.
5   *Is the respondent willing or able to answer the questions?* Non-response or distorted answers are sometimes made by respondents. Embarrassment or loss of face are

strong motivators that influence how a person responds to questions. Ways of alleviating this problem include:

(a) removing or redrafting questions that are likely to create these kinds of problems;

(b) reassuring respondents of the importance of the questions and the confidentiality of the data provided. Anonymity of the responses can help.

When they are first drafted, questionnaires often contain questions that are ambivalent, cumbersome and vague. Instructions may also be confusing: the questionnaire may be too long and questions that should have been included may have been omitted. The pretest is a means of discovering the faults in a questionnaire before it is administered. To pretest a questionnaire a small subsample of the intended respondent group is selected: perhaps a dozen or so people. A good range of respondents is needed. The pretest can be run as a debriefing session or by using the protocol method.

The debriefing method

Here the questionnaire is presented to respondents in exactly the same manner as it would in a real study. After completing the questionnaire, respondents are asked about their thought processes while they were completing it and whether there were any problems with such items as routing and branching instructions, understanding questions, and so on.

The protocol method

This involves respondents thinking aloud as the interview proceeds or as they fill in the questionnaire. In examining the findings of a pretest, particular attention should be given to ensuring that:

- the meaning of the questions is clear;
- the questions are easy to answer;
- the questions flow logically from one to another;
- the routeing/branching instructions are clear;
- the questionnaire is not too long;
- the questionnaire engages and retains the respondent's interest.

There are at least five considerations to be taken into account when conducting a pretest of the questionnaire:

1   All aspects of the questionnaire should be included, most specifically:
     (a) layout,
     (b) question sequence,
     (c) word meaning,
     (d) question difficulty,
     (e) branching instructions.

2   The pretest should be administered and conducted in an environment and context that is identical to the one to be used in the final survey.

3   The majority of the pretest interviews should be undertaken by regular staff interviewers. This should include experienced and relatively new interviewers.

4   Respondents in the pretest should resemble and be representative of the target population. This means that they should be familiar with the topic and possess similar characteristics, attitudes and opinions to those in the target population.

5   The size of the sample used for pretesting will depend on the variation of the target population. The more heterogeneous the target population, the larger the pretest sample required. And the more complex the questionnaire is, the larger the pretest sample should be.

COMPUTER-ASSISTED QUESTIONNAIRES

Computer-assisted programs can handle long and complicated questionnaires of practically any length and can also accommodate very large samples. They can also be personalised or seem to act in an intelligent manner. In the latter respect, answers from previous questions can be inserted automatically into the text of later questions. For instance, a questionnaire about computers may ask whether the respondent has used any particular makes recently and ask them to name the makes. A later portion of the questionnaire may probe into each such computer experience and the program can be structured so that the name of each computer tried is inserted automatically into the questionnaire at the right point. Another useful feature is that the replies to an open-ended question are available to an interviewer for later access, if required. Any interview temporarily terminated at the respondent's request, for instance a telephone interview, can be rescheduled for completion at a later time.

Questions

1   What are the kinds of problems encountered in public sector organisations that marketing research can address. Discuss.

2   What are the advantages of probability sampling over non-probability sampling? Under what circumstances might the latter be preferred?

3   Differentiate between qualitative and quantitative data. What factors govern the preferred method of data collection in a study? Explain.

| Case study 6.1 | The National Fire Service tender |

The National Fire Service is keen to ascertain people's opinions regarding the effectiveness of its service and awareness of the kind of service it offers to members of the public. Four marketing research companies have submitted tenders to undertake the work and you have also been invited to tender. Brief details of the tenders are given below.

Tender	Data collection	Sample size	Areas covered	Cost
1	Questionnaire personal	1,000 (random)	Capital	£ 5,000
2	Questionnaire postal	5,000 (stratified)	South East	£15,000
3	Focus groups	8 × 7 (random selection)	8 locations in different regions	£4,000
4	Telephone survey	1,000 (random)	All country	£3,000

Questions

1 Which, in your view is the most competitive tender?

2 Assuming you have the necessary resources, could you put in a tender that was better than the best of these five tenders? Why or why not?

| Case study 6.2 | Customer satisfaction with the rehabilitation centre |

Eleanor Bron is the manager of a rehabilitation centre for alcohol and drug abuse/addiction. The centre has some 20 resident patients on average whose stay is usually about 1–5 weeks. There are also around 50 outpatients who are regular attenders at the centre. Attendance of outpatients varies from casual calls for half an hour or so once a month to daily attendance for eight hours a day on every day of the week.

Eleanor is not sure about the exact number of outpatients or the exact nature of their specific wants and needs, but feels that she and her staff are doing a good job for the local community. There have been less than 10 complaints from users of the service in the past six months and all of these have been satisfactorily settled.

Eleanor has a small permanent staff of four assistants for the regular 9–5 service offered to outpatients. This figure is augmented by several volunteers who stop by on a regular basis to lend a hand. For the evening and night work she has six qualified staff who work alternating shifts. All employed staff have been trained properly for the kind of work they do and attend updating and further training courses from time to time.

Despite the low level of complaints, Eleanor feels she would like to know more about the kinds of people with whom the centre is dealing and also to have more feedback on the quality of service that the centre is perceived to be providing. In addition she has no information on what happens to people once they stop attending the centre or how successful the centre's treatment is in the long term. Indeed, she would like very much to set up a database of information that could be analysed on a regular basis to provide her with information that would be useful in enabling her to carry out her job more effectively.

Questions

1 What information do you think Eleanor needs to obtain?

2 How should she set about obtaining the required information?

3 What kind of analysis would need to be carried out on the information she would receive?

4 What information should be stored in the database?

References

Hahlo, G. (1992), 'Examining the validity of re-interviewing respondents for quantitative surveys', *Journal of the Market Research Society*, Vol. 34, pp. 99–118.

McKenzie, J. (1988), 'Study of characteristics of ex-directory telephone owners', *Market Research Newsletter*, December.

Semon, T. T. (1994), 'A good sample of accounts may not always be a good sample of your customers', *Marketing News*, Vol. 28, No. 9, pp. 8–11.

Further reading

Carson, D., Gilmore, A., Perry, C. and Gronhaug, K. (2001), *Qualitative Marketing Research*, London: Sage.

Gabor, A. and Grainger, C. (1966), 'Price as an indicator of quality', *Economics*, Vol. 33, pp. 43–70.

Hooley, G. and Hussey, M. (1999), *Quantitative Methods in Marketing*, London: Thomson Learning.

Kent, R. (1998), *Marketing Research*, London: Thomson Learning.

Lehmann, D. R. and Cupta, J. H. (1998), *Marketing Research*, Harlow: Prentice Hall.

Lilien, G. L. , Kotler, P. and Moorthy, K. S. (1992), *Marketing Models*, Upper Saddle River, NJ: Prentice-Hall

McDaniel, C. and Gates, R. (1999), *Contemporary Marketing Research*, Cincinnati: South Western.

McDaniel, C. and Gates, R. (2001), *Marketing Research Essentials*, Cincinnati: South Western.

Malhorta, N. (1999), *Marketing Research: An Applied Orientation*, Harlow: Prentice Hall.

Malhorta, N. and Birks, D. (2000), *Marketing Research*, Harlow: Financial Times/Prentice Hall.

Moutinho, L. and Evans, M. (1992), *Applied Marketing Research*, Wokingham: Addison-Wesley.

Nagle, T. T. and Holden, R. K. (1995), *The Strategy and Tactics of Pricing: A Guide to Profitable Decision Making*, Englewood Cliffs, NJ: Prentice Hall.

Proctor, T. (2005), *Essentials of Marketing Research*, Harlow: FT Prentice Hall.

Shao, A. (1999), *Marketing Research*, Cincinnati: South Western.

Wright, L. T. and Crimp, M. (2000), *The Marketing Research Process*, Harlow: Financial Times/Prentice Hall.

Webb, J. R. (2001), *Understanding and designing market research*, London: Thomson Learning.

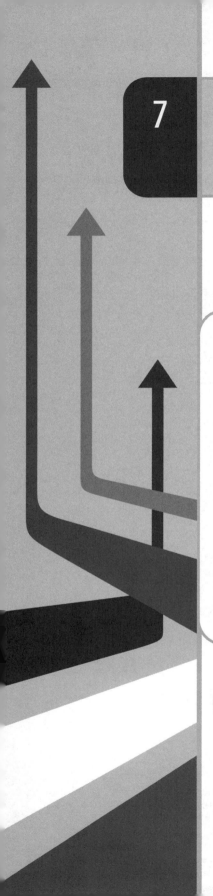

Market measurement and forecasting demand

INTRODUCTION

Planning ahead for service provision requires both knowledge of the current size of existing markets and informed estimates of how the markets are going to change in size and makeup over time. Getting forecasts reasonably correct can spell the difference between success and failure. This chapter looks at methods of assessing market size and outlines various forecasting methods. The usefulness of simulation modelling is introduced to show how different assumptions can affect projected developments.

Forecasting amounts to estimating some future event outside the control of the organisation and that provides a basis for managerial planning. The estimates produced often form the basis of service creation planning, customer contact staff planning, setting advertising appropriations, estimating cashflow and assessing the need for innovation. Marketing plans are only useful if the size of current and future markets is carefully measured and estimated. Such information is a useful starting point from which to determine how resources should be allocated among markets and/or services.

DEFINING MARKET DEMAND

There are many different ways of describing a market. The current number of users of a service and the demand volume they generate constitutes the 'penetrated market'. Secondary data sources may provide information on this or it may be necessary to establish this figure by sample survey. This measure does not take account of those people who have an interest in using the service, but who currently do not. The latter are important, since in looking at future demand they provide a measure of the 'potential market'. A further stipulation is that customers must be able to use the service. In assessing the 'potential market' this too must be established and will lead to a redefinition of the market size. The ability to use a service affects the size of the market. If it is not possible to use a service, this will obviously restrict the market size and taking this into account will define the 'available market'. Finally, an organisation has only a limited amount of resources at its disposal, so it chooses only certain market segments where it feels it has the capacity to compete effectively and where the market size is sufficiently attractive. This becomes the 'served' or the 'target' market.

PREDICTING FUTURE DEMAND

There is no agreement among experts concerning the best forecasting method. This is particularly the case for techniques that use quantitative methods to predict future demand. Even the most complex and detailed quantitative models and methods are not always found to be any better than the simplest ones (see Armstrong, 1986; Schnarrs and Bavuso (1986)). Qualitative approaches depend on subjective judgements, probabilities and scenario writing methods (see Chapter 5 for scenario methods). These are what as known as *uncertain judgements* but by pooling expert knowledge surprisingly good results can be obtained. O'Hagan *et al.* (2006) provide an extensive analysis and extensive suggestions on how expert judgements can be elicited.

CHOICE OF METHOD

The following considerations should be borne in mind when choosing the most appropriate forecasting technique:

- *Time horizon.* The technique must be suitable for use over the period of time required.
- *Technical sophistication.* The people doing the forecasting must be comfortable with the technique used. They must have the knowledge to understand its use and limitations.
- *Cost.* Greater accuracy in forecasting may only be possible at extra cost. We have to assess whether the extra cost of accuracy is worthwhile.
- *The data that can be used.* The extensiveness, currency, accuracy and representativeness of the availability must be assessed before choosing a technique.

When forecasting the demand for established services two approaches are possible, both of which have a number of variants. First, there are methods that rely on asking people questions and, second, there are methods that involve the statistical or mathematical analysis of historical data.

ASKING PEOPLE QUESTIONS

Surveys of users' or buyers' intentions

Some consumer market-research organisations, and even businesses themselves, conduct periodic surveys of intentions. Using the results produced by regular sample surveys, predictions of the likely demand for various items or activities can then be made. This method can be applied effectively by producers of many business services. In the case of the public sector this can be interpreted as the intentions of users of a particular service.

Customer contact opinion

Those in contact with customers are well positioned to provide estimates on potential demand for a service. When making use of estimates produced by them, account needs to be taken of any bias that may exist. They may be biased either in the direction of pessimism or of optimism. We also have to remember that the customer contact staff may not really appreciate the larger economic factors that may influence demand. However, providing we can identify the sources of bias and compensate for them in interpreting predictions, it is possible to make use of these estimates.

Expert opinion

Expert opinion is another method of forecasting. Experts may include marketing consultants. A key factor that influences patterns of demand in a country is the state of its economy. Various economic experts can provide their opinions and a government produces its own economic forecast.

Analysing past data

Organisations tend to base their forecasts on what they have achieved in the past. This approach to forecasting offers few opportunities for mistakes except where there are large variations in demand from one year to the next. There are two basic methods of forecasting, each of which has a number of versions.

METHODS THAT ADOPT A SOLELY TIME-DEPENDENT APPROACH

Classical time-series analysis

The first sets of methods are those based on time-series analysis, which assumes that demand simply varies as a function of time. The time effects are divided into:

- cycle – fluctuations every few years, for example, the effect of trade cycles as various major economies in the world are hit by booms and slumps;
- trend – a general upward, downward or static (no trend) pattern, for example, the upward trend in demand for video-recorders during the growth phase of the lifecycle;
- seasonal – systematic variations at certain times of the year, for example, additional demand for swimsuits in the summer months;
- erratic – unpredictable or random variations, for example, demand interrupted by an industry-wide strike.

Erratic variation is taken into account when making forecasts, but we do not attempt to predict it exactly. We merely express it as the error we attach to the demand forecast. This method is most suitable for forecasting the demand of services where the unexplained variation is small.

The trend component results from developments in a population, the formation of capital and developments in technology. It is evidenced by a general upward or downward shift in the pattern of demand. If there is no such pattern, there is assumed to be no trend.

The cycle depicts the wavelike flow of demand over a number of years and is most useful when examining data for use in intermediate range forecasts (3–7 years). Traditionally, the cycle represents swings in economic activity.

The seasonal component refers to recurrent demand patterns that may exist within the period of a single year. This will reflect elements such as weather factors, holidays and seasonal habits.

Erratic variation comprises such elements as strikes and other unforeseen circumstances. These factors are unpredictable and need to be removed from past data in order to inspect the other three elements. Time-series analysis consists of decomposing the original demand data into its trend, cyclical, seasonal and erratic components. The series is then recombined to produce a demand forecast.

Imagine that Table 7.1 represents the demand data for a particular service in terms of enquiries:

Table 7.1   Demand data in terms of enquiries

Period	Year	Demand
1	2005	436
2		291
3		357
4		529
5	2006	386
6		304
7		333
8		471
9	2007	383
10		336
11		365
12		539

More than one way to forecast time-series data such as these exists. One method is to use dummy variables and multiple regression analysis. Multiple regression is a statistical tool that can be applied to past data to discover the most important factors influencing demand and their relative influence. The dummy variables in this particular case represent the factors influencing sales. The approach consists of creating a variable for each of the four quarters and the following equation is then estimated by multiple linear regression analysis:

$$\text{Demand} = B_0 + B_1 \text{ Time} + B_2 \text{ Winter} + B_3 \text{ Spring} + B_4 \text{ Summer}$$

Multiple linear regression analysis

One of the dummy variables has to be left out so that the regression can be solved by computer: in this case 'Autumn' is omitted (see Table 7.2).
   The values obtained are:

$$B_0 = 510.5 \quad B_1 = 0.3125 \quad B_2 = -110.396 \quad B_3 = -202.042 \quad B_4 = -161.021$$

Substituting values into the equation for subsequent periods enables a forecast of demand to be made. For example:

$$\text{Period 13 forecast demand} = 510.5 + 0.3125 \times 13 - 110.396 \times 1 = 404.167$$

Moving average

This is one of the simplest methods. Trend, seasonal or cyclical patterns are not usually included in it, although in the more advanced methods it is possible to do so.

Table 7.2 Quarterly demand using dummy variables for the seasonal variables

Time	Sales	Winter	Spring	Summer	Autumn
1	436	1	0	0	0
2	291	0	1	0	0
3	357	0	0	1	0
4	529	0	0	0	1
5	386	1	0	0	0
6	304	0	1	0	0
7	333	0	0	1	0
8	471	0	0	0	1
9	383	1	0	0	0
10	336	0	1	0	0
11	365	0	0	1	0
12	539	0	0	0	1

The average demand is the arithmetic mean of demand from a number (N) of past periods.

$$A_t = [D_1 + D_2 + ... + D_{t-(N+1)}]/N$$

The forecast demand for period $t + 1$ is a projection of the past average demand. The number of periods included in the average can be increased to give more importance to past demand (referred to as damping). In order to fine-tune the sensitivity of the moving average to certain periods, a weighting factor W_t can be applied to those periods:

$$F_{t+1} = A_t = W_1 D_1 + W_2 D_2 + ... + W_N D_{t-(N+1)}$$

where $W_1 + W_2 + ... + W_N = 1$

Statistical demand analysis

So far, the statistical or mathematical approaches we have considered treat the factors that seem to influence demand as regularly reoccurring phenomena. The difficulty with this approach is that some patterns do not reappear at regular intervals. For example, while there are economic booms and slumps from time to time, their patterns are not so precise as to enable accurate forecasts to be made.

Statistical demand analysis attempts to identify the source of all influences on demand so that more accurate forecasts can be made. The basic statistical method to take account of such factors is multiple regression analysis. Experience indicates that the factors most commonly considered are price, income, population and marketing promotion (see Pankratz (1991) for a comprehensive overview of this approach).

The first stage in a regression analysis is to build a causal model in which we try to explain demand in terms of a number of independent variables. For example, we might conjecture that demand for a particular service is related to the convenience of accessing the service (C), friendliness of the staff administering the service (F) and promotional effort put into creating awareness of the service (A). We would express this relationship in the form of an equation:

$$D = a_0 + b_0C + b_1F + b_2A$$

We need to estimate the parameters for a_0, b_1 to b_2 and apply them to quantifications of C, F, and A for the period of the forecast. We might use promotional expenditure as an indicator for A, customer satisfaction data for F, and a value representing hours of availability plus number of access points for C.

In principle, demand equations of this variety are acquired by fitting the best equations to historical or cross-sectional data. The coefficients of the equation are estimated according to what is called the 'least squares criterion', according to which the best equation is the one that minimises a measure of the error between the actual and the predicted observations. The better the fit, the more useful will be the equation for forecasting purposes.

Although this is a popular technique, it needs to be used with care. There must always be an adequate number of observations. Independent variables can sometimes turn out to influence each other and are not independent at all. For example, relative price and relative advertising expenditure may well influence each other, since advertising costs can be reflected in the selling price. There are also other pitfalls to be watched out for.

Forecasting take-up of new services

To forecast demand for new services we need some initial demand figures with which to work. Given that early demand data is available, it is usually possible, by using one or other of a variety of mathematical models or 'curve-fitting routines', to make some prediction for demand over a specified time period. Alternatively, it may be possible to look at demand histories of similar new services and make predictions by analogy. There are many examples of these models (see, for instance, Kotler and Lilien (1983)).

Example

The epidemic model of initial demand is a useful tool to have to hand when trying to make a demand prediction for certain kinds of new services. The model developed by Bass (1969), is illustrative:

$$p_t = p + q/m(Y_t)$$

where　p_t = probability of purchase given that no previous purchase was made
Y_t = total number who have tried the service
m = total number of potential buyers (saturation level)
q = parameter reflecting the rate of diffusion of the model
p = initial probability of first-time purchase

The model can be estimated by running a regression of current versus past demand (see Table 7.3):

$$Demand_t = c_0 + c_1 Y_t + c_2 Y_t^2$$

Analysis of the above demand gives the forecasting model:

$$Demand_t = 2.06 + 1.016 Y_t - 0.00464 Y_t^2$$

Note that in the case of public services we simply replace the notion of buyers with that of users of a service.

Table 7.3 Current versus past demand

Year	$Demand_t$ (000s)	Y_t (000s)	Y_t^2 (000s)
1	1	0	0
2	2	1	1
3	4	3	9
4	10	7	49
5	20	17	289
6	36	37	1,369
7	48	73	5,329
8	58	121	14,641

SIMULATION AND SYSTEM DYNAMICS

System dynamics is one approach to modelling the dynamics of complex systems such as population, ecological and economic systems, which usually interact strongly with each other. Systems dynamics was founded in the early 1960s by Jay W. Forrester of the MIT Sloan School of Management with the establishment of the MIT System Dynamics Group. At that time, he began applying what he had learned about systems during his work in electrical engineering to everyday systems. What makes using system dynamics different from other approaches to studying complex systems is the use of feedback loops (see Figure 7.1). Stocks and flows are the basic building blocks of a system dynamics model. They help describe how a system is connected by feedback loops that create the nonlinearity found so frequently in modern day problems. Computer software is used to simulate a system dynamics model of the situation being studied. Running 'what if' simulations to test certain policies on such a model can greatly aid in understanding how the system changes over time.

Clearly, one of the major problems facing the public sector is how best to predict the results or estimate the impacts of various initiatives and measures that emerge

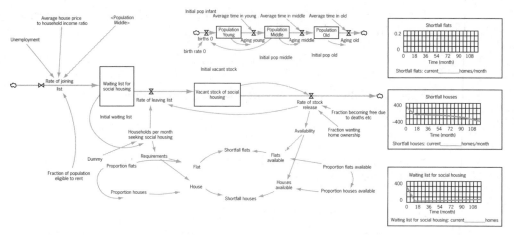

Figure 7.1 System dynamics model – assessing social housing requirements

as part of the process of formulating a policy. One way of testing such initiatives, short of actual implementation, is to develop models of the situation.

In attempting to understand the determinants of behaviour it is fundamental that the complex social systems and causal effects are examined. System dynamics modelling, is one discipline specifically designed to tackle such problems. The past few decades has seen the use of system dynamics increase dramatically, in particular for attempting to model environmental systems.

The use of a system dynamics approach can provide a framework for investigating the likely outcomes of policies if certain initiatives are implemented. Hence, system dynamics modelling may help in assessing the likely impact of different initiatives and in the subsequent formulation of a policy, by providing a model of the major influences. Once developed, it can aid policy makers by allowing them immediate feedback and analysis of how different policies may or may not work.

In Figure 7.1 use is made of the computer simulation package Vensim that makes use of system dynamics modelling to assess likely social housing requirements in an area. The model enables different scenarios and forecasts to be made by varying assumptions about population growth figures, unemployment rates, private housing to average incomes ratios and the available stock of social housing over a projected 10-year period.

There are many applications in the public sector for these kinds of simulations that aim to assess likely demand for services in the future and the capacity of the organisation to supply the requirements to meet the demand.

Questions

1   Forecasting tools are essential to planning. Suggest how you might use the tools illustrated in the text to forecast demand for social housing in an inner city area.

2   How might computer simulations be used beneficially in the area of supported living? What would you see as the main limitations on the use of simulation?

Case study 7.1	Problems and benefits of BPR and forecasting take-up of a new service

The benefits of business process re-engineering (BPR) are expected to be reduced costs, a more efficient and effective organisation, satisfied customers and a more satisfied workforce ... or at least that is the hope. Any new system, however, takes time to settle in and where it involves getting customers to use it then changing people's habits or getting them to take up the service can be a slow process. Creating awareness, interest and desire to use the service is a job for marketing but people may still be slow to respond. One of the biggest headaches facing the public sector is knowing what level of a new service to provide and what implications this will have for staffing levels and other resources.

Of course this all comes back to the age old problem of accurate market measurement and forecasting but unfortunately there does not seem to be an easy solution to the problem. Most evaluation seem to hinge upon a combination of analysis of past data, subjective opinion, potential user surveys and reviewing what has happened elsewhere under similar circumstances. Often, however, this ends up with overly optimistic estimates or ones that greatly underestimate the actual take-up in demand. Yet, marketing theory can offer some good guidelines as to how either of these situations can be avoided through the simple mechanisms of test markets and selected roll-out strategies regarding new service provision. Perhaps there is something to learn from the large retailing organisation after all that maintains that if it cannot produce enough demand in half a day in Central London for its latest lines then it is not worth contemplating launching the product through any of its other outlets. But of course there is always the other side of the coin in that Central London may not be typical of the rest of the country and what works there may not work elsewhere!

Potential user surveys seem to be the most logical answer to the market measurement issue. Why not just ask people whether or not they will make use of a service? Why not ask them how often they are likely to use it? Well, of course, most organisations do precisely that but then people just turn out not to be accurate in what they say. People can have very positive attitudes towards something but whether they will ever make use of it or how often they will make use of it may be a different matter altogether.

It is all a matter of probabilities the statistical experts might argue but probabilities themselves are difficult to assess. So with gloom in their minds the inventors of new systems are forced back to their think tanks to ponder on the issues involved once more. 'What about the product life cycle and the adoption-innovation curve?' a voice might ask. 'Ah, yes,' might come the reply, 'but they are only theoretical notions. Those nicely shaped distribution curves are for the text books only ... their shape in reality is somewhat less uniform and predictable.'

So how then can we predict the demand and take-up for a combination of one-stop shops and a call centre? How can we decide where the one-stop shops should be sited in a large metropolitan area? How can we decide on appropriate staffing levels? What implications does this have for staff training and development and how will it affect their expectations about pay? These are just a few of the issues that such a venture might raise.

Question

1 Consider the issues that arise in planning a new public sector venture such as a call centre and a set of one-stop shops. How would you tackle the various issues and problems that have been raised above?

Case study 7.2 | **Sidchester City – analysing the statistics**

Sidchester is a fairly large northern city with a population of nearly 450,000. The population size is more or less stable though some growth is expected over the next 15–20 years. Experts expect this to be between 5% and 10%. It is estimated that there will be as many people coming into the city as leave it.

The city has over 30 wards (see Figure 7.2) and various data relating to age distributions, household incomes, employment status, housing numbers and prices of different types of houses are shown in Table 7.4.

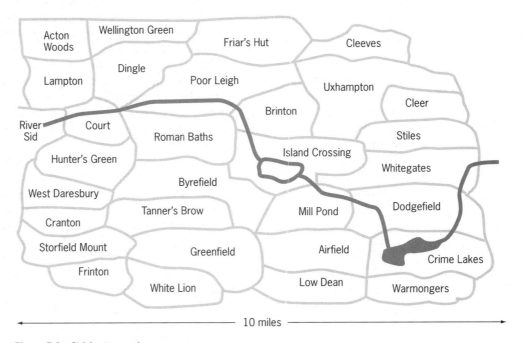

Figure 7.2 Sidchester wards

Use the following assumptions that have been predicted by experts to help answer the subsequent questions:

- Real household incomes will rise by 5% to 15% over the next 15 years. Those households on lowest incomes can expect the lowest percentage rises and those on highest incomes will obtain the greatest percentage rises.

- Prices of properties will rise 2% per annum in the case of the cheapest properties over the next 15 years rising to as much as 10% per annum on the most expensive properties.
- Birth rates will increase by around 1% per annum in the areas where household incomes are lowest and this will change to a decline of around 2% per annum in the areas where household incomes are highest.
- Workless rates are likely to remain the same in all areas.

Questions

1 Each ward, except Airfield, Low Dean and Storfield Mount currently has two primary schools (ages 5–11) that all children irrespective of ethnic origin or creed attend. Airfield and Low Dean both have three primary schools and Storfield Mount has four.

   a Indicate how you would prepare a demand forecast for places required in each of these schools over the next 10 years. Assume none of the schools can house more than 500 children and that is the maximum allowed. Also assume the sending of children to schools outside of the ward in which they reside is not permitted.

   b How would you estimate the effect of allowing children to attend schools in directly neighbouring wards (i.e. those who share the same ward boundary)?

   c How would you determine whether to recommend closing any primary school or build any new primary schools? How would you decide which ones to close or where to build new ones?

2 Assume the city council is under no obligation to provide council housing for its tenants and that it aims to sell off to tenants, or otherwise dispose of the properties to third parties, 80% of the council houses over the next five years. How would you estimate what impact this would have on demand for different classes of property in the various wards of Sidchester, including the declining stock of council owned social housing, over the next 10 years?

3 As part of its strategy of putting the customer first the council aims to introduce a number of one-stop shops to make it easier for members of the community to have their complaints and enquiries dealt with more effectively. How would you decide how many one-stop shops you think it should introduce and where should they be sited on the map? Justify your answer.

   Note: A much lengthier exercise is to actually use the data provided above to come up with specific answers to the questions that have been set.

Table 7.4 Sidchester data (part 1)

Ward	0–4	5–14	15–64	65+	Population	Total houses	Council houses	Workless (%)	Average household income (£)	Detatched: average price (£)	Semi: average price (£)	Flat: average price (£)	Terraced: average price (£)
Acton Woods	756	1,378	10,345	1,234	13,713	5,609	734	19.40	27,480	219,721	81,230	72,678	60,210
Airfield	1,013	2,012	10,200	2,510	15,735	7,623	1,756	41.10	19,312	129,087	99,645	23,467	57,299
Brinton	800	2,023	9,467	3,245	15,535	6,900	3,534	36.80	18,709	108,342	113,150		81,600
Byrefield	300	543	8,800	2,060	11,703	6,234	1,097	25.50	24,022	105,400	97,568	17,245	97,810
Cleves	546	1,834	10,945	1,390	14,715	5,610	380	12.90	30,711	240,000	161,834		125,250
Cleer	702	1,324	9,900	2,345	14,271	5,792	123	10.60	34,194	423,888	239,236	141,500	171,150
Court	930	2,063	9,789	3,023	15,805	6,003	3,345	44.60	17,780		83,800	43,680	63,912
Cranton	800	1,923	9,567	2,345	14,635	7,159	1,479	38.60	18,853		105,611	56,512	63,001
Crime Lakes	700	1,512	10,243	2,143	14,598	6,412	1,267	22.30	27,391	433,000	156,231	141,560	133,104
Dingle	923	2,067	9,046	2,572	14,608	6,456	2,109	25.80	25,699	184,000	114,823	68,000	78,703
Dodgefield	948	1,903	9,790	2,256	14,897	8,512	5,432	64.00	16,411		91,580	104,634	54,511
Frinton	887	2,345	10,321	2,709	16,262	6,800	1,098	23.80	23,991	161,012	99,994	57,000	83,018
Friar's Hut	412	784	10,232	2,123	13,551	5,912	1,082	16.80	24,623	488,500	208,300	141,399	169,076
Greenfield	932	1,800	9,612	2,102	14,446	8,012	2,345	52.50	18,800	216,732	93,821	69,240	62,900
Hunter's Green	834	1,845	11,343	1,612	15,634	8,008	4,157	56.00	18,256	182,711	93,500	151,359	52,027
Island Crossing	856	1,759	9,500	1,943	14,058	6,621	1,794	31.50	22,634	227,925	118,823	90,512	91,750
Lampton	621	1,345	9,456	1,824	13,246	5,079	498	12.70	30,616	326,150	193,324	18,233	145,311
Low Dean	1,234	2,456	12,234	1,956	17,880	7,412	4,260	39.40	17,103		82,524	99,923	77,500
Mill Pond	812	2,234	10,494	2,978	16,518	7,734	1,600	32.40	20,234	122,000	102,673	94,358	91,098

Table 7.4 continued

Ward	0–4	5–14	15–64	65+	Population	Total houses	Council houses	Workless (%)	Average household income (£)	Detatched: average price (£)	Semi: average price (£)	Flat: average price (£)	Terraced: average price (£)
Poor Leigh	987	1,934	11,138	2,071	16,130	8,812	3,124	43.20	17,832		101,120	37,000	71,930
Roman Baths	545	1,543	9,345	1,902	13,335	9,006	6,088	62.80	18,623			141,015	51,760
Stiles	923	2,078	11,027	2,200	16,228	8,167	3,502	50.50	22,910		79,800	174,013	80,800
Storfield Mount	1,654	2,623	12,546	1,782	18,605	8,977	4,444	49.40	17,412		83,000	72,700	69,500
Tanner's Brow	345	1,008	9,600	2,099	13,052	6,712	6,712	29.30	26,390	285,316	128,452	131,600	122,400
Uxhampton	912	2,034	10,600	2,523	16,069	7,700	1,423	42.20	20,917	166,000	108,880	28,200	68,800
Warmongers	756	1,795	9,900	2,308	14,759	6,652	1,067	28.10	23,945	169,432	116,732	67,500	92,700
Wellington Green	712	1,324	10,320	1,534	13,890	6,500	1,009	26.20	25,555	254,000	183,437	94,650	98,600
West Daresbury	750	1,456	9,812	2,690	14,708	6,104	767	17.30	27,610	184,722	145,560	75,900	107,800
Whitegates	534	1,200	9,894	1,772	13,400	6,099	657	13.20	31,400	340,100	206,590	134,950	137,700
White Lion	823	2,456	9,445	2,698	15,422	6,766	2,591	34.20	22,321	199,900	100,800	62,100	76,800
Sidchester	23,947	52,601	304,911	65,949	447,408	209,383	69,474	33.44	23,058	234,906	123,863	86,105	91,267

Table 7.4 Sidchester data (part 2) (written/in person complaints or queries received in a three month period)

Ward	Benefit	Revenues	Rent	Education	Housing	Licensing	Blue Badge	Parking	Environment Services	Total
Acton Woods	3	2	1	6	2	5	5	6	3	33
Airfield	12	14	17	4	14	6	1	7	12	87
Brinton	11	12	15	4	22	5	2	4	14	89
Byrefield	8	7	9	10	8	5	3	2	22	74
Cleves	2	0	1	7	1	2	2	1	17	33
Cleer	3	6	0	12	3	0	2	3	25	54
Court	12	11	14	5	21	5	1	5	18	92
Cranton	9	7	6	13	5	6	1	3	21	71
Crime Lakes	7	5	5	12	2	2	3	4	23	63
Dingle	4	2	3	9	2	3	2	2	21	48
Dodgefield	18	16	17	5	28	4	1	3	22	114
Frinton	7	5	3	8	4	3	2	4	15	51
Friar's Hut	5	5	6	8	3	2	0	3	8	40
Greenfield	3	2	5	9	4	2	1	4	7	37
Hunter's Green	8	9	7	5	3	2	2	3	34	73
Island Crossing	6	5	4	9	6	0	1	4	12	47
Lampton	0	0	0	6	0	0	0	3	11	20
Low Dean	11	12	13	5	9	6	0	7	10	73
Mill Pond	7	5	6	8	4	3	1	6	5	45
Poor Leigh	14	13	15	6	15	7	2	5	34	111

Table 7.4 continued

Ward	Benefit	Revenues	Rent	Education	Housing	Licensing	Blue Badge	Parking	Environment Services	Total
Roman Baths	22	19	25	4	31	9	0	1	21	132
Stiles	3	1	1	7	4	0	1	2	25	44
Storfield Mount	12	14	13	4	16	4	2	2	22	89
Tanner's Brow	5	4	5	8	7	0	1	3	4	37
Uxhampton	9	8	7	10	3	1	3	1	13	55
Warmongers	4	3	5	11	3	0	1	1	18	46
Wellington Green	8	7	8	12	2	0	0	1	23	61
West Daresbury	8	7	7	9	6	1	0	5	15	58
Whitegates	0	1	1	12	1	0	0	2	13	30
White Lion	7	6	6	7	4	0	1	3	11	45
Sidchester	228	208	225	235	233	83	41	100	499	1,852

References

Armstrong, S. (1986), 'Research on Forecasting: A Quarter Century Review, 1960–84', *Interfaces*, Vol. 16, No. 1, pp. 89–103.

Bass, F. (1969), 'A new product growth model for consumer durables', *Management Science*, Vol. 15 (January), pp. 215–227.

Kotler, P. and Lilien, G. (1983), *Marketing Decision Making: A model building approach*, New York: Harper & Row.

O'Hagan, A., Buck, C., Daneshkhah, A., Eiser, R., Garthwaite, P., Jenkinson, D., Oakley, J. and Rakow, T. (2006), *Uncertain Judgements: Eliciting Expert's Probabilities*, Chichester: Wiley.

Pankratz, A. (1991), *Forecasting with Dynamic Regression Models*, New York: Wiley.

Schnarrs, S. and Bavuso, J. (1986), 'Extrapolation Models on Very Short Forecasts', *Journal of Business Research*, Vol. 14, pp. 27–36.

Further reading

Albright S. C., Winston, W. and Zappe, C. J. (2003), *Data Analysis and Decision Making*, Pacific Grove, CA: Thomson.

Chakrapani, C. (2004), *Statistics in Market Research*, London: Arnold.

Hoover, S. V. and Perry, R. F. (1989), *Simulation: a Problem-solving Approach*, New York: Addison Wesley.

Orme, B. and Huber, J. (2000), 'Improving the value of conjoint simulations', *Marketing Research*, Vol. 12 (Winter), pp. 12–21.

Ratner, B. (2003), *Statistical modeling and analysis for database marketing*, Boca Raton, FL: Chapman and Hall/CRC.

Watson, H. J. and Blackstone, J. H. (1989), *Computer Simulation*, New York: Wiley.

Waddell, D. and Sohal, A. S. (1994), 'Forecasting: the key to managerial decision making', *Management Decision*, Vol. 32, No. 1, p. 46.

Yava, U. (1996), Demand forecasting in a service setting, *Journal of International Marketing and Marketing Research*, Vol. 21, No. 1, February, pp. 3–11.

8   The marketing planning process

INTRODUCTION

In this chapter we look at the marketing planning process and how it relates to public services. First we look at the need for systematic marketing planning, commenting on the need for the organisation to keep abreast of changes in the environment and exploiting opportunities for creating value for stakeholders. We then look in more detail at the process of marketing planning. Next we examine in detail ideas relating to market segmentation, targeting and positioning, suggesting how these may be interpreted as far as public sector organisations are concerned. We also consider the step-by-step approach to developing and applying these methods. To aid the process of strategy formulation and to evaluate its *post facto* usefulness we then look at perceptual mapping as a way of enabling us to appreciate stakeholder perceptions of a service or range of services. We review ways in which a service may be evaluated and the final section is concerned with the need to develop creative strategies.

THE NEED FOR SYSTEMATIC STRATEGIC MARKETING PLANNING

Strategic market planning is concerned with adapting the organisation to a changing environment. Public sector organisations are successful when they meet the needs of their stakeholders. The problem is that the needs of stakeholders change and as a result, successful organisations decline if they do not continually adapt and change accordingly. Management has to evolve a strategy and an organisation structure that best fits the environment within which it operates. In such a situation it has to offer services that match or satisfy the needs of its various stakeholders. Changing needs means keeping up with the changing environment is essential. For example, developments in technologies can create opportunities for added value that stakeholders find desirable and these require to be satisfied.

Environmental change takes on two forms: continuous and discontinuous. The former are changes that are slow and fairly predictable. For instance, demographic changes, increasing concern for the environment and problems of growing congestion on the roads are examples of continuous change. With this type of change, affected organisations should have the time to adapt to the problems or opportunities that are being created. However, there is a trend towards change increasingly falling into the discontinuous category and many of the changes in the environment appear sudden, dramatic and unpredictable. It is essentially more difficult to plan for and to adapt to such an environment. To cope with such situations, flexibility has become the name of the game.

STRATEGIC WINDOWS

There are only limited periods during which the 'fit' between the key requirements of the marketplace and the particular competencies of an organisation is at its best. Strategic marketing planning demands both *anticipation* and *response* to changes which affect the marketplace. Resource allocation decisions require a cautious assessment of the future evolution of the market and a precise evaluation of the organisation's capability to effectively meet key market requirements. When sudden environmental changes occur they can trigger major developments in markets. These shocks are often termed 'strategic windows' (Abell, 1978).

Organisations must think about strategic questions, such as:

- Which markets should we be in?
- Do we have the resources, skills and assets within the organisation to enable planned objectives to be achieved?
- Where do we want to be in five or even 25 years' time?
- Can we assume that our current *modus operandi* will be good enough for the future?

These concerns are strategic in nature and have implications for the whole organisation. As such they provide a justification for subsequent actions that are taken. The centre of attention is the future and in particular how the organisation can take advantage of new opportunities and challenges that arise within the changing marketing environment. In this context obtaining relevant information on a regular basis is of paramount importance. It is important to collect, update and analyse information as part of the initial strategic planning and then as a part of monitoring and controlling the implementation of those plans.

While obtaining an appreciation of what is taking place in the external environment is important, as an end in itself it is insufficient. The organisation has to review its internal resources, assets and skills in order to assess whether it is sufficiently well equipped to meet the challenges of the external environment.

At the heart of strategic marketing planning is how the organisation sets about designing appropriate marketing communications in order to inform the various stakeholders in the organisation about what it is seeking to achieve. Whether stakeholders are customers, employees or any other kind of stakeholder they need to be informed and persuaded about the services offered by the organisation. In order to do this the organisation relies on well tried marketing methods to achieve this end.

Let us now turn to examining these methods in some detail.

MARKETING PLANNING

At a strategic level, marketing planning is concerned with identifying and ranking target markets in which the organisation will or might operate. It is also concerned with market positioning, competitive stance where relevant, and the formulation of the organisation's marketing strategy. At a tactical level, marketing planning is concerned with a series of decisions relating to the ways in which the strategy will be implemented. In essence, therefore, marketing planning is to do with the development and coordination of marketing activity. In doing this, it contributes to and takes its lead from the organisation's overall corporate plan.

Marketing planning involves the evaluation or assessment of marketing opportunities and resources, the development of the marketing objectives, the identification of the ways in which these objectives will be achieved, and the creation of the marketing mix to implement and control strategy and tactics. Marketing planning also determines when and how marketing activities will be performed and who is to perform them.

At one time it was the case that plans were typically very formal and highly structured, but many marketing planners today deliberately develop plans that are far less highly structured. Such plans incorporate a much greater degree of contingency thinking.

Relationship to the corporate plan

The relationship which the marketing plan has to the corporate plan is a description of the degree of fit between overall corporate strategies and those which relate directly to the organisation's relationship with its customers and other groups. The corporate plan is usually much greater in scope than the marketing plan and includes statements about the reasons for the organisation's existence, its responsibilities to stakeholders, the customer needs that are met by the organisation's services, the amount of service diversification it expects to encompass, the corporate future, and so forth. Not all of these issues are strictly marketing related, although all will impinge directly or indirectly on marketing activities.

The marketing plan is often seen as being subsidiary to the corporate plan and as stemming from it as a functional part of the overall corporate strategy (McDonald, 1999). This is because the corporate plan will typically be broken down into departmental responsibilities. In fact, the two operate in parallel and the corporate plan should, in any good market-led organisation, be designed around the needs of stakeholders.

Marketing strategy encompasses selecting and analysing the target market(s) and creating and maintaining an appropriate marketing mix that satisfies the target market and the organisation. A marketing strategy articulates a plan for the best use of the organisation's resources and tactics to meet its objectives.

Plan includes:

- an executive summary,
- a situation analysis,
- an opportunities and threat analysis,
- an environmental analysis,
- the company resources,
- the marketing objectives,
- marketing strategies, including financial projections and controls and evaluations.

All plans should have control procedures and permit effective monitoring of how well the plans are adhered to. Marketing control processes consists of establishing performance standards, evaluating the actual performance by comparing it with the actual standards, and reducing the difference between the desired and actual performance. There should also be contingency plans specifying what action should be taken when performance deviates considerably from expectations.

MARKETING CONTROL

Having a marketing control process enables management to know from time to time where the organisation stands in relation to where it wants to be. This requires that progress can be observed, measured and redirected if there are discrepancies between the actual and desired positions. Deviations from the plan need to be compensated for, and corrections applied. The planners need to consider fall-back positions in the event of objectives not being attained, or in the event of more promising objectives presenting themselves in the course of the plan.

Planning and implementation processes should be designed to ensure that appropriate actions are taken to enable the firm to meet its marketing objectives within the context of the environment in which it operates. The marketing plan is developed to cover specifically the organisation's relationships with its stakeholders, other groups and, where appropriate, its competitors. It should prescribe specific action with respect to the 7Ps.

MARKET SEGMENTATION, TARGETING AND POSITIONING

Not everyone's wants and needs with regard to a specific service are the same. Offering a standard service irrespective of the different wants and needs of groups of individuals may therefore satisfy some but leave others unsatisfied (see for example, Zikmund and D'Amico, 1995). Differentiating a service so as to meet the individual wants and needs of different groups can therefore create more overall satisfaction with the service that is offered.

Market segmentation is a systematic approach to analysing markets with respect to different customer characteristics and variations in taste, usage, and so on. In effect a homogenous mass market is partitioned into subsets of customers. Within each subset, customers have similar needs, which are distinct from those in other subsets. The marketing approach used for each segment should reflect the particular needs of customers and potential customers in that segment. By employing different marketing mix approaches to each segment, there should be increased levels of satisfaction in each segment.

We can adopt and modify this approach when we come to look at marketing to stakeholders. Effectively, each group of stakeholders is a market segment so the task of segmenting the market has already been done. Of course, within each group of stakeholders there may well be subsets whose views differ from the remainder of the group. So that within groups further segmentation may still be an issue.

Segmentation can be carried out in many different ways; examples are geographical segmentation, behavioural segmentation and psychographic segmentation. For example, services could be made available at specific times to meet the needs of specific customer groups (e.g. commuters, shoppers, sightseers). This would be an example of *behavioural segmentation*.

In order to be viable, a segment must have the following characteristics:

- It must be substantial, in other words there should be enough people in it to justify producing a service specifically for them.
- It must be measurable and definable. There must be some way of identifying the members of the segment and counting them.
- It must be congruent. Members must have close agreement on their needs.
- It must be accessible. There must be some way of targeting the segment with marketing messages and services.
- It must be stable. The nature and membership of the segment must be reasonably constant.

The above criteria can be applied to delineate all stakeholder groups.

MARKET SEGMENTATION PROCEDURE

There is a common three-step approach that is used by organisations to segment the market:

- Step one – survey stage; the organisation (or a researcher) conducts exploratory interviews and focus groups to gain insight into stakeholder motivations, attitudes and behaviour.
- Step two – analysis stage: the organisation analyses the data in order to categorise the segments based on the identified characteristics.
- Step three – profiling stage: each segment is profiled (described) in terms of its distinguishing attitudes, behaviour, demographics and psychographic patterns/characteristics. Each segment is given a name based on a dominant distinguishing characteristic.

BASES FOR SEGMENTING MARKETS

There are many different ways of segmenting customer markets. Some of these may be applicable to identifying subsegments of specific stakeholders. There is a wide selection of options and no single, prescribed way of segmenting a market. The major segmentation methods are – geographic, demographic, psychographic and behavioural segmentation. In addition, we will also consider segmenting customers in terms of family life cycle.

Geographic segmentation

Geographic segmentation requires the market to be divided into different geographical areas. The organisation can decide to operate in one or few geographic areas or operate in all but pay attention to local variations in geographic needs and preferences. For example:

- area within a community (e.g. Soho in Birmingham);
- population size of the area (e.g. under 10,000, 10,000–20,000, etc.);
- predominant makeup of the area (e.g. urban, rural).

Setting up a number of one-stop shops to provide local government services in different areas of a large metropolitan area is illustrative of geographic segmentation.

Demographic segmentation

In demographic segmentation, the market is divided into groups using demographic variables as follows:

- age (e.g. under 17, 17–21, etc.);
- gender (male or female);
- family size (1, 2, 3, etc.);
- income (e.g. under £10,000, £10,000–£15,000, etc.);
- occupation (e.g. skilled workers, executives, retired people, etc.);
- education (e.g. school leaver, further education college, university);
- religion (e.g. Muslim, Hindu, Christian, Buddhist, etc.);
- race (e.g. Afro-Caribbean, Asian, etc.);
- nationality (e.g. Albanian, Cypriot, Spanish, Greek, Italian, etc.).

Psychographic segmentation

In psychographic segmentation, buyers are divided into different groups on the basis of lifestyle and/or personality (see Lastovicka and Joachimstaler, 1988). People within the same demographic group can exhibit very different psychographic profiles:

- Lifestyle: people's interests and requirements in terms of service may be influenced by their lifestyles (e.g. party-goer, achiever).
- Personality: marketers have used personality variables to segment markets. They endow their services with brand personalities that correspond to consumer personalities (e.g. ambitious, retiring).

Behavioural segmentation

People are divided into groups on the basis of their knowledge of, attitude towards, use of, or response to, a product. Groups may be based on factors such as:

- occasions – regular, special;
- benefits – quality, service, economy;
- user status – non-user, ex-user, potential user, regular user;
- usage rate – light, medium, heavy;
- loyalty status – none, medium, strong;
- readiness stage – unaware, aware, informed;
- attitude toward product – hostile, negative, positive, enthusiastic, indifferent;
- life style – how consumers spend their time.

These factors can be explained in more detail:

- Occasions: people can be distinguished according to the occasions they develop a need, or use a service. Occasion segmentation can help firms expand service usage.

- Benefits: a powerful form of segmentation involves classifying people according to the benefits they seek from the service.
- User status: markets can be segmented into groups of non-users, ex-users, potential users, first-time users, and regular users of the product.
- Usage rate: markets can be segmented into light, medium and heavy service users.
- Loyalty status: a market can be segmented by consumer loyalty patterns.
- Readiness stage: a market consists of people in different stages of readiness to use a service. Some are unaware of the product, some are aware, some are informed, some are interested, some desire the service and some desire to use it.
- Attitude: five attitude groups are found in a market – enthusiastic, positive, indifferent, negative and hostile.
- Life style: this considers such things as how people spend their time, what their beliefs are about themselves and the relative importance of their various possessions (see Plummer, 1974).

Family life cycle

Another useful way of segmenting customers is in terms of family life cycle as shown in Figure 8.1.

People at different stages in the family life cycle have different wants and needs and by tailoring services in order to meet the needs of specific groups a greater degree of satisfaction with the service might be anticipated.

Stage in the family life cycle	Service interests
1. Single and young – away from home	Housing, benefits, cheap travel
2. Young married couples no children	Housing, recreation, leisure
3. Married – small children	Nursery facilities, health, housing
4. Married – children mainly under 13	Education, social behaviour, recreation
5. Married – children mainly teenagers	Education, recreation, drug/alcohol abuse and birth control relating to children
6. Married – children left home, both/one still employed	Part-time courses, supported living for their parents
7. Older – retired	Voluntary work, safety, sheltered housing
8. Solitary survivor	Safety, care, transport, suppport in the home

Figure 8.1   Family life cycle stages and illustrative service interests

TARGETING

A target market is a market or market segments that form the focus of the organisation's marketing efforts. The market segments must be researched and marketers should assess the attractiveness of the segments they want to target. The options include the following:

- Mass marketing strategy: offering one product/service concept to most of the market, across many market segments. Economies of scale may be achieved but there is a possibility that not many customers will be adequately satisfied. The underlying assumption of this approach, referred to as *undifferentiated marketing*, is that all customers in the market have similar needs and wants and can therefore be satisfied with a single marketing mix.
- Single segment strategy: concentrating on a single segment with a product/service. This is relatively cheap in resources, but there is a risk of putting all the eggs in one basket – if there is not sufficient demand from that segment the company's financial strength will rapidly decline. The advantage of this method is that a single strategy permits an organisation to specialise, and to concentrate all its efforts on satisfying the wants and needs of a particular market segment.
- Multi-segment strategy: targeting different product or services at each of a number of segments and developing a marketing mix strategy for each of the selected segments. Although this approach can reduce the risk of being over-committed in one area, it can be extremely resource demanding.

The targeting of segments then leads to the marketer to consider the positioning decisions for the product or service in relation to the characteristics and profile of the target segments.

POSITIONING STRATEGIES

Positioning represents the most important decision that management has to make for the company and its marketing (Marken, 1987). Positioning is the process of conjuring up an image and message so that those within the target segment understand what the organisation, service or brand represents. The process involves identifying the key criteria or attributes that people use to judge the service or organisation and then deciding on those benefits/characteristics that are to be emphasised. These then form the positioning concept and are implemented through the marketing mix.

In working towards finalising the positioning concept research is undertaken to ascertain how consumers perceive the service/organisation. This can lead to the construction of perceptual maps which help to identify the current positioning of the organisation and/or its services. Marketers then have to create an image and message that communicates this information to the target audience.

Positioning strategies may vary considerably or they may have common features. The position of an offering is related to the characteristics and attributes of the service such as its quality and the type of people who use it, its strengths and weaknesses, and the value it represents to users. The whole of the marketing mix is important in developing effective positioning, as attributes of the offering must be closely in line with the target audiences' expectations and needs.

For example, the positioning of a local authority service to young people could be based on the confidentiality and uniqueness of the service. It could be ascertained that the unique nature of the service and the confidentiality of the service are the most important attribute in general but that in the case of younger people, confidentiality is the most important attribute. It might be discovered that in the younger segment of the market there are already similar services but that younger people do not seem to consider them very confidential in nature.

Repositioning strategies

A service will require its positioning to be adjusted from time to time. This is referred to as *repositioning* and it can become necessary if consumer preferences with respect to the product or service have changed. Alternatively, it may be that the original positioning was incorrect

It is possible to reposition services in three ways

- *Among existing users*: by the promotion of more varied uses of a service. A museum may have been positioned in the minds of older people as a venue for educational visits. Repositioning might suggest its use as being suitable for family outings.
- *Among new users*: this requires the service to be presented with a different image to the people who have so far rejected it.
- *For new users*: here one has to search for new uses of the service. A call centre may be used for dealing with local authority enquiries but the service could be run jointly with the fire, police, hospital and ambulance services as well.

TRADITIONAL POSITIONING TECHNIQUES

Each service can be thought of as occupying a certain position in a customer's 'perceptual space'. Perceptual mapping refers generally to techniques used to represent this product space graphically. In the context of public services the objective of perceptual mapping is to help identify service attributes that are determinant in influencing customers' attitudes. Often the determining aspects of a service are latent and perceptual mapping can be very useful in uncovering these latent dimensions. Throughout this process, managers are seeking customer relevant dimensions to show that they are customer focused.

Methods of analysis used in service positioning include factor analysis, multi-dimensional scaling (MDS) and cluster analysis. Factor analysis is essentially a data reduction technique in which the objective is to represent the original pool of attributes in terms of a smaller number of underlying factors. After the factors have been identified, the services' ratings on these factors are used to position the services in perceptual space.

For example, suppose that data have been collected on customer service encounters in a local authority via questionnaires. Analysis of the data shows that the two principal dimensions underpinning customers' perceptions of the encounters are friendliness of the encounter and efficiency in terms of conducting business. Perceptual mapping methods enable these to be shown graphically in a 2 × 2 matrix as show in Figure 8.2.

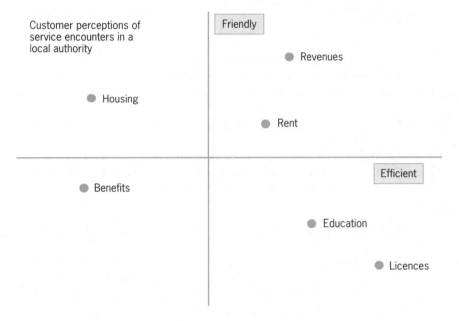

Figure 8.2   Perceptual map of customers' perceived service encounters in a local authority

Interpetation of the map shows that encounters with regard to revenues and rent are perceived to be friendly and efficient, which is the desired state. All other encounters however are perceived to be lacking somewhat in this respect.

CRITICAL EVALUATION OF POSITIONING TECHNIQUES

Perceptual mapping can require a high level of data input. This input must be detailed and taken from a large sample group, which can lead to difficulties in collection, management and analysis. The large number of stimuli required increases the complexity of respondents' tasks giving rise to possible judgement errors on their part. Once gathered, the data only provide a snapshot of time, enabling short-term planning at the most.

Each perceptual mapping technique serves a different purpose, and rarely does one technique alone provide a reliable basis for product positioning. As such, a series of techniques must be used, the complexity of which often requires managers to engage research professionals to perform this analysis, which precipitates additional costs. When managers do take on the responsibility themselves, software programs may be required to assist analysis and these have their own associated pitfalls.

VALUING THE STRATEGY

Once the strategy has been developed, management have to demonstrate that it is the best strategy for creating stakeholder value. The strategy valuation process should enable business unit managers to answer questions such as:

- Does the proposed marketing strategy create value for the organisation's stakeholders?
- Would alternative marketing strategies create more value?
- How sensitive is the strategy to the marketing assumptions *and* to unexpected changes in the industry environment?

Evaluating results in the light of stakeholder value

The main concern in evaluation is the extent to which the various stakeholders are satisfied as a result of a specific marketing campaign and the degree to which there is still stakeholder resistance regarding the subject matter of the marketing campaign. Essentially we have to assess this in terms of the objective of the marketing efforts. Here we can take the hierarchy of effects models and see how much attitudes have changed in terms of awareness, knowledge, liking and preferences shown with respect to the objective of the marketing efforts.

This is best shown by an illustration. Suppose a new local authority service has been launched despite misgivings of employees. Stakeholders with an interest in the service might be identified as top management, senior management, the union, councillors, employees delivering the service and customers. The main objectives for marketing were to create knowledge about the service in the minds of the respective groups where this was required. Pre-measurement data is shown in Table 8.1.

The campaign requires letters to be sent to employees supported by detailed information on the local authority intranet. In addition an information reception/buffet was organised to which representatives of all the local authority-based interested stakeholders were invited. At the reception a talk was given by a member of the top management team, supported by a video/lap-top presentation explaining the benefits of the new service to the customer. The presentation also

Table 8.1 Pre-measurement data

Stakeholder group	Percentage having detailed knowledge of the proposed service	Percentage having some knowledge of the proposed service	Percentage having no knowledge of the proposed service	Objective of the campaign
Top management	100	–	–	–
Senior management	100	–	–	–
Councillors	100	–	–	–
Union	100	–	–	–
Employees	10	60	30	Gain 60% detailed awareness of the proposed new service
Customers	1	5	94	Not directed specifically at customers in this instance

explained how the service would operate from the employees' point of view and the steps management would take to make sure staff would be adequately compensated for delivering the new service.

Following the programme the information shown in Table 8.2 regarding employee knowledge was collected by survey.

In terms of creating stakeholder value marketing's contribution is in terms of the information it gives the employees. There is clearly an increase in detailed knowledge for many of the employees but it has not reached the proportion that had been hoped for in the campaign. In addition, among those who had previously no knowledge at all there has only been a relatively small change from 30% to 25%. It would seem that the marketing campaign has been relatively ineffective in terms of reaching this particular group of stakeholders.

Further marketing efforts need to be directed at planning a campaign to reach those who have no knowledge – a different approach seems necessary. In addition the campaign will also have to address those who still do not have detailed knowledge of the service.

Table 8.2 Old and new levels of employee knowledge

	Detailed knowledge	Some knowledge	No knowledge
Old level	10%	60%	30%
New level	45%	30%	25%

DEVELOPING CREATIVE MARKETING STRATEGIES

The previous section underlined the need for developing creative marketing strategies. In the profit-making commercial sector much effort has been put into developing new and innovative ways of marketing products and services to customers. The messages in advertisements are usually considered to be one-sided arguments delivered by the marketer. Receivers, however, are ultimately responsible for interpreting consumer messages and constructing meaning, but the ability to discriminate between communicator assertions and implications is complicated. One needs to consider the information processing responses of the receivers as they perceive and interpret messages and images in advertisements.

Common sense suggests that any formal assertion or claim made in a marketing message should be backed up with substantive evidence to avoid claims of misrepresentation or be rejected outright by receivers. As a consequence, marketers tend to moderate claims. Creators of messages expect receivers to perceive and process these messages into favourable inferences that may result in behavioural reaction in terms of getting attention, developing interest and stimulating desire for what is being advertised. This is a safe marketing tactic since originators of messages are morally and often legally responsible for information they formally assert.

It can be argued that advertisers are not responsible for any inferences drawn by the receivers since not everyone may infer the same meanings. Perception and interpretation is not under the control of the marketers so they are only liable for a literal interpretation of their advertisements. As a result, weak and fragile claims can be easily changed into convincing sales arguments that can potentially mislead consumers to infer more meaning than is actually proffered. Many marketers in fact pursue a more positive approach providing information to customers which is not misleading and which will reinforce customers' perceptions and comprehensions about the product or service being offered.

Marketers prefer a suggestion rather than a definite statement when promoting a product or idea. Through weak implications, attempts are made to influence and direct behaviour using language that is slyly constructed. There is an effort by marketers to control inferences that can be drawn by receivers by both delineating message parameters and using their insights into the audience's prior knowledge. Receivers of messages are then more likely to construct inferences that were intended. Marketers can manipulate the critical comprehension abilities of receivers by 'asserting less and implying more'. Research findings appreciate the effects that ambiguous implications have on cognitive processing and the methods to construct such manipulations are highly valued since efforts simply to persuade consumers of a product's attributes and value are no longer considered sufficient.

Questions

1 'Segmentation, targeting and positioning are the cornerstones of modern marketing strategy.' Discuss this statement in relation to the kinds of issues that need to be addressed by marketing in the context of the public sector.

2 In what ways and for what reasons might you want to reposition a public sector service in the mind of the user? Suggest how this might be best achieved.

3 'Marketers can manipulate the critical comprehension abilities of receivers by "asserting less and implying more".' How might one apply this argument to corporate advertising of an emergency service?

Case study 8.1 | Vandals

The city council and police are calling on the community to remain vigilant and help combat vandalism in the area. In a recent act of vandalism large fences were destroyed and serious damage was done to the cricket pitch and playing surface. As a result, the city council will have to replace the cricket pitch at a cost of up to £5,000. The cost of replacing the fence, between £5,000 and £7,000, and the fact that it is a regular target of vandals has forced the city council to consider pulling it down altogether

On three separate occasions over the past three years, the amenities building has been burnt out by vandals. Given the rising cost of insuring the amenities facility, which includes a canteen, changing rooms, a store room and separate male and female toilets, the city council is looking at downsizing the amenities building to a simple toilet block.

The city council is particularly distressed that the vandals' actions may mean that the athletics club will have to be relocated from the site to another sporting ground. The city council's administrator said that it was working closely with the police on the matter but was also seeking the community's cooperation to help combat vandalism in the area.

'Sporting grounds such as this are for the whole community to enjoy. It's a real shame that a minority of people are hindering the growth and development of local clubs and spoiling recreational opportunities for the majority of people,' she said. 'The city council is committed to providing the best possible sporting facilities and opportunities for the community, particularly its young people, and so we're calling on people to remain vigilant and report vandalism to the Police or phone the Council as soon as possible.'

Question

1 Assume that you work in the marketing department of the city council and the above report has been brought to your attention. You have been asked to design and plan a marketing campaign that has a bearing on vandalism problems within the various

communities of the city. Draw up such a plan indicating in particular what will be its objectives and messages, and how it will be portrayed in your chosen media. You should pay specific attention to which audience or audiences you are addressing, whether it is necessary to apply segmentation in your campaign and what implications this has for the message and images that need to be conveyed.

Case study 8.2   Social housing

Spiralling house prices have taken the cost of buying a home beyond the reach of many families unless they are prepared to burden themselves with very heavy debts. In parts of the North West of England average house prices were ten times average household income and a factor of six times average household income was very common in most areas. Compared with 50 years ago the cost of buying a house is astronomical and even small interest rate increases can push people into extending the period of repayments beyond retirement.

The Housing Act of 1980 enabled council tenants to purchase their homes from the council and this turned out to be extremely popular. Purchasers of social housing tended to be established residents living in more attractive and marketable properties that they intended to continue to live in. However, it seems that the majority of purchasers buy with the intention of moving on to more expensive properties. The encouragement of home ownership has produced cultural changes within society that have affected the social rented housing market. Owning a house is now a determinant of status in British culture.

Rapid house price inflation has, however, made social housing seem an attractive alternative to people in many areas and there is a growing move back into what had become a much less attractive proposition. The definition of 'social rented housing' is housing that is provided by local authorities or registered social landlords to meet the needs of vulnerable households.

During the 1990s the customer base of the social rented sector changed so that households new to social housing had different characteristics to those leaving it. In general, those that are economically active try to move into the owner occupied sector. However, in the 1990s households entering the social housing sector were mostly young, lone parents who were likely to be unemployed or unable to work. Socially rented stock seems to be disproportionately concentrated in areas with low demand for housing and where there are fewer opportunities for employment.

Question

1 Identify the different market segments for social housing in the current economic climate. What marketing strategy should be employed to make sure that customers' wants and needs with respect to social housing are best met?

References

Abell, D. F. (1978), 'Strategic Windows', *Journal of Marketing*, Vol. 42, No. 2, pp. 21–26.

Lastovicka, J. L. and Joachimstaler, E. A. (1988), 'Improving the detection of personality-behaviour relationships in consumer research', *Journal of Consumer Research*, March, pp. 583–587.

McDonald, M. H. B. (1999), *Marketing Plans: how to prepare them, how to use them*, Oxford: Butterworth-Heinemann.

Marken, A. (1987), 'Positioning key element for effective marketing', *Marketing News*, Vol. 21, No. 4, pp. 7.

Plummer J. T. (1974), 'The concept and application of lifestyle segmentation', *Journal of Marketing*, January, pp. 33–37.

Zikmund, W. G. and D'Amico, M. (1995), *Effective marketing: creating and keeping customers*, St Paul, MN: West Publishing Company.

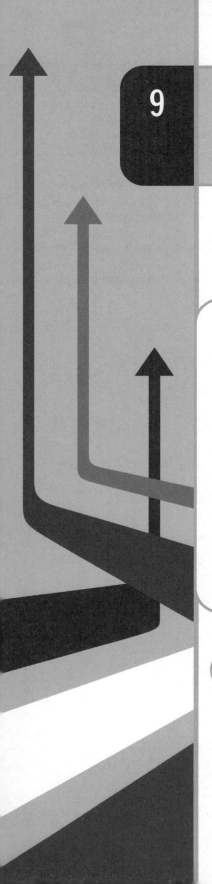

9 Corporate brand building and delivering the service

INTRODUCTION

In this chapter we look first at the nature and the concept of branding before examining how a brand can create value for stakeholders. We distinguish between service or product branding and corporate branding, noting the shift in recent times in favour of corporate branding as a means of creating value for customers and other stakeholders. The values in building brand extensions are also explored.

Establishing a corporate identity and projecting this to customers and other stakeholders is seen as a key component of marketing management. This is particularly the case in services marketing where the service encounter plays such an important role in expressing the quality of the brand. Customer focus and customer brand relationships are seen as determinant of brand equity. We look at the importance of people, processes and physical evidence in assisting the marketing effort at service encounters and comment specifically on the advent of one-stop shops (or citizen shops) as a means of enhancing this process.

NATURE OF THE BRAND

The purpose of brands is to put across the image of a service or an organisation. This takes the form of a name, term, symbol, sign or design used by an organisation to differentiate what it does or offers to customers from those of other organisations (see for example, Czinkota and Ronkainen, 1995). Using our imagination, we can think of a brand as a cluster of purposeful and expressive values. In the case of service industries, and particularly the not-for-profit organisations, the brand communicates the idea that such organisations are values driven. Values of service brands are delivered by staff in their interactions with the customer and other stakeholders (see, for example, Ind, 2001; Nguyen and Leblanc, 2002) and the focus of attention is on paying attention to internal organisational values. Hence, the notion of people in the organisation and organisational cultural values are intimately tied in with the notion of a service brand. Furthermore, the notion of organisational culture can be reflected in the processes and physical evidence that are associated with the service organisation.

ORGANISATIONAL CULTURE

'Organisational culture' can be defined as an organisation's values, beliefs, principles, practices and behaviours. We can find evidence of the organisational culture in its public language: the printed documents, such as brochures, that describe the organisation's vision, values and mission, and the policy and procedures manuals. Organisational culture changes very slowly. The deeper values and beliefs implied in the language of the organisation's culture may not be within the conscious awareness of the organisation's members and leaders (Denison, 1990).

Hofstede *et al.* (1990) identified six independent dimensions to organisational culture that provide a useful framework for understanding how it affects, in this instance, service delivery and ultimately brand associations. Aspects of these dimensions and how they may affect customer service and interaction with other stakeholders are summarised in Table 9.1. In the table aspects of the dimensions to be found in organisations are contrasted from one extreme to the other.

How an organisation or parts of it are perceived in terms of the polarised views shown in Table 9.1 by customers and other stakeholders will influence how this group perceives the brand. In a customer-focused organisation the emphasis should be on those factors that are most likely to be perceived as serving that point of concern.

This raises a very important point when considering how an organisation wants to develop the brand. If the messages it gives out by non-personal means, such as advertising, reports, newletters and so on, are not supported by the kind of customer encounters that reinforce these messages then the brand will become tarnished.

Table 9.1 Organisational culture factors influencing how the staff/brand are perceived during the service encounter

From one extreme ...	to the other
Following procedures	**Getting results**
Avoid taking risk	Comfortable in unfamiliar situations
Staff spend little effort on things	People spend maximum effort
Dominated by technical and bureaucratic routines	Dominated by common concerns for outcomes
Getting the job done	**Keeping staff happy**
Pressure for getting the job done	Attention to personal problems
Important decisions taken by individuals	Important decisions by groups
Long-term solution focus	**Short-term solution focus**
Think well in advance about matters	Do not think far ahead
Transparent communication	**Opaque communication**
Organisation and people are transparent to outsiders	Organisation and people are closed and secretive even to insiders
Control conscious	**Laissez faire**
Everyone is cost conscious	Nobody cost conscious
Meeting times kept punctually	Meeting times only kept approximately
Pragmatic solutions	**Normative solutions**
Emphasis on meeting the needs of customers	Emphasis on correctly following procedures
Results more important than procedures	Correct procedures more important than results
Pragmatic not dogmatic in matters of ethics	High standard of ethics even at the expense of results

HOW BRANDS CREATE VALUE FOR STAKEHOLDERS

In the marketing of fast-moving consumer goods (FMCGs), consumers often purchase products because of the brand names and not because of who owns the brand name. Indeed they may very well be unaware of who this is. However, it seems likely that consumers who do not distinguish between different brands are in fact influenced by corporate brands and make their purchases taking account of the producer of the goods or services. Corporate brands reflect reputation and not the actual products or services on offer (Branson, 1996).

Establishing a good brand reputation enables organisations to market other services effectively (see De Wit and Meyer, 1995). In doing so, positive attributes of the corporate brand are transferred to the new service and it is the brand associations that influence the consumer's perceptions.

Brands make it easier to position services in people's minds (see Ambler and Styles, 1995) and by increasing scale of operation they can also lead to better utilisation of resources. They can also create shareholder value (Kerin and Sethuraman, 1998) and support growth (Broniarczyk and Alba, 1994) and innovation (de Chernatony and Dall'Olmo Riley, 1998). From the customer's perspective brands can make decision making easier (Jacoby and Kyner, 1973), lessen search costs (Jacoby *et al.*, 1977), and even provide emotional, hedonic and symbolic benefits (Srinivasan, 1987).

A brand has to be differentiated from others in the marketplace so that it achieves a distinctive or even unique appeal to users. It also needs to be developed in line with customer needs. The strength of a brand is a combination of its esteem and familiarity, and its likely success in projecting its associated image reflects its differentiation from other brands and its ability to satisfy stakeholder perceptions. When considering using a new service, lack of familiarity and a high level of uncertainty regarding performance are of concern to consumers.

Established successful brand names help to reduce customer concerns and by introducing services under the same brand name – brand extensions – organisations can reduce the uncertainty for the customer (Roselius, 1971; Sheth and Venkatesan, 1968). Customers are thought to use their experiences with other products or services associated with the brand in place of actual experience with the new product. Brand extension strategies are often used in the services sector and this is partly accounted for by the fact that the goodwill in the parent's corporate name overcomes the perceived risk in purchasing an intangible benefit (Iacobucci, 1998).

CORPORATE IDENTITY

The *corporate identity* of an organisation is 'what an organisation is' and this sets it apart from other organisations, making it uniquely recognisable to its various stakeholders. Corporate identity is looked upon as a strategic activity involving the communication of an organisation's corporate vision and strategy (see, for example, Markwick and Fill, 1997; Van Riel and Balmer, 1997). It is argued that an organisation presents itself and is perceived internally and externally through the three elements of the corporate identity mix – symbolism, communication and behaviour (Birkigt and Stadler, 1986)

Corporate image reflects both what the organisation purposefully projects to its various target groups or stakeholders and what is actually in the minds of these target groups. *Corporate reputation* is linked to image and refers to the perception of an organisation that is built up over time in contrast to corporate image which consists of the most recent beliefs about an organisation.

Corporate communication enables an organisation to project its identity to its various stakeholders. It may use advertising, public relations, visual identity and various behavioural codes to achieve this end. Unintentional communications may also have the same effect, for example, the throwaway comment of the disgruntled employee or the unexpected additional help given to a supplier (see Balmer, 2001).

CHARACTERISTICS OF BRAND RELATIONSHIPS

Understanding how value is created for customers is clearly important (Berry, 2000). How well a service is performed influences the value that customers and other stakeholders put upon a service. A strong service brand increases stakeholders' trust in the service and makes it easier to understand what the brand symbolises. The emphasis in service organisations should be on producing distinctiveness in performing and communicating their services and branding should be used to define an organisation's purpose and connect the organisation emotionally with customers (Berry, 2000). A brand may thus be seen as something which helps to build relationships with stakeholders. Hence, one might draw the conclusion that the close links between the rationale for relationship marketing and the rationale for branding suggests that branding and relationship marketing are interdependent and could possibly be seen as two stages of the same process (de Chernatony and Dall'Olmo Riley, 2000).

We have argued that brand images are produced through formal communication activities and also that service personnel are important in building reputable service brands. Van Riel and Balmer (1997) argue that an organisation has to take into account its historical roots, personality, corporate strategy and the three parts of the corporate identity mix (behaviour of organisational members, communication and symbolism) in the search for a favourable brand reputation. Fombrun (1996) and Rindova (1997) also acknowledge the importance of the organisation's strategy and identity and how they are communicated to the stakeholders as factors that influence the images that the organisation projects to its publics and hence, in the long-term, the reputation of its brand.

Developing effective graphics and visual representations of the brand are insufficient in themselves for representing and managing a service brand. The reality of the organisation – the attitudes and behaviour of service personnel during the service encounter – has to be commensurate with the brand values that the organisation is projecting to its publics. Service organisations should use internal marketing to communicate brand values internally within the organisation. In this way they can encourage employees to understand better the corporate identity and improve commitment, enthusiasm and consistent staff behaviour in delivering the organisation's core values.

DELIVERY OF CUSTOMER SERVICE TO REFLECT THE CORPORATE BRAND

Often, the public sector is constrained in terms of the services it can provide and may be unable to implement a customer-led approach strictly in line with the philosophy of good marketing. Constraints may include:

- legislative restrictions,
- political philosophies,
- lack of physical resources,
- lack of financial resources.

Since public sector organisations normally provide services as opposed to products the typical local authority must place high emphasis on the actual service and servicing (people and processes). Marketing success cannot as a rule be measured in terms of increased revenues and profits but in increased user awareness of service provision and other measures of performance. Among these may be the aim to increase usage, demonstrate value for money, educate users, raise profile, demonstrate quality and gain a positive image in the marketplace

Public sector finance is limited and most public sector organisations cannot afford to engage specialist marketing personnel. As a consequence, marketing is often undertaken as part of an employee's duties. This puts responsibility for building the corporate brand image firmly on the shoulders of all people coming into contact with customers and other stakeholders. Marketing activities may be wide ranging in scope as a result and include activities such as:

- creating the right type of public image (e.g. caring, quality oriented, professional);
- justifying certain decisions (e.g. cuts, closures, reduced services);
- promoting key social issues (e.g. crime prevention, environmental protection);
- raising customer awareness (e.g. promoting new services, encouraging take-up of services);
- raising funds (e.g. business and private investment, loans, donations);
- encouraging volunteering (self-help schemes, carers).

Some of these efforts can be controlled by factors beyond the service deliverers' influence. For instance, marketers argue that 'the customer is always right' but in the public sector this principle is sometimes compromised because the customer can sometimes be wrong *and* the public sector organisation always has to adopt the best professional practice whether the customer agrees or not. In addition, many public sector organisations are providing services for the public good that are often restrictive and controlling in nature, where the user is far from happy with the service, for example, enforcement of legislation.

In the public sector, one of the key marketing activities is to educate the public (and all stakeholders in fact) with respect to:

- what is and is not available for them;
- the factors that govern how certain services have to be delivered;
- the reasons for there only being a limited number of options;
- what is best in the public interest;
- the difference between needs and wants;
- the reasons for reduced or inadequate service provision.

Using marketing methods this information can be communicated in a manner that helps develop a good relationship with customers and other stakeholders so that even if they are not totally satisfied with the outcomes they at least appreciate many of the reasons for them.

Services have to be continually updated to ensure that the corporate image of the organisation is viewed as doing its best for all stakeholders. Continuously reviewing, developing and enhancing services, and taking account of customers' opinions, complaints, comments and suggestions is an important means of achieving this end. Often it may be achieved by changing how services are provided or replacing them with alternative ones.

PEOPLE, PROCESSES AND PHYSICAL EVIDENCE

We have argued that creating a brand has much in common with forging a relationship and that relationship marketing and branding have much in common. The people concerned with delivering the service, the processes involved in delivering the service and handling customers, and the physical evidence of the service are key elements of relationship building. Since it is the attitudes and behaviour of the organisation's staff that perhaps best underpins and reflects its corporate brand image this should receive the prime attention.

Arguably, establishing an organisational culture that supports the brand is the key. Organisational culture is permeated downwards from the top of the organisation and is disseminated throughout so that all staff understand the marketing objectives that need to be achieved. If the organisation wishes to be seen as a caring one, for instance, then staff have to adopt a caring attitude in all aspects of their work. This extends to direct verbal and written communication with the public, but should also reflect how colleagues relate to each other. Very importantly, organisational culture can be reflected in the management style that predominates in the organisation and the manner in which services are delivered both internally and externally.

Last, but not least, the physical environment has a huge impact on image formation in the minds of all stakeholders. An agreeable, orderly and fresh environment creates an impression of professionalism and a notion of efficiency. Figure 9.1 shows how the brand image is projected as one that is concerned about providing convenience of place and time in serving customers' interests. In this case the end result is the one-stop and citizen shops.

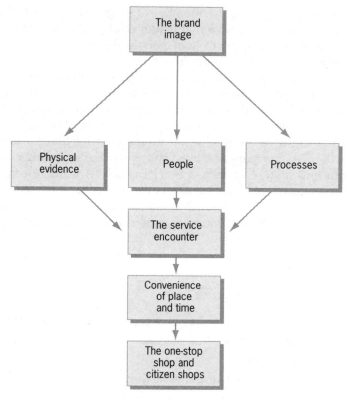

Figure 9.1   Projecting the brand image

ONE-STOP SHOPS

One way of trying to improve customer service is to make it more convenient for customers to use the services provided. In this context, convenience of place and time are important. Rather than having the customer come to the service provider to have queries and matters attended to, the provider tries to go at least part way towards bringing the service to the customer at a convenient location and time. In the UK, the one-stop shops provide face-to-face contact between customers and those responsible for delivering council and partner services. The intention of one-stop shops is to provide a high-quality experience for customers. One-stops shops have grown in popularity over the past few years and are now widely used in local government as a way of bringing the service to the user.

Investment has been made in the business environment and perhaps, more importantly, in the training and development of the one-stop shop staff. Staff are trained to provide a generic service to customers, i.e. they can deal with any and all customer enquiries but to differing degrees depending on first point of contact resolution for a particular service, access to service legacy systems and the level of experience/training the member of staff has received. The vision of the one-stop shop is that of a service that is universally acknowledged as consistently providing value added support to managers in delivering services that achieve the organisation's overall vision and aim.

The notion of the one-stop shop is not confined to the UK or to Europe for that matter. Under different names they are to be found offering a wide range of services to the public worldwide. For example, 'citizen shops' were created in the Brazilian state of Bahia and were introduced in Portugal by the late 1990s to implement the administrative modernisation undertaken by the government (Patricio and Brito, 2006). The Portuguese citizen shops are like shopping centres where the consumer can find a large variety of services such as water, electricity, gas and telephones; banks; certificates and registrations; post offices; personal documents; taxes; labour relations and professional training; social security; health services; services for public servants; and communications and transport (*Ibid.*).

Questions

1   How would you seek to establish a brand image for a city council?
2   Examine how a brand image creates value for stakeholders in an organisation of your choice.
3   In what ways does the delivery of customer service reflect the corporate brand of a public sector organisation?

Case study 9.1   Sports centre – letter of complaint

The following letter found its way into the offices of the municipal council:

Dear Sir/Madam

I would like to take this opportunity to write to you concerning the sports centre and the fact that I have been informed it will be closing to the public during weekdays from 9.00am to 5.00pm.

As a regular user of the facilities I find this proposal to be really out of order as absolutely no consultation has been conducted with the general public concerning this matter. I understand that the reason for these changes is to reduce the operating costs at the centre. May I point out that the facilities are a public service which are already funded through the council tax system.

Whilst using the facilities I have always found the staff to be very helpful and friendly and this complaint has nothing to do with the running of the centre.

I look forward to your response.

(Name and address supplied)

Question

1 The council regularly get letters of complaint from users of its services, many of whom are ratepayers. While the council appreciates that the delivery of customer service reflects the corporate brand, it does not appear to have any systematic procedures in place for dealing with such complaints or for preventing them from occurring in the first place. Draw up an action plan to remedy this situation.

Case study 9.2	Corporate branding issues

The executive directors of the city council met with the Chief Executive Officer (CEO) to discuss what role marketing should have in the organisation. The first item on the list was a proposal that the organisation should put effort into establishing a corporate brand image.

'I know', said the Director of Regeneration, 'that there is a tendency in the public sector to see branding is as a rather frivolous activity but I believe it is important for two very good reasons. In the first instance, people using our service need to know what it is and what it does, and accurate branding can make this easier to appreciate.

Second, a well-defined brand makes it easier for employees to comprehend what their service represents to users and helps keep them focused on achieving this end. What I am suggesting is that we hire an advertising agency that specialises in this sort of thing and get it to help us design and market an image of ourselves that will create meaning for all our stakeholders. This will enable us to project our identity and working culture.'

'I'm not so sure that I agree with you,' said the Director of Finance. 'These notions of culture and identity don't really mean much to anyone. Those who work for the organisation are only interested in their take-home pay and ratepayers are only interested in keeping costs down and having their complaints sorted out. Is there any point in spending more of the latter's money on such frivolous activities as branding? We would be better spending that kind of money on improving services, increasing salaries or reducing council tax bills.'

The CEO looked thoughtful. 'Well what I suggest is that for the next meeting both of you prepare a statement with evidence to support your viewpoints. I don't think we should fritter away the council taxpayer's money and any ideas like this would have to be put before the councillors.'

Question

1 Draw up the case for both points of view. How would you decide corporate branding was worth investing in?

| Case study 9.3 | Revenues and benefits |

In focus group studies conducted on behalf of the revenues and benefits section of a local authority it was indicated that less than 40% of its customers are happy with the service they receive. The same study identified some 14 different attributes customers thought important in the service encounter.

A further survey of customers was then conducted. In this survey respondents were asked two questions about each of the identified attributes in the focus group studies:

1 How important is the attribute?
2 How well did revenues and benefits perform in terms of this attribute?

Mean importance and mean performance rating from some 311 of the 682 contacted previous buyers are shown in Table 9.2.

A five-point rating scale was used. In terms of importance, the scale ran from extremely important (5) to not important (0). In the case of performance rating, the scale ran from excellent (5) to poor (0).

Table 9.2   Mean importance and mean performance ratings

No.	Attribute	Mean importance rating	Mean performance rating
1	Query or problem completed at first interview	3.79	2.68
2	Complaints dealt with speedily	3.61	2.78
3	Immediate attention given to dealing with unresolved queries after interview	3.57	3.11
4	Competence displayed in dealing with queries	3.59	2.96
5	Service available when required	3.42	3.02
6	Friendly/courteous service	3.36	3.28
7	Actions agreed/implemented satisfactorily	3.33	3.00
10	Pleasant surroundings in which interviews conducted	3.22	2.97
11	Convenient for home	2.46	2.21
12	Convenient for work	2.39	2.47

Question

1 How would you interpret the findings of the studies and what actions would you suggest are taken by revenues and benefits?

References

Ambler, T. and Styles, C. (1995), 'Brand Development: Towards a Process Model of Extension Decisions', Pan'agra Working Paper No. 95–903, Centre for Marketing, London Business School.

Balmer, J. M. T. (2001), 'The three virtues and seven deadly sins of Corporate Brand Management', *Journal of General Management*, Vol. 27, No. 1, pp. 1–17.

Berry, L. L. (2000) 'Cultivating Service Brand Equity', *Journal of Academy of Marketing Science*, Vol. 28, No. 1, pp. 128–137.

Birkigt, K. and Stadler, M. M. (1986), 'Corporate identity, grundagen, funktionen fallbeispiele, verlag, moderne industrie', *Landsberg an Lech*, pp. 9–63.

Branson, R. (1996), *Brand New World*, London: Economist Publications.

Broniarczyk, S. M. and Alba, J. W. (1994), 'The Importance of the Brand in Brand Extension', *Journal of Marketing Research*, Vol. 31, pp. 214–228.

Czinkota, M. R. and Ronkainen, I. A. (1995), *International Marketing*, Chicago, IL: The Dryden Press.

de Chernatony, L. and Dall'Olmo Riley, F. (1998), 'Expert Practitioners' Views on Roles of Brands: Implications for Marketing Communications', *Journal of Marketing Communications*, Vol. 4, pp. 87–100.

de Chernatony, L. and Dall'Olmo Riley, F. (2000), 'The Service Brand as Relationship Builder', *British Journal of Management*, Vol. 11, pp. 137–150.

de Wit, B. and Meyer, R. (1995), *Strategy: Process,Content, Context, An International Perspective*, St Paul, MN: West Publishing Company.

Denison, D. (1990), *Corporate Culture and Organizational Effectiveness*, New York: Wiley.

Fombrun, C. J. (1996), Reputation: Realizing Value from the Corporate Image, Boston, MA: Harvard Business School Press.

Hofstede, G., Neuijen, B., Ohayv, D. D. and Sanders, G. (1990), 'Measuring Organisational Cultures', *Administrative Science Quarterly*, Vol. 35, pp. 286–316.

Iacobucci, D. (1998), 'Services: What Do We Know and Where Shall We Go? A View from Marketing', *Advances in Services Marketing and Management*, Vol. 7, pp. 1–96.

Ind, N. (2001), *Living the brand*, London: Kogan Page.

Jacoby, J. and Kyner, D. B. (1973), 'Brand Loyalty vs. Repeat Purchasing Behavior', *Journal of Marketing Research*, Vol. 10, pp. 1–9.

Jacoby, J., Szybillo, G. J. and Busato-Schach, J. (1977), 'Information Acquisition Behavior in Brand Choice Situations', *Journal of Consumer Research*, Vol. 13, pp. 209–216.

Kerin, R. A. and Sethuraman, R. (1998), 'Exploring the Brand Value-Shareholder Value Nexus for Consumer Goods Companies', *Journal of the Academy of Marketing Science*, Vol. 26, No. 4, pp. 260–273.

Markwick, N. and Fill, C. (1997), 'Towards a framework for managing corporate identity', *European Journal of Marketing*, Vol. 31, Nos 5/6, pp. 396–406.

Nguyen, N. and Leblanc, G. (2002), 'Contact personnel, physical environment and the perceived corporate image of intangible services by new clients', *International Journal of Service Industry Management*, Vol. 13. No. 3, pp. 242–262.

Patricio, C. and Brito, C. (2006), Managing Public Services Delivery – The Case of Citizen Shops, Academy of Marketing Conference, Middlesex University Business School, 3–6 July.

Rindova, V. P. (1997), 'The image cascade and the formation of corporate reputations', *Corporate Reputation Review*, Vol. 1, Nos 1 and 2, pp. 188–194.

Roselius, T. (1971), 'Consumer rankings of risk reduction methods', *Journal of Marketing*, Vol. 35, No. 1, pp. 56–61.

Sheth, J. N. and Venkatesan, M. (1968), 'Risk-reduction behavior in repetitive consumer behavior', *Journal of Marketing Research*, Vol. 5, No. 3, pp. 307–310.

Srinivasan, T. C. (1987), 'An Integrative Approach to Consumer Choice', in *Advances in Consumer Research*, (eds) Wallendorf, M. and Anderson, P., Association for Consumer Research, pp. 96–100.

Van Riel, C. B. M. and Balmer, J. M. T. (1997), 'Corporate Identity: the Concept, its Measurement and Management, *European Journal of Marketing*, Vol. 31, Nos 5/6, pp. 340–355.

10 Pricing services

INTRODUCTION

First we discuss the relevance of pricing in public sector organisations pointing out than in some instances there is latitude to charge customers a price but in others there is not. We quickly review some economic aspects of pricing before going on to look at its practical aspects. We then discuss cost-oriented approaches to prices which in the main reflect the basis on which 'prices' may be set in the public sector, and we look specifically at the usefulness of breakeven analysis as a tool in the context of setting prices for new services. We also look at an alternative view of price where opportunity cost is taken into account. Price perceptions and price changes are briefly considered followed by dynamic pricing and price boundaries/price flexibility. Finally, we also look briefly at pricing in a social marketing context and finally we look at local government pricing practices.

THE IMPORTANCE OF PRICE

Price is often described as a measure of the value exchanged by the buyer for the value offered by the seller. It seems reasonable to expect then the price set will reflect the costs to the seller of producing the service and the benefit to the buyer of consuming it. However, this is not always the case since price along with other elements of the marketing mix also contributes to the overall image created for a service or product and customers may be prepared to pay much more for it than it actually costs the seller to produce.

However, when we come to look at public sector service offerings price may have different dimensions since as far as the consuming public is concerned services may appear to be free. When viewed from the perspective of stakeholders, however, it will become apparent that this is not the case since in the long run the cost of services are met by taxpayers either directly through council tax charges or indirectly through central government taxes that are then passed on to local authorities to provide services.

The extent to which the consumer or user of public sector services has choice in the matter of the price they pay for services is restricted. It is only through exercising votes in elections (in the case of a local authority) that the consumer can influence the pricing mechanism. In many instances in a public sector context, price is something which is effectively determined by the organisation in conjunction with central government and with the advice of elected councillors representing the interests of the users of the services.

Nevertheless, the pricing of services is important and has a strategic dimension to it in terms of one set of stakeholders, the organisation, and its negotiations with other sets of stakeholders, notably users and central government. There are occasions, too, when public sector organisations may want to exact charges for their service – homes for the elderly, pest control for houses and business owners being examples. Colleges and universities charge for courses and these also illustrate this point. There is thus a mixed approach to pricing in the public sector: sometimes the customer using the service is charged and at other times no charge is levied at all.

PRICING FROM AN ECONOMICS PERSPECTIVE

Classical economics takes the view that price determines both the supply and the demand for goods and services in the marketplace, formulating the 'law of demand' to explain this phenomenon. The law of demand states that the quantity demanded per period of time is inversely related to price. That is, as the price increases, demand will fall, and as price falls then demand will increase.

A key concept in understanding how demand shifts with respect to changes in price is the elasticity of demand. Price elasticity is defined as the ratio of the percentage change in demand to a percentage change in price. While, by definition, the ratio usually has a negative sign – this is because as price rises, demand usually falls – it is customary, in illustrating elasticities, to drop the sign. A price elasticity equal to one signifies that demand rises (falls) by the same percentage that price falls (rises). In this case, total revenue is not affected by price changes. However, when the elasticity is above or below one, then total revenues will be affected by changes.

Knowing the price elasticity of demand for its products or services enables an organisation to determine whether its price is too high or too low.

Price elastic demand occurs where a rise in price reduces total revenue and a fall in price raises total revenue. This is because if demand is price elastic, any change in price will cause a large change in the number of customers wanting to buy. This is good news from a revenue point of view if you are looking to reduce prices, as you will attract a lot of new customers and revenue will rise. But it is bad news if you want to put prices up, as you will lose a large proportion of your customers and revenue will consequently fall.

Price inelastic demand occurs where a rise in price raises total revenue and a fall in price reduces total revenue, because demand is price inelastic, and the customer base will not change much when prices are changed. If the organisation drops its prices, it will gain some customers, but not too many, and consequently its total revenue will fall. If the organisation increases its prices, it will not lose many customers and its total revenue will increase. This is why the Chancellor of the Exchequer always adds duty to the same products in budgets (e.g. alcohol, cigarettes and petrol) because he knows that demand for these is relatively inelastic and consequently we will still buy them even at the higher price.

PRACTICAL PRICING

The classical economic approaches to price setting over-simplify reality and cannot be readily implemented. What is really required is a consideration of all the practical and theoretical guidelines that are available when one is setting prices. Pricing should have objectives, and these should result from marketing and organisational objectives. We will now look at various methods that organisations can use to set prices.

COST-ORIENTED PRICING

Many organisations set prices mainly or even completely on the basis of their own costs. The most common and the most basic types of cost-oriented pricing are *standard cost pricing* and *mark-up pricing*. In applying both methods a fixed percentage is applied to the unit cost to arrive at a preliminary price. A comparison is then made between the preliminary price and the going market price for a similar service, and an adjustment is made if necessary. If the pricing is simply intended to cover costs of providing the service then there is no mark-up on costs involved.

BREAK-EVEN ANALYSIS

Break-even analysis is a useful technique for helping to set prices for new services. The production and marketing of every service acquires a cost on the one hand, and yields revenue on the other. Two kinds of costs are associated with a service. There are those that are readily identifiable such as labour and materials put into running the services. These are usually referred to as *variable costs* since they vary in accordance to the level of service provided. The second kind of costs are *fixed costs*, which do not vary with the level of service provided. If the organisation only produces one service then clearly all the fixed costs can be charged to the one service. Since organisations usually offer many services, they tend to allocate the fixed costs across services. Fixed costs are also known as *overheads*, and do not vary with output. Rent, heat, interest, etc. are examples of fixed costs. In applying break-even analysis the idea is to estimate how much revenue is needed to recover the fixed costs associated with the service and at the same time cover variable costs. Break-even point is where the total revenue equals the total cost.

Figure 10.1 shows the situation where the organisation is able to charge the customer a price for the service offered. The total revenue received is equal to number of people using the service multiplied by the price (assuming that only a single price is charged).

Figure 10.2 below shows the situation where local government revenues from central government and council taxpayers is allocated to cover costs.

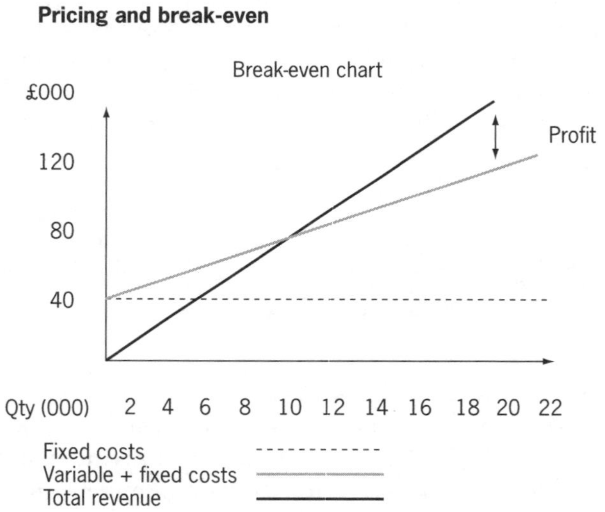

Pricing and break-even

Figure 10.1   Pricing and break-even

PRICE: AN ALTERNATIVE VIEW

Price may be considered as 'what is given up, from the customer's point of view, to obtain the product or service' (Zeithaml, 1988). For example, the price of setting up and running a new service is not just the actual cost in terms of using up allocated revenues, for example, but also involves the opportunity cost associated with how

Pricing and break-even

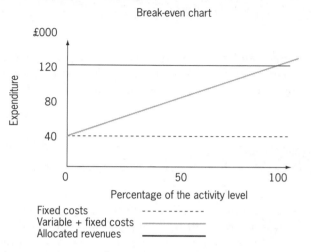

Figure 10.2   Local government revenue allocation to cover costs

else the money might be spent. In other words, it is the cost of the package plus the cost of not being able to buy something else.

This gives rise to several new perspectives on pricing. First, the issue is raised of a possible inconsistency between *objective* and *perceived* prices. Second, price is not simply a single monetary value paid for a specific item because additional expenditure on repairs, maintenance and energy consumption may be required. In addition, price can entail *non-monetary considerations* (e.g. ethical, legal or moral issues) and there may also be 'time costs' resulting from travel, shopping, waiting, search and transaction time. Price also includes a 'risk' component, such as the risk of failure or of poor technical and delivery support. It may also be social or psychological in nature, an example being the risk of signalling low social status.

PRICE PERCEPTIONS

Understanding how consumers judge prices is important. Consumers may use a simple heuristic, for example evaluating a price by determining its relative position *vis-à-vis* prices charged for what they consider to be similar products (see, for example, Janiszewski and Lichtenstein, 1999). On the other hand, consumers may compare a price in relationship to what they think is in a range of acceptable prices (see e.g., Petroshius and Monroe, 1987).

PRICE CHANGES

Price changes and consumer perceptions of price change are also of considerable interest to marketers. Consumers may judge a price increase to be more painful than a price discount of equal value is pleasurable (see, for example, Heath *et al.*, 1995).

DYNAMIC PRICING

Price levels vary in accordance with the stage of the product life cycle. In dynamic pricing, these factors will be taken into account. In the case of *price skimming*, for example, an organisation may introduce a service at a high price in order to 'skim' the high willingness to pay of innovators and early adopters, and gradually lowers the price in later stages of the life cycle. On the other hand, an organisation adopting a *penetration pricing* strategy may charge low prices in the introduction stage in order to secure a solid customer base, when the organisation will increase prices.

Dynamic pricing is productive in generating cost advantages (*vis-à-vis* future competitors). When pricing in accordance with the experience curve, an organisation charges low prices initially in order to encourage consumption and obtain high usages. There are also external dynamic changes, such as new technological developments, that can influence reduce costs and thus influence price setting.

PRICE FLEXIBILITY AND BOUNDARIES

An important aspect of pricing concerns *pricing flexibility*, or the extent to which an organisation has freedom in setting prices. Pricing flexibility can be assessed through the analysis of price boundaries: minimum and maximum price levels that an organisation can charge for a service. Certain factors, such as costs, set the price floor. The price should enable the organisation to cover the various costs incurred in providing customers with the service. In addition, legal constraints, or the fact that customers associate low price with low quality, may prevent the organisation from charging prices below a minimum level. Other factors set an upper boundary on price. Government regulations may impose an upper boundary on price in certain markets. However, the maximum price that can be charged tends to be mainly dependent on customers' willingness to pay for the service.

PRICING IN THE CONTEXT OF SOCIAL MARKETING

In the context of social marketing price can be regarded as the monetary cost associated with adopting a change in behaviour (Sargeant, 2005). Attending a rehabilitation programme may require the person concerned to fund some of the treatment that may be required. For example, an alcoholic may seek intensive treatment to enable withdrawal from alcohol abuse which involves staying in a clinic for an extended period of time, and they may have to pay for the stay and the treatment. There is obviously an implied associated opportunity cost involved in that the alcoholic may have preferred to spend the money concerned on a more pleasurable experience such as a holiday or the purchase of things for the house or garden.

The costs of an a change in behaviour, however, tend to be social in nature (Sargeant, 2005). Reducing alcohol consumption may make a person less acceptable to their associates or friends and can even make them the subject of ridicule. It is important therefore to identify all the social costs involved when undertaking social marketing campaigns and attempt to minimise them.

LOCAL GOVERNMENT PRICING PRACTICES

Local government pricing has been described as a 'seat-of-the-pants' activity for most managers with few clear guidelines as to how to approach pricing problems (McCarthy and Perrault, 1993). It has been recommended, however, that the process should involve the participation of councillors and their involvement in the development of the charging policy has, according to the Accounts Commission for Scotland (1998:13), a number of clear advantages:

- Councillors are allowed to discuss the overall impact and inform the political judgements necessary on ability to pay.
- Councillors are able to develop their understanding of the reasons for the prices, and can be in a position to justify their imposition to their constituents.
- Discussion of proposed prices take place in committee.
- Potential public relations problems can be minimised.

The Audit Commission (1999) found that in most local authorities pricing was not connected to particular objectives and knowledge about the impact on service users. In the main, pricing was found to be budget driven, with little monitoring or evaluation being undertaken. Pricing was not related to a corporate charging mechanism designed to deliver best value. Councils are apt to price on a service-by-service basis and do not take account of common issues in a corporate manner. Moreover, some departments within a council have well-developed processes in place while others do not (Accounts Commission for Scotland, 1998:12).

Local governments are able to charge only in accordance with legislation established by central government (CIPFA, 2006). This tends to be prohibitive, in the sense that it sets out those services for which local authorities are prevented from imposing charges. However, under the terms of The Local Government Act 2003 local authorities can impose 'reasonable' charges for new services. Reasonable is defined as having regard to the financial circumstances and so as not to cause financial hardship.

COMPLEXITY OF PRICING

Trying to get to grips with 'what is the right price?' is a complex challenge for most in the public sector. The reason behind this is reflected in difficulties in determining the exact selling price and the presence of differing pricing schemes such as cost-based, demand-based, competition-orientated and differential pricing methods (Cannon and Morgan, 1990). In addition, councils seek to achieve a wide range of objectives and provide a wide range of services. In some cases, the council is the only provider and has a geographic monopoly while for others it competes openly with the private sector for custom. These complications mean that a large number of different factors present themselves when councils try to decide whether the price is right.

NATIONAL LEGAL FRAMEWORK FOR CHARGES

The national legal framework for council charges further complicates the picture in that a wide variety of specific duties, powers and restrictions on local authority charging have been introduced piecemeal for over 100 years. The result is a complex array of differing degrees of national control over local government policy. The current position is that councils can charge for a service only if they have an express power or duty to charge for those services. For some services, charges are mandatory and government sets the specific fee but sometimes a council is obliged to provide a service, but is prohibited from charging. In the remaining instances, councils may be permitted to charge for a service but are constrained in some way, such as:

- They must take into account the ability of the user to pay.
- They may charge only what is necessary to cover 'related' costs.
- They must have regard to the cost of provision when setting the charge.

Last but not least, legislation in 2003 identified that income from charges must not exceed the costs of provision.

In summary, pricing methods in operation are highly variable, involving flat-rate charges, means-tested charges, concessions and exemptions from charges. Irrespective of the nature of the charge, the extent to which charges recover the costs of service provision vary from service to service.

Questions

1   How does pricing in the public sector differ from that in the private sector? Illustrate your answer.

2   Assuming that a public organiation wants to exact a charge on users of a new service, how should it set a price level for the service? Should it offer any discounts? If so what might these be and what would be the rationale for such discounts?

3   The legislation passed in 2003 that identified that income from charges must not exceed the costs of provision is not in the best interests of all stakeholders in a public sector organisation. Discuss.

Case study 10.1   Charging for library information facilities

The library in a large town has decided to introduce a 24-hour library and intends to include 'Britannica Online' at a variety of appropriate reading levels, from 5 to 18+, each with a separate user-friendly interface. Library members will have access to some of the most popular online information sources via the website. The development means that members will have access to a huge range of dictionaries, encyclopaedias, back and recent copies of newspapers, and many other information sources in their own homes and places of work or study, 24 hours a day, seven days a week. It will also allow members to check their borrower details and permit them to renew and reserve items from the library catalogue.

Access to the 24-hour library

After selecting a website link, members will be taken to an interim page asking them to confirm borrower number and personal identification number (PIN). After supplying this information they will be taken to a further page asking them to confirm the name of the information source they wish to access. Clicking on the relevant link will gain access to the information source of choice

Information sources

Information sources available include:
- *Oxford Reference Online*: This comprises Oxford's unparalleled collection of reference books covering the entire subject spectrum from accountancy to zoology. Over 200

titles are available. As well as standard works of reference in the arts, humanities and sciences, many general interest titles are also included: dictionaries, including bi-lingual and visual dictionaries, encyclopaedias, books of quotations, companions to food and drink, names and places, and many more. Users will be able to search each title individually or cross-reference the entire online database.

- *Oxford English Dictionary*.
- *Grove Music Online*: This contains the full text of *The New Grove Dictionary of Music and Musicians*, *The New Grove Dictionary of Opera*, and *The New Grove Dictionary of Jazz*. Enhanced features unique to the online edition include regular updates and audio musical examples.
- *Cobra* (Complete Business Reference Adviser) The Cobra database has hundreds of small business ideas and business opportunity profiles, practical how-to guides, reports, checklists and fact-sheets.
- *Oxford Dictionary of National Biography*: This is an illustrated collection of 50,000 specially written biographies of the men and women who shaped all aspects of Britain's past, from the fourth century BC to the year 2000. It was compiled over a 12-year period by some 10,000 experts, who have produced a 60 volume, 60 million word reference work, and a website of over 100,000 pages.
- *Newsbank*: This is a full-text content of selected national, regional and international English language newspapers: the *Guardian*, *The Times*, the *Daily Mirror*, the *Daily Mail*, and the *Daily Express*. This database also includes the international newspapers: the New *York Times*, the *South China Morning Post* (Hong Kong), the *Times of India*, the *Nation* (Islamabad), and the *Irish Times*.
- *Times Digital Archive*: This delivers every page of *The Times* newspaper, as published, from 1785 to 1985.
- *New Britannica Online*: The online edition contains many enhanced features and is now available at a variety of appropriate reading levels, each with a separate user-friendly interface. It comprises: Encyclopedia Britannica Online Academic Edition, Encyclopedia Britannica Online Library Edition, Encyclopedia Britannica (18+ reader-ship), Britannica Student (age 12–18 readership) and the Britannica Junior (age 5–11 readership).
- *Grove Art Online*: Full access to the entire text of *The Dictionary of Art* (1996, 34 volumes), plus extensive image links are available. Grove Art Online is the most com-prehensive and authoritative online resource for all research into the history of the visual arts.
- *whichbook.net*: This is a completely new way to help find exactly the right kind of book. This website allows a user to choose whether they want a happy or sad book, a long or short read, easy or demanding material, and even books with lots of or hardly any sex! When the title of choice has been found the site will redirect the user to the library catalogue to check whether the item required is on the library shelf.

Question

1 Should the library charge for this service? Why or why not? If it were to exact a charge for the service what would be the basis of the charge levied? Might there be higher charges for some users than others? Discuss.

Case study 10.2 | Local Government Consultants – pricing issues

Local Government Consultants (LGC) is profit-making partnership company set up as joint venture between a city council, a business school of a university, a firm of management consultants and a chamber of commerce. Its aim is to offer advice on all management matters relating to local government and other public sector organisations, and to provide short course training in advanced management topics to executives working in public sector organisations.

LGC has a core staff of 25 personnel who manage the business but all advisory expertise is bought in from experts working for one or other of the four parent organisations. At present it has no training facilities of its own but can buy space from the university and city council at slack periods or run courses in one or more of a number of local or regional conference centres depending upon where the client organisations are situated.

The organisation is in the course of revising its existing pricing policies and is considering what might be the best approach to take. The staff of LGC are concerned with making contacts and getting business. Once a firm lead has been established experts are then brought in to look at the job that needs to be done and to indicate what they would want in terms of remuneration for the work. LGC prepares an estimate for the job adding 25% to the cost to contribute to overheads and make it a profit. In the past this method has worked well and LGC has carried out the work identified in 65% of the cases where negotiations have taken place. In the 35% of cases where work has not ensued from initial enquiries and estimates this had led to some bad feelings on the behalf of the experts since they felt that their time and energy has been wasted in following up unfruitful leads. This has made many of them reluctant to want to be involved further with LGC.

LGC operated at a loss in its first year but achieved an after-tax return on capital employed of 5.2% in its second year of operation.

Question

1 In what ways might LGC alter its approach to pricing so that both profitability and expert satisfaction may be improved?

References

Accounts Commission for Scotland (1998), The Challenge of Charging: A Managed Response, Edinburgh: Accounts Commission for Scotland

Audit Commission (1999), *The Price is Right? Charges for Council Services*, London HMSO.

Cannon, H. M., and Morgan, F. W. (1990), 'A strategic pricing framework', *Journal of Services Marketing*, Vol. 4, pp. 19–30

CIPFA (2006), 'Charging', retrieved from http://www.tisonline.net.fis/18.2_charging on 15 May 2006.

Heath, T. B., Subimal, C. and France, K. R. (1995) 'Mental Accounting and Changes in Price: The Frame Dependence of Reference Dependence', *Journal of Consumer Research*, Vol. 22, p. 90.

Janiszewski, C. and Lichtenstein, D. R. (1999), 'A Range Theory Account of Price Perception', *Journal of Consumer Research*, Vol. 25 (March), pp. 353–368.

McCarthy, E. J. and Perrault, W. D. (1993), *Basic Marketing: A Managerial Approach*, Homewood, IL: Irwin.

Petroshius, S. M. and Monroe, K. B. (1987), 'Effect of product-line pricing characteristics on product evaluations', *Journal of Consumer Research*, Vol. 13, March, pp. 511–519.

Seargeant A, (2005) *Marketing management for non-profit organisations*, Oxford: Oxford University Press.

Zeithaml, V. A. (1988), 'Consumer Perceptions of Price, Quality and Value: A Means–End Model and Synthesis of Evidence', *Journal of Marketing*, Vol. 52 (July), pp. 2–22.

Further reading

Kotler, P. and Keller, K. L. (2006), *Marketing Management*, Upper Saddle River, New Jersey: Prentice Hall.

11 Communicating values

INTRODUCTION

In this chapter we consider how different forms of communication, which we broadly define as being under the umbrella of external and internal marketing activities, create stakeholder value. An important pre-requisite for this is to understand something about the decision-making processes engaged in by customers and other stakeholders. We therefore turn to what has been written about consumer behaviour and to models that have been developed, in particular those relating to the influence that marketing communications have on consumer behaviour. While our main interest is on consumer behaviour many of the ideas and concepts involved have a direct bearing on communicating with stakeholders more generally.

We stress the importance of *people*, *processes* and *physical evidence* as a means of communicating with stakeholders and employees in particular. Preparing employees to be envoys of the organisation is seen as a most important strategy and we consider how employees acquire the values we want them to communicate to other stakeholders.

HOW EFFECTIVE COMMUNICATION CREATES STAKEHOLDER VALUE

Marketing communications may be thought of as a management process through which an organisation enters into dialogue with its various audiences (Fill, 1999). Dialogue entails creating, transmitting and interpreting messages to and from identified stakeholder groups with the aim of positioning or repositioning the organisation and/or its offering in the mind of each member of the stakeholder audience. In this context, ethics and trust are extremely important (Jones, 1995). Dialogue is about the spirit of communication (Pearson, 1989) and reflects being prepared to listen and change practices where appropriate in the interests of consensus.

The process of communication, dialogue and consensus reaching can be represented in descriptive models. These can be used to help explain customer buying behaviour for example. They permit customer decision-making processes to be expressed in a form where the role of marketing communications and its influence on behaviour can be comprehended and evaluated. The simplest form of communication can be represented by the following model whose elements include:

Sender → Message → Encoding → Media → Noise → Receiver → Decoding → Response → Feedback

In this model:

- The *sender* is the source of the message.
- The *receiver* is the person or persons receiving the message.
- *Encoding* sees the meaning of the message placed in an appropriate symbolic form (signs, words, sounds, etc.).
- The *media* are the communication channels the message moves through.
- The *decoding* process is carried out by the receiver who interprets the message from symbolic form into a form understandable by them.
- The *response* is the reaction the receiver gives once the message is decoded.
- *Feedback* is that part of the receiver's response that is communicated back to the sender.
- *Noise* represents other messages and distractions that may distort the message sent.

The model can also be represented diagrammatically as shown in Figure 11.1.

In Figure 11.1 the sender selects an effective medium to communicate with the receiver and sets up a means of receiving feedback. The sender has to design the message (encoding) so that the receiver or audience will interpret correctly through the decoding process. Noise in the model reflects the fact that messages may be competing for the attention of the receiver and there are many distractions, which could prevent the message from being correctly received.

Models of the communication process may assist an organisation in understanding the buying behaviour of its customers. Among these models are the response hierarchy models. There are several such models and they all adopt the principle that customers pass through a sequence of mental stages on the way to making a purchase. Figure 11.2 displays four of these models.

Marketing communication gives out information about a product or service and shows how it will benefit the user. At the same time, it tries to persuade customers that they should have a liking or a preference for the product or service that is featured in the communication. In other words, a marketing communication tries to influence a person's attitude towards the object featured in the communication. Having a positive attitude towards something is considered to be essential before a

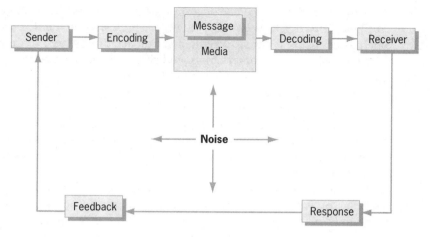

Figure 11.1 The communication process
Source: Croft R. (1999), 'Audience and Environment: Measurement and Media', in P. J. Kitchen (ed.) *Marketing Communications: Principles and Practices*, London: ITP Business Press.

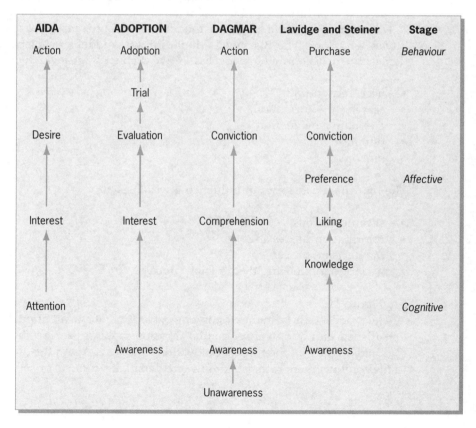

Figure 11.2 Response hierarchy models
Source: AIDA, see Strong (1925); for ADOPTION, see Rogers (1995); for DAGMAR, see: Colley (1961); Lavidge and Steiner, see Lavidge and Steiner (1961).

person will buy or make use of certain products or services. However, such thinking applies primarily to what are known as 'high-involvement' products or services – such as choosing a house, buying a car or deciding where to go abroad on holiday. In such instances customers may well search around for a lot of information before making a decision to purchase the product or service.

Where the service is 'free' – which is generally the case with local authority services – the involvement may well be 'low' so that it is not necessary to pass through all the stages indicated in Figure 11.2 prior to making use of the service. Indeed, as is the case with all low-involvement products or services positive attitudes are created after trying or using the product or service. The key is therefore to achieve trial of the product or service.

In profit-making organisations trials are often induced through giving away free samples of a product or by demonstrations at the point of sale where consumers have the opportunity to try out the product for themselves. This is more difficult to achieve in the case of publicly provided free services. We therefore have to find mechanisms for inducing potential customers to visit the place where the services are made available (special events which people would find interesting, for example) and once there to use sales promotion and possibly personal selling methods to evoke customer interest and trial of what is on offer.

More comprehensive or 'grand' models also exist to map all of the complexities of buyer behaviour. The Blackwell–Miniard–Engel model (See Blackwell *et al.*, 2001) depicts the decision-making process as five distinct stages which occur over time:

- need recognition,
- search for information,
- alternative evaluation,
- purchase,
- outcome.

The four main categories of influencing variables are:

- stimulus inputs,
- information processing,
- the decision process,
- variables influencing the decision process.

See Figure 11.3.

The model starts with the customer's perception of a want or problem which must be satisfied and adopts a sequential decision-making process showing the factors that may impact on the final decision along the way. Again this model is applicable to high-involvement rather than low-involvement products or services.

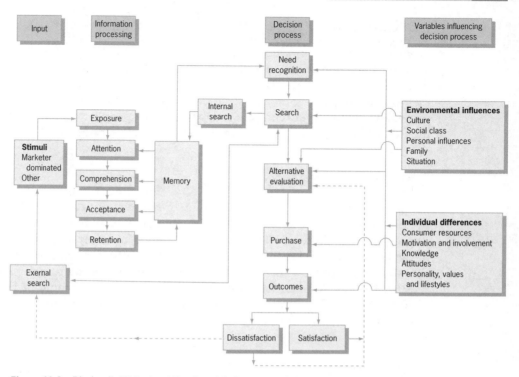

Figure 11.3 Blackwell, Miniard and Engel model of consumer behaviour
Source: Blackwell, R. D., Miniard, P. W. and Engel, J. F. (2006). Exhibit 4.1 from *Consumer Behavior*, 10th edn. Reprinted with permission.

COMPONENTS OF THE PROMOTION MIX

The marketing mix of the 4Ps may not be entirely appropriate for public sector services marketing. An alternative marketing mix – that of the 7Ps – is advocated by Booms and Bitner (1981). By adding the variables of:

- participants (the people who deliver the service),
- physical evidence (the tangible clues used to assess the quality of the service), and
- procedures (the process by which the service is acquired),

it is argued that this presents a more complete paradigm of the generic marketing mix.

Participants

Systems need to be in place and evidence shown that regular team meetings are taking place where key issues are discussed and information disseminated to show that the opinions and needs of staff are valued. Staff also need to be made aware of their role in supporting the organisation's objectives and relevant training should be provided for this. The organisation depends on its people to deliver the service, and they should be equipped to deliver the best possible service.

Physical evidence

Physical evidence is the buildings, the features and facilities and if this is poor then the promotion will be impaired. Poorly maintained buildings give a negative first impression. In addition, leaflets, correspondence and newsletters should be well-designed. A well-designed and informative leaflet or booklet should be available, containing photographs of facilities available plus performance figures and annual reports. The development of a website linked to the service would be beneficial and should contain all essential documents and encourage customers to contact and interact with the organisation.

Processes

How people are treated in the course of receiving a service has a substantial impact on their attitude towards that service. Establishing customer-friendly procedures for processing enquiries and dealing with complaints is also very important and projects the image and culture of the organisation to members of the public.

INTEGRATED MARKETING COMMUNICATIONS STRATEGY

Integrated marketing communications (IMC) reflects the advantages of combining different media so that they are all projecting very similar messages and images about a product, service or organisation. Three broad conceptualisations of IMC can be discerned (Nowak and Phelps, 1994):

- 'One voice' marketing communications, or 'seamless' marketing communications involves the maintenance of a consistent, clear image, position, message and theme across all marketing communications.
- 'Integrated communications' suggests that this conceptualisation is micro-oriented. Marketing communications should both develop an image and directly influence consumer behaviour.
- 'Coordinated marketing communication campaigns' in which IMC means coordinating marketing communication disciplines. Unlike the 'one voice' approach,

the separate disciplines do not necessarily work under a single brand positioning; rather multiple positionings on multiple target audiences is the norm, with each discipline working to its own objectives, whether they be image-related or behavioural.

Thoughts and ideas about the role of IMC have extended the concept to apply beyond the conventional promotional mix. Ind (1998), for example, has argued that if strong corporate brands are desired, then internal communications should be considered as important as external communications.

STAKEHOLDER VALUE ANALYSIS OF COMMUNICATION STRATEGIES

Rokeach (1973) defined a value as an enduring belief that a specific mode of conduct or end-state of existence is personally or socially preferable to an opposite or converse mode of conduct or end-state of existence (1973:5). In this section we will examine how the values of an organisation are communicated to staff and consumers via corporate communication. Three primary types of corporate communication have been identified (van Riel, 1995):

- *organisational* – which covers all other communications based within an organisation, such as PR, public affairs, environmental communications, investor relations and internal communication;
- *management* – which refers to messages conveyed by management to both internal and external stakeholders;
- *marketing* – which is directly aimed towards the consumer (e.g. advertising, direct mail, personal selling and sponsorship).

Arguably, communicating values to staff takes place primarily through a combination of management and organisational communication, whereas customers learn about the organisation's values mainly through marketing and organisational communication. We next consider in more detail the ways in which values are communicated to employees and consumers.

COMMUNICATING ORGANISATIONAL VALUES TO STAFF

Organisational communication occurs at both recruitment and selection and in the various channels through which socialisation occurs once an employee has joined the organisation (e.g. human resources (HR) processes, mentoring, story-telling, rites and rituals, and the encoding of values into a values statement). Recruitment and selection convey the initial communication of values via the recruitment processes and literature (Davidson, 2002). 'Socialisation' is the name given to the process by which individuals absorb organisational values once they have joined an organisation. It is commonly referered to as *learning the ropes*, that is the the process of learning what is important in an organisation (Schein 1988). Such learning is acquired in different ways. While HR processes can be used to assist socialisation, processes such as hiring methods, performance management systems, criteria for promotions and rewards, dismissal policies (Lencioni, 2002) and story-telling can also be used to transmit values to employees. Employees may also gain clues about the organisation's values from advertisements intended primarily for the attention of customers (Wolfinbarger and Gilly, 1991).

Management communication in the form of the example set by senior managers and their function as role models have great potential in communicating values to employees (Dauphinais and Price, 1998; Giblin and Amuso, 1997). In this context, naturally, the behaviour of senior management should be congruent with the values of the organisation (Griseri, 1998:202). It is common for *roadshows* to be used to express values to employees and these commonly involve the CEO and/or senior managers (Hallam, 2003). However, as Dobni *et al.* (2000) recommend, managers do need to check that employees understand the values that have been communicated. This is often achieved through surveys and focus discussion groups.

Marketing communication in the form of advertising can play a role in creating stakeholder value for the customer. The corporate image of the organisation is a reflection of stakeholders' interpretations of organisational values. Van Riel (1995:73) defines image as the set of meanings by which an object is known and through which people describe, remember and relate to it. Nguyen and Leblanc (2002:244), in considering the factors that influence corporate image, conclude that organisational communication *via contact elements* represent an important channel by which customers gain information about values. Such contact elements include both staff dealing with customers and the physical environment in which the service is provided. In addition they noted that marketing communications also play a role in the communication of values to consumers.

Customer and other stakeholder interactions with employees during service encounters lead to communicating values (Davies and Chun, 2002). However, customers and other stakeholders receive communications about values in a variety of different ways, including the corporate name, communications strategy, external marketing activities and word of mouth (Nguyen and Leblanc, 2002).

It is important to bear in mind, however, that since an organisation's values are communicated to stakeholders through employees and other channels, there is the question of the extent to which these are integrated. It is safe to conclude that corporate image may not reflect corporate identity if complementary values are not being communicated. Hatch and Schultz (2001) identified a number of gaps where the undesirable occurs, including the 'image–culture gap', which produces confusion among customers, employees and other stakeholders about what an organisation actually represents. Gaps usually signify that an organisation does not practise what it preaches (Hatch and Schultz, 2001:131).

Questions

1   How might one make use of the hierarchy of effects model and the Engel, Blackwell and Miniard model to influence opinions and attitudes of stakeholders with regard to projects where there is a conflict of interest or opinion?

2   What is meant by integrated marketing communications? How might a public sector organisation such as the police make use of such an approach?

3   Describe and discuss the way in which organisational values are communicated to staff in your organisation. Is there a role for marketing communications? Explain.

Case study 11.1   The call centre – a commercial partnership

A municipal council entered into a commercial partnership with a telecommunications company to set up a call centre. The call centre was envisaged to be primarily for use by members of the public wanting to communicate out of office hours and in times of emergency with the council. In addition it was also seen as an alternative way of dealing with personal queries by phone, which would obviate the need to make unnecessary journeys that might be inconvenient to the service's users. The telecommunications partnering organisation also saw it as an opportunity to provide a service to other organisations in the area and even to some commercial companies.

Take-up of the service has been excellent though its capacity is somewhat underutilised and the organisation is unable to expand its existing capacity to the level it first envisaged Not all of the council's departments actively engage in the service which means that some enquiries have to be referred to other numbers that can only be accessed in normal working hours. In addition, the call centre service is only utilised by the council and no other external organisations make use of it.

The chief executive of the call centre is keen to expand the service and is wondering how she can make best use of marketing communications to pursue this objective.

Question

1 How would you advise the call centre's chief executive?

Case study 11.2   Work routes for parents and carers

W4PC was set up in the 1990s in a disadvantaged area of the Midlands to support families via a range of services. It aims to provide routes into work or training for parents and carers, removing barriers to finding or staying in work. The support it offers includes childcare, training and support to families. W4PC employs 34 full- and part-time staff. Its most recent annual income was just under £1 million.

W4PC is a user-led organisation with an exceptional track record for involving and engaging the local community, including families who have otherwise proved hard to reach. There is widespread community commitment to its expansion and development plan. W4PC works in partnership with local people, current service users and agencies working in the area to develop new projects. Services are managed in three sections:

- neighbourhood nursery,
- community development, and
- learning centre (training programme).

The activities of W4PC are focused around the needs of local women who were trapped on benefits and unable to take advantage of training or employment due to the high costs of childcare, particularly lone parents. The organisation is looking ahead in its business planning towards achieving 60% of funding through contracts and moving away from grant funding. It sees this as the way forward because there is a need to replace about £50,000 of funds each month.

Question

1 Identify how marketing communication methods can help W4PC to obtain its funding objectives.

Case study 11.3   The training department – rethinking its strategy

The training department operates with a very limited budget and most of this is spent on sending people off to courses run by universities, colleges and other providers. While this has proved satisfactory from a training quality point of view, recent pressures to cut back on the training budget have forced the department to rethink its strategy.

The department has limited training experience of its own but can call on short inputs from managers and executives within the organisation who are well qualified to talk about specialised aspects of their work and general management issues. All managers and senior executives have to undertake a compulsory course in communication so that in theory all should be competent to express a viewpoint on their specialist or generalist interests.

The training department can also call on part-time lecturers who are retired or those who are be willing to take on additional paid work over and above their university or college duties. This would supplement any shortfalls in general management experience among executives and managers.

There are many opportunities and demands for training from staff and the department has conducted a survey among all members of staff to ascertain what they think are their training needs. In addition, it has available a consultant's report that has identified aspects of general management training in which it is felt that staff at all levels up to middle management would benefit.

Questions

1 Enumerate what you think may be the areas of training in which staff at all levels up to middle management would benefit.

2 Identify the Strengths, Weaknesses, Opportunities and Threats that might have a bearing on the training department's ability to deliver necessary training.

3 Construct a SWOT matrix in which you identify objectives to be achieved based on the above SWOT analysis.

4 Suggest strategies for achieving what you consider to be the more urgent objectives.

5 Identify specific marketing communication objectives and programmes to enable the objectives and corresponding strategies you identified in questions 3 and 4 above to be accomplished.

Case study 11.4 | A question of traffic lights

Dear Sir/Madam

New traffic lights

Since the introduction of the new traffic lights at the road junction close to my house, I cannot get out of my property, either in the morning or in the evening, due to traffic waiting across my driveway. If the signals are not removed I will be taking the matter further with my solicitor.

No one informed us that new traffic lights were being introduced!!

(name and address supplied)

The above letter arrived on the highways manager's desk a few days after the installation of new traffic lights at what had become known as a notorious black-spot for accidents. In the past five years there had been several serious accidents involving motor vehicles and pedestrians, including two fatalities.

The highways manager was considering the best way in which to reply to the letter. Clearly, he thought, the council was acting in the best interests of people by installing lights at the crossing and believed that the complainant would not be able to bring a case against the council on any grounds though of course he recognised there was the problem of temporary obstruction of access to the complainant's property. He also recognised that it was not in the council's best interest to simply brush aside the complaint since the complainant might find avenues of publication that brought the issue of proper consultation into focus.

Question

1 How might the highways manager take advantage of this situation and gain good publicity for the council along with satisfaction for the complainant?

References

Blackwell, R. D., Miniard, P. W. and Engel, J. F. (2006), *Consumer Behavior*, 10th edn, Belmont, CA: South Western College Publishing/Thomson Learning.

Booms, B. H. and Bitner , M.-J. (1981), 'Marketing Strategies and Organisation Structures for Service Firms', in *Marketing of Services*, J. H. Donnelly and W. R. George, (eds), Chicago: American Marketing Association.

Colley, R. H. (1961), *Defining Advertising Goals for Measured Results*, New York: Association of Advertisers.

Croft, R. (1999), 'Audience and Environment: Measurement and Media', in P. J. Kitchen (ed.) *Marketing Communications: Principles and Practices*, London: ITP Business Press.

Dauphinais, G. W. and Price, C. (1998), 'The CEO as psychologist', *American Management Association International*, September, pp. 10–15.

Davidson, H. (2002), *The Committed Enterprise*, Oxford: Butterworth-Heinemann.

Davies, G. and Chun, R. (2002), 'Gaps between the internal and external perceptions of the corporate brand', *Corporate Reputation Review*, Vol. 5, Nos 2/3, pp. 144–158.

Dobni, D., Brent Ritchie, J. R. and Zerbe, W. (2000), 'Organisational values: The inside view of service productivity', *Journal of Business Research*, Vol. 47, pp. 91–107.

Fill, C. (1999), *Marketing Communications, Contexts, Contents and Strategies*, Harlow: Prentice Hall.

Giblin, E. J. and Amuso, L. E. (1997), 'Putting meaning into corporate values', *Business Forum*, Winter, pp. 14–18.

Griseri, P. (1998), *Managing Values*, London: Macmillan Press Ltd.

Hallam, R. (2003), 'Delivering the brand promise at Washington Mutual', *Strategic Communication Management*, Vol. 7, No. 4, Jun/July, pp. 18–21.

Hatch, M. J. and Schultz, M. (2001), 'Are the strategic stars aligned for your corporate brand?', *Harvard Business Review*, February, pp. 129–134.

Jud, N. (1998), *The Corporate Brand*, London: Macmillan Press.

Jones, T. M. (1995), 'Instrumental stakeholder theory: A synthesis of ethics and economics', *Academy of Management Review*, Vol. 20, No. 2, pp. 404–437.

Lavidge, R. J. and Steiner, G. A. (1961), 'A model for predictive measurements of advertising effectiveness', *Journal of Marketing*, 25, October, pp. 59–62.

Lencioni, P. M. (2002), 'Make your values mean something', *Harvard Business Review*, July, pp. 5–9.

Nguyen, N. and Leblanc, G. (2002), 'Contact personnel, physical environment and the perceived corporate image of intangible services by new clients', *International Journal of Service Industry Management*, Vol. 13, No. 3, pp. 242–262.

Nowak, G. J. and Phelps, J. (1994), 'Conceptualizing the integrated marketing communications' phenomenon: an examination of its impact on advertising practices and its implications for advertising research', *Journal of Current Issues and Research in Advertising*, Vol. 16, No. 1, Spring, pp. 49–66.

Pearson, R. (1989), 'Business Ethics as Communication Ethics: Public Relations Practice and the Idea of Dialogue', in *Public Relations Theory*, Botan, C. H. and Hazelton, V. (eds), Hillsdale, New Jersey: Lawrence Erlbaum Associates.

Rogers, E. M. (1995), *Diffusion of Innovations*, New York: The Free Press.

Rokeach, M. (1973), *The Nature of Human Values*, New York: The Free Press.

Schein, E. H. (1988), 'Organizational socialization and the profession of management', *Sloan Management Review*, Fall, pp. 53–65.

Strong E. K. (1925), *The psychology of selling*, New York: McGraw-Hill.

van Riel, C. B. M. (1995), *Principles of Corporate Communication*, Harlow: Prentice Hall.

Wolfinbarger, M. F. and Gilly, M. C. (1991), 'A conceptual model of the impact of advertising on service employees', *Psychology and Marketing*, Vol. 8, Fall, pp. 215–237.

Further reading

Duncan, T. and Caywood, C. (1996), 'The concept, process, and evolution of integrated marketing communication', in Thorson, E. and Moore, J. (eds), *Integrated Communication: Synergy of Persuasive Voices*, Mahwah, NJ: Lawrence Erlbaum Associates, pp. 13–34.

Klein, H. J. and Weaver, N. A. (2000), 'The effectiveness of an organizational-level orientation training program in the socialization of new hires', *Personnel Psychology*, Spring, Vol. 53, No. 1, pp. 47–66.

12 Social marketing

INTRODUCTION

In this chapter we will look at aspects of social marketing and its good practice. First we will explain what is meant by social marketing. Social marketing is often associated with health issues and is integrated with other forms of bringing about changes in habits among the population. Social marketing faces many challenges and we explore some of these. Its prime aim is to change behaviour and basic marketing techniques such as segmentation can be used to aid this process. Based on experience we look at what best practice has to offer in the way of suggesting a strong basis for successful social marketing. Finally, we suggest social marketing should be viewed within the setting of relationship marketing rather than viewed as a transactional process.

DEFINITION OF SOCIAL MARKETING

There are many definitions of what social marketing entails but this one has a good practical basis to it. Social marketing is:

> 'the systematic application of marketing concepts and techniques, to achieve specific behavioural goals, to achieve a social or public good.' (French and Blair-Stevens 2006, http://www.nsms.org.uk/public/default.aspx? Accessed 13 August 2006)

A good deal of social marketing is aimed at preventing the occurrence of acute illness in the community. In this context, health-related social marketing is:

'the systematic application of marketing concepts and techniques, to achieve specific behavioural goals, to improve health and reduce inequalities.' (*Ibid.*)

Definitions vary but three key elements commonly appear with regard to social marketing:

- Its first purpose is to achieve a particular 'social good' (rather than commercial benefit) with specific behavioural goals clearly identified and targeted.
- Second, it is a systematic process phased to address short-, medium- and long-term issues.
- Third, it employs marketing methods.

Since social marketing is often associated with health it may be integrated with overall health promotion strategies (e.g those relating to tobacco, diabetes, healthy pregnancy). Communication of ideas and information on what is good for a healthy life style or what should be avoided to prevent ill health occurring are central to social marketing in this context. In carrying out marketing activities many functional aspects of marketing may be employed, including marketing research, strategic planning, partnerships and strategic alliances and delivering all elements of a communication campaign in conjunction with agencies.

Typical health campaigns relate to:

- substance abuse – tobacco, alcohol and drugs and their effects on drivers;
- healthy living – physical activity, nutrition, diabetes and cardiovascular disease (CVD) prevention;
- healthy pregnancy – taking folic acid, tobacco and alcohol in moderation to avoid fetal alcohol syndrome (FAS);
- children – injury prevention, immunisation, SIDS (sudden infant death syndrome);
- communicable diseases: hepatitis C, severe acute respiratory syndrome (SARS), AIDS and other sexually transmitted diseases (STDs);
- other factors – healthy environment, organ and tissue donation, seniors issues.

Social marketing is not the only way in which people can be targeted on important matters such as those outlined above and it can often be integrated with other aspects of health promotion strategies, including:

- training,
- education,
- community mobilisation,
- legislation,
- research.

Social marketing is used to establish themes and provide a focus/profile for a health promotion strategy. Its great advantage is that it can reach many people sumultaneously (see Figure 12.1). Informing or reassuring people of matters that are of grave concern to society are an issue for central government and social marketing presents

Violence

Anti-social behaviour

Abuse

Health

Figure 12.1   The scope of social marketing

an opportunity for it to inform the public that it is concerned about a specific issue. The main task for such marketing activities is to influence behaviour change (long term).

UNIQUENESS OF SOCIAL MARKETING

While social marketing has much in common with other forms of marketing it does differ from public education and other communication/health education strategies in that its ultimate goal is to influence and change behaviour, not just to increase knowledge and/or change attitudes. Central to this mission is the aim to change values and attitudes as a means of influencing behaviours.

This task represents major challenges of social marketing since many attitudes and behaviours are well entrenched and extremely difficult to influence. For example, it is much more difficult to change behaviours that are high involvement (e.g. smoking) as opposed to those that are lower involvement (e.g. flossing) or one-time-only decisions (e.g. donating blood).

There is also the problem that there may be low situational involvement for most people and many are just not interested in social and health causes. Even when people are aware of a social or health problem they feel helpless and ineffective in ameliorating or solving it. Attitude change is difficult to achieve and the less palatable the behaviour change, the more difficult it is to change. The key problem seems to be the lack of immediate reinforcement to effecting a change of attitude. Indeed, often solutions to problems depend on the collective action of many people to reduce the sense of self-efficacy.

Influencing behaviour recognises the need for consumer orientation and analysing behaviour from the point of view of target audiences. It takes cognisance of the fact that markets are comprised of market segments requiring different marketing strategies to generate behaviour change. Key to this is the notion that analysing social behaviours and segmenting markets requires innovative marketing research.

Segmentation offers many different ways of identifying subgroups within a market. Two key ways to segment the target market for social marketing communications are:

- demographic – age, gender, occupation, income, marital status, etc.;
- psychographic – life style, social class, values, personality.

A combination of these categorising variables offers a basis for creating meaningful messages and for accessing the targeted groups via appropriate media.

Marketing, of course, costs money and there may be a reluctance on the part of public sector organisations to spend money from the public purse on marketing communication messages and other efforts to get people to do what many would rationally regard as common sense behaviour. However, there is a justifiable rationale underlying social marketing campaigns. They make a substantial contribution to the reduction of social costs generated by undesirable social behaviours (see Figure 12.2). The costs would be borne by society, which justifies the investment of government resources to reduce them.

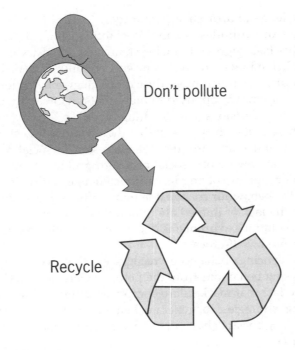

Figure 12.2 Don't pollute! Recycle!

The stages of change

When devising social marketing plans one has to bear in mind that people do not change their behaviour overnight. Behaviour changes only gradually so that different kinds of marketing effort have to be expended to progress the different stages in the change process that are being experienced by the target audiences. We can visualise five stages of change:

- *Pre-contemplation*: no intention to change behaviour in the foreseeable future.
- *Contemplation*: people are aware that a problem exists and are thinking about changing but have not made any commitment to take action.
- *Preparation*: combines intention and behavioural criteria, individuals intending to take action in the next month.
- *Action*: individuals modify behaviour, experiences or environment to overcome problems.
- *Maintenance*: people work to prevent relapse and consolidate the gains attained during action.

Marketing communications and other efforts have to be designed to move people through these stages and different kinds of messages, images and marketing ploys have to be used at these stages. However, consistency is also required to move target audiences through the various 'stages of change'.

Social Marketing for Fair Trade

The development of a more sustainable global economy is currently being badly hampered by a growing crisis linked to collapsing prices in commodity markets in poorer countries. According to UNCTAD, the economic, social and environmental consequences of this crisis directly impinge upon the livelihoods, well-being, dignity and independence of one billion people in developing countries. One proposed pathway to finding a solution to this crisis is a growth in Fair Trade, and for an increasing proportion of global commodities to be marketed on a Fair Trade basis. This will involve developing consumer markets for Fair Trade labelled products, to harness the perceived willingness of consumers in industrialised countries to purchase 'ethical' products that promote progress towards sustainable development. BRASS (Business Relationships, Accountability, Sustainability and Society) is therefore seeking to take a lead in exploring the potential of social marketing to promote Fair Trade products and markets, with a particular emphasis on coffee (which currently accounts for 60% of Fair Trade sales globally).

Social Marketing for Sun Safety

One health issue where social marketing has not previously been fully applied is that of skin cancer prevention for 'sun safety'. This is an area where there is a significant business interest, since it is sunshine-based holidays that pose a significant risk to UK consumers in terms of the risk of sunburn and the resulting risk of skin cancer. One element of BRASS's research has investigated the role that a social marketing approach to sun-safety for children could be used to create changes to commercial products (such as holidays, clothing and sun-screens) and to other aspects of children's lives including school and leisure activities to promote sun-safety and reduce the risks of skin cancer.

Source © 2005 The ESRC Centre for Business Relationships, Accountability, Sustainability and Society.

SOCIAL MARKETING IN PRACTICE

There is no doubt that placing a focus on an issue of personal relevance to each member of the target audience is likely to be the most productive way of bringing about change but this, of course, could prove quite expensive. Focusing on the audience segment and crafting a message via the most appropriate medium offers a less expensive and acceptable alternative. Whatever approach is taken it is important to find a means of specifying the desired outcome and action required in the message and imagery used and if possible providing a means by which positive reinforcement can be effected.

Getting the attention of a specific audience may prove to be quite a difficult task so it is important to adapt creatively a style to appeal to specific audiences. Variety in creative approach from one period to another and one group to another is required to keep the attention grabbing power of the campaign (although the overall message has to be consistent). Messages and imagery should portray people with whom members of the target group can identify and in this respect it is crucial to pre-test a marketing communication appeal or whatever marketing mechanism is to be used.

Appeals may be based on arousing emotions and focusing attention on immediate, high-probability consequences of positive behaviour. Marketers should not moralise or use pity/altruistic appeals since these do not work well. Guilt messages can be effective in certain circumstances but again usually do not work well. As with most forms of promotion humour should only be used with caution. It is important to communicate the benefits of changing behaviours and celebrities and popular figures can be used effectively. Alternative behaviours should also be promoted as substitutes for undesirable present behaviours: for example; designated driver in drink–driving campaigns, or suggesting daily actions (use stairs, not elevators) as ways to be physically active, or promote the benefits of mass transit rather than the car. Showing the desirable behaviour serves as a guide to appropriate behaviour.

With young audiences there are additional elements that may need to be taken into account. Young people are prone to want to defy authority so highlighting that the communication comes from an authority body or figure, or presenting it from an adult viewpoint or in the form of a 'lecture' will not be successful. Nor should high-risk youth be shown in a negative light or the young talked down to or made to feel inadequate. When choosing people to put forward the communication use self-confident, attractive actors that look a few years older than the target. Also remember that the web and e-mail are important tools in getting messages over to this target group.

Bear in mind the length of time it may take to bring about the desired change. Only long-term cumulative efforts can produce significant measurable changes and this could be within a 3–5 year time frame. The period for achieving results depends on various factors. It is customary for campaigns to adopt a phased approach, each phase building on the results of the preceding one. Intermediate goals are used to measure impact: awareness of campaign, attitude and preference changes, intermediate changes in behaviour, and/or behavioural intent. Small increases are the norm.

However, some confusion about marketing's role in these matters may be evident since marketing in the public sector is, to quite a large extent, different to what it is in the public profit-making sector. Apart from the confusion which may exist about marketing there is often confusion about the difference between social marketing and:

- health education,
- public education,
- strategic communications,
- community outreach,
- reaching the 'hard to reach' (e.g. low income families).

Indeed, we have to bear in mind that often social marketing initiatives are not designed or led by marketers and tend to be strategic communication/public relations initiatives.

A social marketing approach to increasing breast cancer screening rates

This study used a social marketing approach to identify factors that influence women's breast cancer screening behaviors and to guide the development of strategies to increase breast cancer screening utilization rates among underserved women in Florida. Qualitative and quantitative methods were used to gather data regarding women's perceptions of breast cancer screening, frequency of mammography use, screening motivations and barriers, and recommendations for screening promotion. Thirteen percent of women surveyed had never had a mammogram, whereas 26% were irregular users and 51% were regular users of a mammography. Factors significantly associated with mammography use included frequency of clinical breast examinations, insurance coverage, physican referral, knowledge of American Cancer Society recommendations for annual screening, and misperceptions of the potential for mammography usage to cause cancer. Results were used to develop a comprehensive social marketing plan that would motivate irregular users of breast cancer screening services, specifically underserved women 40 years of age and older, to be screened annually. The plan included recommendations for increasing physician referrals, modifying service delivery, developing client education materials, creating a public information campaign, and initiating public policy efforts to address financial barriers to mammography use.

Source: *Journal of Health Education* (2000), Vol. 31, No. 6, pp. 320–330.

SOME IMPORTANT REMINDERS

The advent of partnerships with the private sector may bring social marketing into contact with commercial enterprise. Strategic alliances are extremely important in order to facilitate more cost effective ways of providing services but it is very important to have guidelines and policies. Partnerships with the private sector can produce differences of opinion and conflicts of interest since, with rare exceptions only long-term, multi-year campaigns can produce measurable changes . . . but management/funders always want immediate results.

There is often too much emphasis in campaigns on behaviour change (individual rather than the community) instead of placing much more emphasis on creating a social climate/consensus conducive to social change. Moreover, it should always be borne in mind that the messenger in many cases can be much more important than the message.

SOCIAL MARKETING IN THE CONTEXT OF RELATIONSHIP MARKETING AND TRANSACTIONAL MARKETING

Social marketing is concerned primarily with changing attitudes. While there is no guarantee that a change of attitude will produce the desired behaviour it is an important step along the way. Certainly it is the usual rule that people's behaviour reflects their attitudes even though having positive attitudes does not in itself mean that we can predict behaviour from this. Two of the primary components of attitudes are cognitive and affective. To have a strong attitude towards something we must not only have information about it (the cognitive dimension) but we must also have definite feelings about it (the affective dimension). Thus in the Lavidge and Steiner (1961) hierarchy of effects advertising model in order to have a positive attitude towards an advertised product or service it is suggested that both knowledge and liking have to be developed in the target audience. The credibility of the information source is highly important and the development of trust in that source of paramount importance. It is perhaps not surprising then that the building of trusted relationships seems to be a critical aspect of social marketing.

Relationship marketing presents a paradigm within which social marketing might be viewed. Concentrating on relationships can bring about behavioural change and this can be viewed as a key social marketing goal. Adopting a relationship approach to social marketing is more likely to enable change to be effected (see Hastings, 2003). The paradigm shift away from visualising social marketing within a transactional framework to a relational one has considerable implications for social marketing and represents a new approach to thinking about social problems.

Relationship marketing sometimes entails a highly proactive organisation interacting with a relatively passive client (see Bennet and Barkensjo, 2005). Under such circumstances, the organisation must take the initiative in starting a relationship. The same argument also applies in situations where social marketing is involved. This argument is underlined by Brenkert (2002) who argues that, because social marketers target people who may not believe they suffer from a problem, social problems are identified independently of what any particular person or people may or may not believe. An outcome of this is that the criteria and standards by which social problems are identified should result from inviting people to become part of a process of change to enhance their welfare rather than treating them as recipients or targets of efforts to change their behaviours.

There is a tendency for social marketers to regard their audience as being in need of persuasion, rather than needing to be engaged in a process whereby they need to recognise that change is required. However, what is much more the case is that in order to begin to build meaningful and sustained relationships with clients people need to make healthy choices, rather than having decisions imposed on them (Department of Health, 2004).

THE MARKETING MIX EXTENDED

We have with regard to services marketing shown how the marketing mix has been extended to include an additional 3Ps in the form of people, processes and physical evidence. Social marketing redefines the basic 4Ps (and a number of other Ps as well) as follows:

- *Product* – What does the customer receive? What is offered to the customer?
- *Price* – How much will it cost the customer? Not just in money terms, but also in terms of time, effort, emotional costs, etc.
- *Place* – Where does the relevant behaviour take place? Where are there opportunities to reach the customer?
- *Promotion* – What package of incentives can be offered that will be valued by the customer?

And in addition we have (Department of Health and The National Consumer Council, 2005):

- *Proposition* – how is it envisaged the customer can be assisted and supported to move towards the desired behaviour?
- *Partnerships* – identifying common goals and working together in genuine partnerships.
- *Purse-strings* – looking at ways to maximise resources by engaging across all sectors, including human resources as well as financial.
- *Politics* – recognising the political drivers and potential constraints and looking at ways to inform, influence and engage the relevant political players.
- *Policy* – using social marketing to help link and connect different policy agendas – maximising its impact across the whole system.
- *People* – public, professionals, politicians – recognising the customer can be any or all of these and gearing efforts accordingly.

An example of the extended marketing mix

Behaviour change required – less speed on the roads

Product – What does the customer receive? What is offered to the customer?
Here we are looking primarily at what benefits are offered to the consumer. These are: greater personal safety; lower insurance costs; less inconvenience relating to damage to cars plus the associated financial benefit; greater safety to other people on the road and pedestrians; freedom from guilt and punishment as a result of causing an accident.
Price – How much will it cost the customer? Not just in money terms, but also in terms of time, effort, emotional costs, etc.
   In terms of money very little at all. There will be a slight increase in the time it

takes to travel from A to B. It will involve more concentration of effort to ensure that speed limits are adhered to. Emotional costs will be much less since the driver is unlikely to suffer as much anger and frustration in traffic.

Place – Where does the relevant behaviour take place? Where are there opportunities to reach the customer?

The relevant behaviour takes place on the roads in urban areas. Opportunities to reach the customer include roadside billboards, TV advertising, magazine and newspaper advertising, editorial releases in car magazines as well as general TV and newspaper reporting.

Promotion – What package of incentives can be offered that will be valued by the customer?

Proposition – How is it envisaged the customer can be assisted and supported to move towards the desired behaviour?

Partnerships – identifying common goals and working together in genuine partnerships.

The nature of the behaviour which it is hoped to change is of interest to the community in general. However, in terms of public bodies the police, ambulance service, health service and fire service would all have an active interest in this problem. It offers the opportunity for a collaborative partnership between these various bodies. Such an approach would help considerably in deferring the cost of social marketing campaigns.

Purse-strings – looking at ways to maximise resources by engaging across all sectors, including human resources as well as financial.

We have indicated in the previous section how a collaborative effort between the public services mentioned lead to maximisation of resources both in terms of human resources and financial ones.

Politics – recognising the political drivers and potential constraints and looking at ways to inform, influence and engage the relevant political players.

There are various intervention strategies that can be employed to reduce speed on the roads in urban areas. These include cameras, physical traffic calming obstacles, and realistic speed limits that reflect the dangers inherent in particular areas. All of these measures require financial investment on the behalf of local government. Part of the funding may have to come from central government sources.

Policy – using social marketing to help link and connect different policy agendas, maximising its impact across the whole system.

There are many issues to do with motoring that are in the public eye. These include drink driving, the high number of accidents on the roads, congestion in towns and cities, environmental pollution and spiralling oil prices. By way of example, a connection can be shown between speeding and accidents on the roads, excessive fuel consumption and subsequent environmental pollution. With a little creative thought connections may also be made with the other issues.

People – public, professionals, politicians – recognising the customer can be any or all of these and gearing efforts accordingly.

Not only are these diverse people possible recipients of the message that is central to the issue but they may themselves participate in the process of persuasion with respect to the target audience.

Speeding on the roads is a consumption habit. In the marketing of fast moving consumer goods (FMCGs) marketers try to change habits by encouraging customers to switch brands. In the case of social marketing and the issue of speeding, intervention strategies are implemented to make it difficult for habitual speeders to carry out their undesirable consumption habit. Social marketing efforts have to be aimed at getting the message across to those who can be influenced in this way. Moreover, among the consumers we might identify a number of different market segments. There may be those who never speed and never will, and there may be those who are prone to speed from time to time. Alongside these are those who drive fast and unintentionally often exceed imposed speed limits. Finally, there may be those who deliberately disregard both the speeding regulations and common sense safety. Arguably, from a marketing standpoint, a different marketing mix approach is probably required in addressing each segment.

Question

It is argued that social marketing is in the social good and that any expenditure in this area will reap dividends by saving much greater expenditure at a later date in trying to deal with the problems that have accumulated through anti-social behaviour of one form or another. Imagine you wanted to gain evidence to support this argument. How would you set about collecting it?

Case study 12.1 | The AIDS pandemic

The incidence of AIDS and its negative effect on the lives of communities worldwide continues to rise almost unabated. More and more it is becoming the central concern of governments and gives rise to various far-reaching means of combating a disease that has the potential to take on the dimensions of a worldwide plague in its detrimental effect on the human race. Tackling the issue requires substantial investment in terms of people's time and a great deal of money. Many view the resources that are being made available as inadequate and often used ineffectively because of inadequate consideration of how the money should be spent and resources allocated. Allocations need to be thought through carefully and attention given to strategic and consultative issues. Accountability is also an issue – it has to be demonstrated how money distributed is used to optimum effect. This can be extremely difficult since with all social marketing campaigns change occurs only slowly and in the case of AIDS measurement of change is extremely difficult to accomplish. The overemphasis on simple indicators and short-term results, at the cost of long-term change, is viewed by some to be detrimental to the whole process of what is being sought to be accomplished in fighting AIDS. The disease is a long-term and complex problem requiring approaches that are not simple to measure.

As well as the need to look carefully at the measurement of change there is also the need to look closely at the means by which change may be effected. Some argue that approaches should change so that it is not just simply a case of projecting messages but one of nurturing an atmosphere where the voices of those most affected by the pandemic can be heard. This shift in emphasis would be a fundamental and radical shift in the response to AIDS. Giving out HIV/AIDS information and key health messages are of course still vitally important but it is important to go further than this and help to develop environments where lively dialogue can flourish.

Question

1 What would be the implications for marketers of the suggested change in policy?

Case study 12.2 | The problem of obesity

Media reports indicate an increase in the number of people classed as being obese in the UK. It is thought that the potential problems of obesity are so devastating that they could cause the total demise of the National Health Service. At some time in the future the NHS would be rendered totally incapable of dealing with health problems if no action is taken to do something about obesity now.

One lobby suggests that attention should be focused on the responsibility of the food industry in the way that it markets its products and the information it gives out to customers. Improved labelling of food products to inform people is essential. In particular, attention should be directed to informing parents and producers should avoid marketing their products at vulnerable groups like children. In addition, there have been demands for the removal of vending machines that sell sweets, crisps and fizzy drinks in schools together with a review of the food being offered in school canteens. This raises an important question: Do such measures represent a sensible approach to dealing with the problem of obesity or are they just another example of the state interfering with the rights of individuals to choose their own life styles?

It seems unlikely that attempts to educate parents and children about the nutritional value of different foods and recommended dietary intakes will make a substantial impact on the problem of childhood obesity

Much more needs to be done. This may extend to assisting parents to get to grips with their desire to avoid confrontation with their children in promoting the positive aspects of healthy food choice. Social marketing, with its emphasis on understanding the consumer and addressing issues of competition, offers a promising intervention approach capable of providing the practical assistance required.

Question

1 Indicate how a programme of social marketing might address the identified issues.

| Case study 12.3 | The fire service – using social marketing tools |

The fire service in the town, like that in many other towns, receives many hoax 999 calls. In addition, it is sometimes called out to incidents and situations where its services are inappropriate. The worst time for the fire service, however, is around November 5th and at New Year when people set alight dangerous bonfires and the service also receives hoax calls.

In recent years a new trend has also had a worrying impact on the running of the service. In certain areas of the town, fire service staff have been attacked while attending fires. Youths have hurled stones and bottles at them and several staff members have received quite serious injuries. The trend is not restricted to the local fire service, it is also evident in other towns and cities.

The fire service offers advice to members of the public on how to lessen the risk of accidental house fires occurring but this is not carried out on a pro-active basis. Deliberate house fires resulting from arson attacks are not unknown in the town though their occurrence is rare. The same applies to arson attacks generally, though the incidence of these on private and business premises has more than doubled in the past 10 years.

The fire service's duties in the community go beyond dealing with and putting out fires, extending to all kinds of situations where there is a risk of fire from cutting people free from cars in accidents to monitoring conditions on local moor lands to assess the risk of fire outbreaks close to residential properties.

The fire service is keen to ensure that it is making use of effective ways of both communicating with the public and, where necessary, influencing miscreant behaviour that has dangerous consequences for the public. It has heard that social marketing is a possible means of doing this and wants to investigate what use it might make of the tools of social marketing in the context of the problems it faces in communicating with the public.

Question

1 Draft a report indicating how social marketing might help the fire service with its communications with members of the public.

References

Bennet, R. and Barkensjo, A. (2005), 'Relationship quality, relationship marketing and client perceptions of the levels of service quality of charitable organizations', *International Journal of Service Industry Management*, Vol. 16, No. 1, pp. 81–106

Brenkert, G. G. (2002), 'Ethical challenges of social marketing', *Journal of Public Policy & Marketing*, Vol. 21, No. 1, pp. 14–25.

Department of Health (2004), 'Choosing Health: Making Healthy Choices Easier', London: The Stationery Office.

Department of Health and The National Consumer Council (2005), *Social marketing pocket guide*, London: National Social Marketing Centre for Excellence.

Hastings, G. (2003), 'Relational paradigms in social marketing', *Journal of Macromarketing*, Vol. 23, No. 1, pp. 6–15.

Lavidge, R. J. and Steiner, G. A. (1961), 'A model for predictive measurements of advertising effectiveness', *Journal of Marketing*, Vol. 25, October, pp. 59–62.

13 Internal marketing

INTRODUCTION

Local government exists to serve the community and has to find ways and means of satisfying the wants and needs of its customers and other stakeholders. Internal marketing provides a way of ensuring a customer focus in the way in which employees of an organisation go about their work and in particular how they interact with customers and other stakeholders. It also provides a means of engendering employee trust, commitment and loyalty to the organisation and is a means of creating employee satisfaction through empowerment. Internal marketing can help to project the corporate entity, both internally and externally, and tackle problems of low morale within the organisation. Most public bodies tend to be traditionally bureaucratic in nature but over recent years many have been the object of rationalisation and change, providing an opportunity for internal marketing to be used effectively.

THE NATURE OF INTERNAL MARKETING

It has been suggested that the term 'internal marketing' is used to refer to the activities an organisation must implement in order to 'woo and win over the hearts and minds of its employees to achieve service excellence' (Rust *et al.*, 1996). An alternative definition of internal marketing views it as treating both employees and customers with equal importance through proactive programmes in order to achieve organisational objectives (Woodruffe, 1995). Payne (1993) suggests that the key aims of internal marketing are the development of internal and external customer awareness and the removal of functional barriers to achieving organisational effectiveness.

The main argument behind internal marketing is that employees should feel that management cares about them and tries to meet their needs. The successful application of this concept is translated into positive employee attitudes towards their work including organisational commitment, job involvement, work motivation and job satisfaction (Tansuhaj *et al.*, 1987). There is empirical support for a significant relationship between internal marketing and consumer satisfaction. There is also evidence of a relationship between internal marketing and service quality. Through applying internal marketing it is hoped that employees will input maximum rather than minimum effort, thereby better satisfying the needs and wants of external customers (Berry, 1981; Donnelly *et al.*, 1985; George, 1990; Sasser and Arbeit, 1980). Lack of commitment from employees can be detrimental, resulting in poorer performance arising from inferior service offerings and higher costs. Hogg (1996) has suggested that internal marketing could be the answer to gaining employee commitment, succeeding where traditional internal communications programmes have failed.

This leads us on to consider what exactly internal marketing is and how is it practised in an organisation. In the first instance, internal marketing is about informing the internal market (employees) about the organisation's mission and its role within it. Employees need to know what the organisation is trying to achieve and how they fit into the overall scheme of things. Any vagaries in this context mean that employees are at a decided disadvantage when they are confronted with enquiries from the organisation's stakeholders. In order to address this shortcoming internal marketing conducted by senior management has to ensure that the internal information and communications channels work effectively in order to promote and sell ideas and services internally. Using staff manuals, bulletin boards and meetings to disseminate knowledge about policies, plans and actions is a productive way of doing this.

Staff also have to feel motivated in order to put policies and procedures into effect and the organisation has to implement special motivation programmes directed at front-line service providers. Motivating employees through reward incentives to provide excellent service is of paramount importance. At the same time, too, it becomes necessary to develop internal audits to assess critically organisational performance with respect to the internal service and to determine where performance gaps occur.

Managers at all levels in the organisation have to accept the need to understand employee capabilities – their attitudes, know-how and skills – and also need to participate in an internal marketing strategy. The aim is to create an internal environment that enhances employee–customer interaction. This can be done by establishing an open information climate in order to improve interpersonal interactive communication channels and to apply the internal marketing programme. To achieve this goal there are many different mechanisms available. These include using mass communication techniques (e.g. newsletters and videotapes about new marketing strategies, etc.) to provide employees with helpful information. Initiating a programme to educate employees on important council issues can also be an effective mechanism. It is important to teach employees 'why they should do things' and not simply 'how they should do things'.

Continually conducting internal market research and keeping employees informed of new developments within the organisation are both necessary and essential features of good internal marketing practice. Employees need to be encouraged to innovate without fear and to use quality management techniques across the organisation. Getting feedback from employees regarding their concerns is necessary and establishing a network service that answers employees' questions, fields their complaints, remedies situations and alerts top-level management to potential trouble spots in employee concerns should receive priority. Seeking employee suggestions as to changes and improvements that would also be beneficial in improving the level of customer service and taking actions based upon what is learned from an internal marketing research survey provide positive reinforcements for further collaboration.

Many organisations have adopted internal marketing in order to achieve a 'people' orientation that is conducive to the achievement of service quality and customer satisfaction. Many of the activities that are an integral part of the internal marketing practice are geared towards the achievement of:

- high quality in internal and external service interactions; and
- internal and external customer satisfaction.

The emphasis placed on the rigid rules and procedures in an organisation creates an environment that is not supportive to customer-oriented and high-quality service operations. The flexibility of the staff delivering the service to the internal/external customers is restricted by the rigidity and formality of the structure. If staff are governed by a pattern of rules that is intended to restrict and structure their behaviour it creates employee dissatisfaction, frustration and low motivation that results in slow delivery and potential dissatisfaction in internal and external service encounters.

Internal communication is an important integral part of internal marketing practice and is one of the core elements of implementing internal marketing. It is important to develop a formal, coordinated and organisation-wide internal communication system that facilitates the implementation and practice of internal marketing. Internal marketing can be used to change the attitudes and behaviour of staff towards being more service and customer oriented, and it is necessary to create awareness and understanding about internal marketing in a structured and consistent way. A lack of an internal communication system regarding internal marketing suggests that internal marketing information is not properly communicated to staff, which could hamper its effective implementation.

Trust, commitment and loyalty can be developed with the help of internal marketing and empowerment of employees can be facilitated. However, the kind of information that is presented by management and the manner in which it is presented may be key determinants of whether internal marketing succeeds in the workplace.

The bureaucratic nature of organisations and the difficulty of developing trust, commitment and loyalty can all work against the implementation of internal marketing within an organisation. While employee empowerment may be a very desirable outcome its realisation represents a difficult challenge where conditions work against it. There is a need for trust, commitment and loyalty in an organisation and in this chapter it is pointed out how this might be achieved with the aid of internal marketing. However, It also shows how such progress might be stymied in conditions where bureaucracy prevails and there is mistrust in the first instance.

The increasing recognition of the importance of the employee's role in the service industry has led organisations to adopt the internal marketing concept and hence treat their employees as 'internal customers'. The rationale for the adoption of internal marketing is that it leads to higher employee satisfaction and, subsequently, to the development of a more customer-conscious, market-oriented and sales-minded workforce.

Trust, commitment and loyalty are much valued in organisations. Moreover, it is through effective communication and employee empowerment that these values can be nurtured and developed. Empowerment helps break down the problems created by excessive bureaucracy and it is through the medium of effective internal marketing that high morale and a motivated workforce can be engendered (see Figure 13.1).

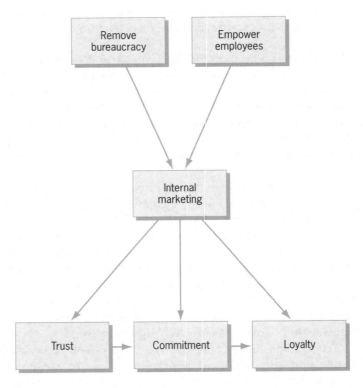

Figure 13.1 Moving the employee through the stages of trust to loyalty using internal marketing

TRUST

Trust may be thought of as not deliberately or accidentally, consciously or unconsciously taking unfair advantage of a person. It means that you can put your current situation, status and self-esteem in the group, relationship, job, career, even life in the other person's hands with complete confidence (McGregor, 1967). Trust means a belief that those on whom we depend will meet our expectations of them (Shaw, 1997). Trust can take a number of different forms (Mink *et al.*, 1993). It may be the confident expectation that people will do what they say they are going to do, which can be achieved by making and keeping simple day-to-day agreements, including meetings and deadlines. Alternatively, it may be reflected in a willingness to engage in reciprocal sharing and openness, to share relevant information when it is needed. The latter form of trust requires a willingness and ability to be open and share relevant information while meeting the needs of oneself, team members and the organisation. Trust can also be associated with the confidence that other people care about our physical and psychological well-being, a certainty as to the safety of our environment. This last kind of trust can be threatened by personal criticism hence open discussions between management and employees is essential in producing a setting where this kind of trust can occur.

While organisations may demand commitment and trust from their employees this is not necessarily a reciprocal arrangement. To build commitment and loyalty managers within an organisation need commitment and loyalty from people towards their own team, which embraces themselves, their supervisor and their internal or external customers. High commitment to customer expectations automatically generates a desire to improve the quality of products and services to those customers and that is where team morale starts to be good. Building commitment to meeting customer expectations requires action and loyalty develops after commitment has been established.

EMPOWERMENT

Empowerment to act is a motivating factor in achieving commitment from people. It involves training, communication, recognition and motivation. It requires the acceptance of responsibility by employees for their own actions. It also demands allowing people to make mistakes without fear of reprisal. It is about trust and accountability. Empowerment simply gives individuals bigger pieces and removes close supervision by superiors and unnecessary rules. It enables people to get on with the job without interference from above. Empowerment is often hampered by the presence of bureaucracy that operates by dividing work into small pieces and building walls between them. Bureaucracy can block the responsiveness and continuous innovation that are essential in modern day organisations.

BENEFICIAL EFFECTS OF COMMUNICATION

Good internal communications helps to improve the likelihood of an organisation being successful. Clampitt and Downs (1993) undertook a wide review of the evidence on the effects on organisations of communication. They concluded that the benefits obtained from quality communications included improved productivity, a reduction in absenteeism, increased levels of innovation, a reduction in the number of strikes, higher quality of services and products, and a reduction in costs. Kanter (1988) argued that higher levels of innovation can be achieved by good communication within and between organisations and sections of organisations. More specifically, the thrust of Kanter's (1988) conclusion is that contact between as many levels in an organisation as possible is important to achieving enthusiastic, widespread involvement in the achievement of organisational goals and the creation of a supportive climate for innovation.

Communication involves individuals sharing meaning. It provides the means of creating and implementing behavioural changes both within and without an organisation (see, for example, Cheney, 1991). When dealing with the external market, the role of the marketing communicator includes the facilitation of a sense of shared understanding with external customers about the organisation itself, its values, the identity of its brands and the specific benefits of its products/services. At the intra-organisational level, however, the communication process has been shown to have a variety of additional roles including:

- encouraging the motivation and commitment of employees by ensuring an understanding of the company's objectives and goals (McDonald, 1995; Foreman, 1997);
- enhancing overall levels of service quality by ensuring that an understanding of the needs of the customer is fostered at every level within the organisation (Acito and Ford, 1980; Reukert and Walker, 1987; Wolfinbarger and Gilly, 1991).

The above themes have been developed in the internal marketing literature: see, for example, Greene et al. (1994), Sargeant and Asif (1998), Caruana and Celleya (1998). Both the internal marketing and the more specific internal communications literature concur that a variety of benefits could accrue to an organisation from the effective management of its communication processes.

MANAGING INTERNAL COMMUNICATIONS

Management needs to ensure that its service delivery staff is in a position to honour the service promises made to external customers through marketing communication (see, for example, Parasuraman et al., 1988; Zeithaml, 1996). Marketing concepts directed exclusively at external customers may fail to accomplish their objectives if internal subsystems and processes are not properly focused onto the customer-related objectives, and if employees lack the necessary customer-oriented attitudes and behaviours. The organisation needs to integrate the overall approach it takes to both internal and external communications. From an internal perspective there is a need to take full account of the complex nature of the relationships that develop between individuals and departments at all levels within the organisation.

In applying the marketing concept internally the instrument of communication policy is highly relevant. It consists of all channels that have an impact on knowledge, attitudes and behaviours of internal customers on different hierarchical levels (George, 1990). This does not suggest that employee communication should be one-sided top-down communication. Planned bottom-up (or feedback) communication and lateral communication between employees on the same hierarchical level are also essential.

The goals that can be achieved through managed employee communication are quite significant. These can include improving profits by reducing costs and/or increased revenues from upward communication while downward communication can aim to affect the knowledge, attitude and behavioural level of employees.

Questions

1   Internal marketing is just another name for efficient management and offers nothing new in its approach? Discuss.

2   How are trust in and loyalty to the organisation linked to being customer focused? What role does internal marketing play in this linking operation and how might it seek to achieve this end?

3   Internal communications seem to lie at the heart of effective internal marketing. What would constitute an internal communication system and how might internal marketing be employed to maximum effect within such a system?

Case study 13.1   A need for internal marketing

The municipal authority commissioned a study to identify the quality of its communication processes with employees. The senior management of the organisation had felt that there was room for improvement both in terms of communication and management style but was unsure as to what this should be. The actions it had taken were a response to these feelings. It hired the services of a firm of consultants and they undertook the brief. The consultants' study took the form of a survey and questionnaires were sent to the home addresses of employees of the authority. The overall response rate was just over 30% and over 1,000 completed forms were returned.

The findings indicated that employees liked working with and for the public and their community. In particular they felt that they wanted to work for an establishment that provided excellent services and that was respected and trusted. However, in recent times, difficulties caused by change and uncertainty had led to low job satisfaction and pride in the organisation and had left staff feeling that they were under-valued/uncared for. Moreover, cuts in resources had left staff feeling pressurised.

Staff understood there was a need for change but believed there had been a focus on financial objectives at the expense of services and staff. Management style was viewed as 'macho', 'uncaring', 'remote' and 'secretive'. There was a feeling that there was a 'veil of secrecy' over everything that was happening in the organisation.

The process of cutting staff numbers was seen as indiscriminate and poorly managed. There was a feeling that management just wanted to pay people off and could not be bothered with the detail. Management, it was thought, had a target of so much to trim from its budget and was not concerned about whom it was going to get rid of and what skills it would lose as long as it met its target. As a consequence, a culture of fear existed within the organisation and people did not know whether their name was on the list of people to be cut.

Poor communication was seen as a key driver of negative feelings among the authority's employees and it was considered that the only way to find out what was happening was either from the rumour mill or local newspaper. Employees did not feel that the senior management team had a clear vision or that communication was open or honest. Staff called for a more managed approach to communication including a schedule for change that is adhered to, and, more than lip service paid to staff consultation.

Some line managers were recognised for their knowledge and commitment to the authority but there was felt to be a general lack of key people management skills, particularly regarding feedback on performance (good or bad), policies for promotion and development, and handling poor performing staff. It was felt that there was too great an emphasis on management by exception and not enough praise given for work done. People who worked hard were given more work (and no praise), yet those who did little continued without any reprimand.

Nearly all staff believed that it was necessary for the organisation to undergo change but that there should be more openness and honesty about the changes occurring. Senior managers needed to trust their staff, so that staff could trust them. Staff needed to be recognised as a key resource.

Finally, it was also felt that there was a need to give feedback on performance in order to improve the standards of middle management, and for staff (especially management) to be more accountable.

Question

1 Indicate a programme of internal marketing that would help to remedy the situation.

Case study 13.2	Sidchester NHS Trust – aiming for effective internal marketing

A communication audit was carried out in the Trust and as preparation for this audit, and in line with normal procedures, a meeting was held between the audit team and the senior management team. At this meeting the main intention was to work through the basics of an effective communication strategy, the need for an adequate flow of information on key corporate issues and the need to explore the attitude of the senior management team to these issues. All members of the team were keen to discuss these issues, all were committed to the principles of effective communication; all agreed that a steady flow of good-quality information on key issues was a vital prerequisite to effective organisational functioning.

During the subsequent communication audit interviews and focus group discussions were held. Results indicated the need for more communication. A significant number of people, even when critical, felt that genuine efforts had been made to improve communication within the trust in recent months. However, positive comments about the current situation were in a minority.

The majority of people in the focus groups, who came from all levels of the trust, felt that internal communications required further improvement. The perceptions were not confined to the issue of information being transmitted downwards from managers. Many felt that bottom-up communication needed more development.

Specific comments included:

- 'Getting your views across to senior management is a problem.'
- 'There is a lack of face-to-face communication.'
- 'When we receive information it is often insufficient or even inaccurate ... and mistakes occur.'
- 'There is a lack of communication. We don't know what's going on. We hear things on the grapevine rather than from supervisory staff.'
- 'Communication is not good. Sometimes there is no communication on very major things. Or information arrives too late for us to take appropriate action.'
- 'Major decisions are made without consultation. I don't blame senior managers. They are under pressure from the department to do various things, sometimes far too quickly.'
- 'When money is allocated to the trust we read about it in the paper rather than hearing about what is going on from management.'
- 'We rely a lot on informal communication.'
- 'There is no formal strategy for communication, no policy document or anything else. This could set out a process for everybody. It would also assign and clarify roles relating to communication.'
- 'When I joined the trust last month I just did not know where to get the information I needed.'

Question

1 Assume you want to implement an effective system of internal marketing in this trust. How would you overcome the problems highlighted above?

| Case study 13.3 | The police corporate communications team |

The county police's corporate communications team serves the needs of the force, the media and the general public. The team is divided into the News Desk and Press Office, eCommunications, Marketing and Corporate Communications. The Corporate Communications and Marketing Officer is concerned with marketing and communications requirements for the Citizen Focus Programme covering 'Safer Neighbourhoods', 'Improving User Experience' and 'Organisational & Cultural Change'. The role presents an opportunity to draw on internal and external marketing skills, ensuring that key messages are relevant and coherent to both internal and external audiences.

The Corporate Communications and Marketing Officer deals with all internal and external marketing and communications not linked to eCommunications. From posters and leaflets to bus and billboard campaigns, from banners and the staging of marketing and PR events to editing the force's magazines. It is a job that requires creative skills to keep up with the changing environment and demands that messages sent out are clear, accurate and create a strong impact.

The Senior Press Officer manages the work of the News Desk and News Desk staff to ensure accurate details of incidents and crimes are released to assist police enquiries through public appeals for information. She works with senior officers to ensure the force works effectively with media partners to prevent and detect crime and encourage the public to come forward with information to assist enquiries. Maintaining a strong working relationship with the media to ensure the public has a positive understanding of the work of the force is important.

Question

1 Discuss the role of internal marketing in the force. How might it be associated with 'organisational culture and change' and what might be the role of internal marketing in this context?

| References |

Acito, F. and Ford, J. D. (1980), 'How advertising affects employees', *Business Horizons*, Vol. 23, February, pp. 53–59.

Berry, L. L. (1981), 'The employee as customer', *Journal of Retail Banking*, Vol. 3, No. 1, March, pp. 33–39.

Caruana, A. and Celleya, P. (1998), 'The effect of internal marketing on organisational commitment among retail bank managers', *International Journal of Bank Marketing*, Vol. 16, No. 3, pp. 108–116.

Cheney, G. (1991), *Rhetoric in an Organizational Society*, Columbia: University of South Carolina Press.

Clampitt, P. and Downs, C. (1993), 'Employee perceptions of the relationship between communication and productivity: a field study', *Journal of Business Communication*, Vol. 30, pp. 5–28.

Donnelly, J. H. Jr., Berry, L. L. and Thompson, T. W. (1985), *Marketing Financial Services: A Strategic Vision*, Homewood, IL: Dow Jones Irwin, pp. 229–245.

Foreman, S. (1997), 'IC and the healthy organisation', in Scholes, E. (ed.), *Handbook of Internal Communication*, Aldershot: Gower.

George, W. R. (1990), 'Internal marketing and organizational behaviour: a partnership in developing customer-conscious employees at every level', *Journal of Business Research*, Vol. 20, No. 1, January, pp. 63–70.

Greene, W. E., Walls, G. D. and Schrest, L. J. (1994), 'Internal marketing: key to external marketing success', *Journal of Services Marketing*, Vol. 8, No. 4, pp. 5–13.

Hogg, C. (1996), 'Selling your soul', *Human Resources*, Vol. 96, No. 25, pp. 88–90.

Kanter, R. (1988), 'Three tiers for innovation research', *Communication Research*, Vol. 15, pp. 509–523.

McDonald, M. (1995), *Marketing Plans*, Oxford: Butterworth-Heinemann.

McGregor, D. (1967), *The Professional Manager*, New York, NY: McGraw-Hill.

Mink, O. G., Owen, K. Q. and Mink, B. P. (1993), *Developing High Performance People: The Art of Coaching*, New York, NY: Perseus Press.

Payne, A. (1993), *The Essence of Services Marketing*, Harlow: Prentice-Hall International, pp. 37, 166–167.

Parasuraman, A., Zeithaml, V. A. and Berry, L. L. (1988), 'SERVQUAL: a multiple item scale for measuring consumer perceptions of service quality', *Journal of Retailing*, Vol. 64, No. 1, Spring, pp. 12–37.

Reukert, R. W. and Walker, O. C. (1987), 'Marketing's interaction with other functional units: a conceptual framework and empirical evidence', *Journal of Marketing*, Vol. 51, January, pp. 1–9.

Rust, R. T., Zahorik, A. J., and Keiningham, T. L. (1996), *Services Marketing*. New York: Harper Collins.

Sargeant, A. and Asif, S. (1998), 'The strategic application of internal marketing – an investigation of UK banking', *International Journal of Bank Marketing*, Vol. 16, No. 2, pp. 66–79.

Sasser, W. E. and Arbeit, S. P. (1980), 'Selling jobs in the service sector', *Business Horizons*, Vol. 23, No. 1, January–February, pp. 58–9.

Shaw, R. B. (1997), *Trust in the Balance*, San Francisco, CA: Jossey-Bass.

Tansuhaj, P., Wong, J. and McCullough, J. (1987), 'Internal and external marketing: effect on customer satisfaction in banks in Thailand', *International Journal of Bank Marketing*, Vol. 5, No. 3, pp. 73–83.

Wolfinbarger, M. F. and Gilly, M. C. (1991), 'A conceptual model of the impact of advertising on service employees', *Psychology and Marketing*, Vol. 8, Fall, pp. 215–237.

Woodruffe, H. (1995), *Services Marketing*, London: M & E Pitman.

Zeithaml, V. A. (1996), 'The behavioral consequences of service quality', *Journal of Marketing*, Vol. 60, April, pp. 31–46.

Further reading

Brenkert, G. G. (2002), 'Ethical challenges of social marketing', *Journal of Public Policy & Marketing*, Vol. 21, No. 1, pp. 14–25

Donovan, J., Tully, R. and Wortman, B. (1998), *The Value Enterprise: Strategies for Building a Value-Based Organization*, Toronto: McGraw-Hill/Ryerson.

Duncan, T. and Moriarty, S. E. (1998), 'A Communication-Based Marketing Model for Managing Relationships', *Journal of Marketing*, Vol. 62, April, pp. 1–13.

Hastings, G. and Saren, M. (2003), 'The critical contribution of social marketing, theory and application', *Marketing Theory*, Vol. 3, No. 3, pp. 305–322.

14 Marketing via the Internet and intranet

INTRODUCTION

Information technology (IT) has changed the way in which business is conducted in the public sector. Linked with marketing it creates a 'one-to-one market', providing individuals with vast of amounts of information on whatever interests them. In this chapter we look at ways in which information technology can be used in marketing. We also examine how recent trends in local government have led to an increasing use of information technology in the drive to be more customer focused. E-government has arrived and should continue to grow at a substantial pace over the coming years. What applies to marketing in terms of service provision applies also to e-government since the electronic service encounter is a central feature of both. Assessing just how satisfactory this encounter is requires some thought and we point to the SERVQAL tool as an assessment mechanism. We conclude the chapter by stating some reservations regarding the likely take-up of e-government and e-marketing by members of the public at large. These reservations are based on the difficulties that some people may encounter in making use of online services.

INTRANETS AND INTERNAL MARKETS

Initially, internal marketers employed the same kind of communication media as externally orientated marketers when interacting with target audiences. The media that were initially employed, such as bulletin boards, in-house magazines and newsletters, all suffered from the same kind of limitations as television, newspapers, radio and magazines in that it was one-way communication. Additionally, in face-to-face communication tools, such as meetings, briefings and interviews, there were similar efficiency limitations as were encountered in personal selling. Internal marketers however have recognised the interactivity and efficiency potential of internet technology. Intranets can become powerful tools for management in organisations that are increasingly fragmented and at the same time subject to discontinuous change.

IT AND MARKETING

There is a wide range of software and systems that can be used in marketing, and internet and telecommunication-based IT applications abound. While it is not possible to draw up a list of specific marketing-related applications many general-purpose applications can be used in a marketing department, for example.:

- customer databases,
- customer relationship management systems,
- e-commerce applications,
- data analysis packages,
- intranets,
- electronic data interchange (EDI),
- internet survey – design and application,
- e-mail,
- video conferencing,
- executive decision support systems,
- help lines,
- marketing planning systems,
- marketing modelling,
- mobile communication devices,
- computer links with suppliers,
- decision support systems,
- computer links with customers,
- project management software,
- networked computers,
- word processing,
- spreadsheets,
- laptops,
- presentation software.

While this is only a short list of the types of IT applications to be employed in marketing activities it does reflect the wide range available.

DRIVERS OF THE NEW E-MARKETS

The UK 'Modernising Government' programme began in 1999. It required high-quality public services to be delivered, seven days a week, 365 days a year. One result was a central portal through which people could gain ready access to services and information from many different and varied sources. It represented the government's commitment to utilising information and communication technology (ICT) in order to improve communication between itself and members of the public. The implication of this was the need to establish a regulatory and legislative environment to support e-commerce. The government wanted to be a prime mover in this direction by taking the lead and providing quality services electronically to citizens and businesses. Such an approach reflected a desire to make services available at any time and in the most convenient manner.

MODERNISING GOVERNMENT

The Modernising Government paper outlined an e-Government Strategic Framework that focused attention on delivering better services for people and businesses and more effective use of the government's information resources. Making this operational implied using e-business methods throughout the public sector. The strategy enunciated four guiding principles:

- building services around citizens' choices;
- making government and its services more accessible;
- social inclusion; and
- using information more efficiently.

The UK Online Citizen Portal (www.ukonline.gov.uk) is a single point of entry to a wide range of government information and services. It is organised around people's needs, making dealing with government as easy and seamless as possible. Information is focused around 'Life Episodes', which enable users to access all the information they need about a particular event, such as 'Having a Baby' or 'Learning to Drive', without having to understand the workings of government or departmental delivery structures. The portal provides a structured way of accessing existing information available online.

E-GOVERNMENT METADATA FRAMEWORK: THE E-GMF

The main drivers behind the framework – abbreviated to e-GMF – were:

- the need to make government information easily available to businesses, members of the public, and indeed to civil servants themselves, without having to be familiar with the structure of government or know what each organisation is responsible for;
- the need to develop electronic records management systems in line with the guidelines laid down by the UK Public Records Office;
- the requirements of the UK Freedom of Information Act and the Data Protection Act;
- the continuing need to improve efficiency.

Traditionally, information resources have been stored in a number of different locations and treated differently in each case. It is not unknown for one document to exist on the Internet, an intranet, in the organisation's electronic network and in hard copy in an organisation's official record-keeping system. In each of these circumstances different information needed for the retrieval and handling of the resource would have been created, often by different staff.

E-MARKETING

Organisations possess different media vehicles through which to communicate with their various publics and stakeholders. However, the use of the Internet for this purpose has created a medium that has altered the ways in which organisations now communicate with different audiences. Indeed, the Internet enables one-to-one communication with potentially huge audiences. It does, nevertheless, require a well-designed website in order to do so.

WEB-ENABLED COMMUNICATIONS

Websites have users with varying information needs. This means that organisations usually have to develop their websites to meet the differing needs of their stakeholders who may access these corporate websites to varying degrees. The responsibility for communicating with various publics can fall under the remit of a number of different departmental functions within an organisation.

Perceived advantages of using the intranet/extranet include improvement in collaboration and knowledge sharing, improvements in the quality of work, the enabling of better decision making, and improvement in communications with suppliers and customers thus enabling speedier service and a reduction in costs.

CUSTOMISATION

The Internet enables customers to have services personalised to their requirements. This can be achieved either in terms of how the offer is communicated or in terms of whether service attributes are personalised.

- *Cosmetic* customisers present a standard service in various ways to different visitors. For example, many websites give a personalised greeting to regular visitors, but the content of the site is unchanged.

- *Transparent* customisers provide individually customised services, but do not explicitly communicate this personalisation. For example, the latest sites make 'smart offers', personalised presentations of services, based on the visitor's history. The idea is to work out the visitor's needs and preferences without asking.
- *Adaptive* customisation uses the same service and message but the service has multiple settings, allowing the visitor to customise it.
- *Collaborative* customisation is the ultimate one-to-one marketing. It involves the organisation conducting a dialogue with individual visitors to help them define their needs, identify the precise offering that fulfils those needs and then to make customised services for them.

Dealing with people on-line offers convenience since customers can shop from their offices or at home whenever they want. Most sites offer 24/7 access and service and there is no difficulty about parking the car or being disappointed that they cannot get served. The Internet offers customers almost unlimited information about services for very little cost. Before making enquiries, customers can consult consumer guides for comparative ratings, visit specialist websites for opinions and enter online communities to discover the views of other users. They can even check services and features.

Web-based dealings may give customers greater confidence that their requirements will be satisfied. Sites on the Web retain information about previous visits and requirements, forming the basis of a continuing relationship. They can also introduce services that specifically reassure customers that their business is on track.

Improvement-based benefits from the Web create stakeholder value in three ways:

- by cost savings,
- by enhancing the brand image, and
- by greater marketing effectiveness.

Having online manuals and customer support documents can produce big savings and this works out much cheaper than any other form of interaction for all concerned. In principle, facilitating customer self-service lies behind many of these savings and makes it easier for customers to do more of their own searching and problem solving.

There is general agreement that creative, high-quality websites can help build stronger relationships with customers and hence enhance the brand image. The Internet enables an organisation to do new things and to do old things better. For example, marketing effectiveness can be improved because the use of the intranet or Internet allows a closer dialogue with customers. It also enables the spreading of information about customers throughout the organisation. Digitisation and networks enable organisations to collect and hold detailed information about their customers and it is through holding consumer information and achieving direct interaction that a real relationship management programme can be developed.

One advantage of using the Internet is that marketing promotions can often be directly evaluated in terms of their financial payoff. One can then assess with considerable accuracy whether marketing spending has created value. It also enables organisations to assess which types of marketing ploys are best at producing specific results.

IMPLICATIONS FOR MARKETING STRATEGY

At the core of marketing strategy is segmentation and positioning. In the new information environment both these dimensions have to change significantly. Doyle (2000) suggested there is an imminent shift from segmentation to personalisation. Traditionally, information about consumers had been obtained through sampling. A few hundred or thousand consumers were interviewed about their attitudes, wants and buying processes and the results partitioned and averaged by profilers such as age, sex, income or, sometimes, lifestyle characteristics. The aim of market research was to group customers into a handful of market segments with similar wants and characteristics. This enabled communications to be aimed at each of these segments. The result produced was mixed – services and messages would meet the needs of some consumers better than others. How good or bad the fits were was often not clear since organisations did not obtain direct feedback from individual consumers. Digitisation and networks take away the need for compromises. Dialogue with individual customers can be achieved but, of course, for organisations with thousands or even millions of customers, investing in detailed interaction with all of them is not cost effective. Hence segmentation is still a necessary marketing tool but digitally stored databases allow organisations to tell customers apart and remember their individual requirements.

THE CHANGING MARKETING MIX

Getting marketing strategies to work now and in the future may require organisations to adapt their marketing mix to suit the needs of evolving IT. Evidence of this is to be found in changes taking place already. Marketers making use of the Internet recognise that customers want less choice. They require a single offer that fits exactly with their requirements and expectations. They do not want to have to consider a vast range of services that only fit imperfectly with what they are looking for. In this context it is personalised communications and customised solutions that seem more appropriate for both customers and organisations.

The Internet makes possible interactive, multimedia one-to-one communication. Unlike conventional advertising where the message is sent by the seller to customers, in the case of online communications the customer has to seek out the supplier's message. Online communications are self-selecting and the customer must be motivated to want to read the supplier's communication and is more likely to be interested in what the message has to say.

Online advertising makes it possible for the advertiser to target the most valuable customers and avoid advertising to all and sundry. The banner advertisement on the Internet can facilitate this appearing only to customers who key in relevant words when using search engines. Technology is making the targeting of promotions and advertisements on a one-to-one basis possible. Potentially, it has the ability to build valuable interactive relationships with users on an individual basis. Web communication also has the ability to give considerable service information, unlike traditional media. It also creates the opportunity for immediate interaction with customers, either by providing more information or even completing an online transaction. Moreover, using the Web enables services to be delivered direct to the customer where the transaction can be completed by filling in an electronic form.

In the e-marketplace, people and organisations interact to simplify complex business processes and benefit from a more efficient way of doing business. New technology has enabled an e-marketing medium that can build strong personal connections with individuals in a variety of market segments. It enables the marketer to:

- profile market segments efficiently;
- gain valuable marketplace intelligence;
- individualise communications and incentives effectively.

While this method of communication has a very low cost of entry, the strategy requires careful planning and a good knowledge of the target markets.

EVALUATING THE VALUE OF E-SERVICE FOR STAKEHOLDERS

Let us first consider what is meant by e-service and then what it means in the context of government. In seeking to define e-service in a public sector context it seems sensible to draw on both private sector e-service and e-government sources. This suggests that:

- the e-service encounter (as defined by Boyer *et al.*, 2002) 'is the initial landing on the home page until the requested service has been completed or the final service has been delivered and is fit for use';
- e-government is the provision of government information to citizens and the facilitation of active participation and consultation for citizens (e.g. electronic voting);
- e-public service is the delivery of public services to citizens, business partners and suppliers, and those working in the government sector, by electronic media including information, communication, interaction and contracting, and transaction.

There appears to have been little in the way of discussion regarding e-service quality in the public sector. Indeed, while considerable literature exists to date in the area of e-government service delivery it has tended to focus on ideal standards rather than actually examining the realities of delivery (Kaylor *et al.*, 2001). However, Parasuraman (2002) offers the following definition:

> 'e-Service Quality is the extent to which a Website facilitates efficient and effective shopping, purchasing and delivery of goods and services.'

Moreover, Parasuraman argues that his initial research in the area suggests that there are eleven dimensions of e-service quality:

- access;
- ease of navigation;
- efficiency;
- customisation/personalisation;
- security/privacy;
- responsiveness;
- assurance/trust;
- price knowledge;
- site aesthetics;
- reliability; and
- flexibility.

Based on a sample of 540 internet users he concluded that there were four key dimensions: efficiency, fulfilment, reliability and privacy. Essentially four measures of e-service quality seem to be indicated: efficiency; reliability; privacy; and user satisfaction, measured by instruments such as SERVQUAL.

USEFULNESS OF THE INTERNET TO PUBLIC SECTOR ORGANISATIONS

Public sector organisations can provide vast quantities of information and guide customers towards other sources of information through the medium of the Internet. Customers can also be moved out of long queues into web-based interactions, thus reducing the strain on physical and human resources.

Public sector enthusiasm for the possibilities offered by the Internet mirrors that of the private sector. However, there are notable differences between the 'markets' of public and private sector organisations that may affect the successful introduction of the Internet as a service outlet. In particular, the breadth of client groups including those in lower socio-economic groups, and older citizens, may affect the likely take-up of services provided via the Internet.

Parasuraman (2002), addressing the issue of technology readiness, i.e. 'people's propensity to embrace and use new technologies for accomplishing goals in home life and at work', indicates that older consumers are less likely to transact business on the Internet, in particular with government organisations. Additionally, Buckley (2003) highlights the low levels of technology ownership and access among those in the lower socioeconomic groupings.

E-MARKETING GUIDELINES

Computer internet and intranet technology facilitates one-to-one marketing and thus has the potential to build strong personal connections with individuals in a variety of market segments. Such marketing does of course require planning, target segmentation and setting up a database.

The first step involves identifying audience segments. In an intranet situation where organisational members represent the target audience, the segments might reflect the department or position of people within the organisation (e.g. Human Resources, Finance, Marketing, Chief Executive, Director of Regeneration). Segments might be further defined by other variables such as influencer, gatekeeper, decision maker, etc.

The next step is to set up a database template consisting of e-mail addresses with information about each person that reflects the segment to which they belong. This

Figure 14.1   Directing the newletters to different e-market segments

Source: 'Directing the newsletter to different e-market segments'. Clipart from GSP Pictures 5000. Reprinted with permission.

constitutes the initial database construction and it should be noted that building and maintaining a database is an ongoing process and is never completed. This should be followed by developing audience profile fields – initially perhaps half a dozen specific interests, job functions or characteristics that can provide insights that will influence strategic marketing decisions. It is important to ensure that these profile characteristics are served within the content categories that have to be created next. These separate content categories should appeal to the specific segments. Resources need to be made available to inform the target audiences about the subject matter on a regular basis. A graphic newsletter template should then be created that can present the content categories – usually a headline and an opening paragraph – to each segment (see Figure 14.1).

Over time, new information can be introduced onto the database. Each publication should furnish new information that can sharpen audience profiling. This can be achieved by including electronic questionnaires that can derive useful information. Target audience members should be willing to furnish survey responses if it means that the content of newsletters will be more aligned with their needs and interests. Examining the feedback obtained in this way should provide invaluable insight into evolving trends and interests that can be used effectively in subsequent newsletters and communications strategies.

Questions

1   To what use might each of the following put an intranet?
    a The police
    b A local authority
    c A hospital
    d A GP surgery
2   Repeat question 1 above but with respect to the Internet.
3   How might one evaluate the usefulness of communication via the intranet and the Internet to stakeholders in an organisation?

Case study 14.1   Local government websites

The city council employs many thousands of people, many of whom work unsocial hours. In addition it serves an area containing around a million inhabitants. It is about to implement an intranet and internet sites for its major services and has engaged designers for this purpose.

The designers indicate that the installation of these facilities will present the council with an excellent opportunity to market itself to its stakeholders and to help establish and develop its brand image in the minds of stakeholders. The designers have asked the council to work closely with site developers in order to ensure that this opportunity is not missed.

Question

1 How can the council aim to ensure that marketing opportunities presented in this way are fully exploited? Illustrate your answer with examples.

Case study 14.2	Oldfield Borough Council – using ICT

Oldfield Borough Council has 51 councillors representing 22 wards. Elected for four years, their job is to decide overall council policy and manage the services provided. Oldfield has a population of 129,959 and the council's ambition is to help people to live a better life by increasing opportunity, encouraging education and business confidence, reducing dependency, encouraging responsibility and fostering community involvement.

Since people matter in the council's view, it is working towards customers having their enquiries dealt with at a single point of contact, getting right answers first time from the first person they speak to, whenever possible. It wants to provide help at a wide range of access points with services delivered and supported electronically. In order to realise this vision, the council is committed to supporting and developing strategies using innovative ICT.

The councillors at Oldfield are based at various locations across the borough, with many of them working from home. In order for them to communicate with each other and with the citizens of the wards they represent, they use an internet connection. This provides them with e-mails and an intranet containing shared documents to work on. This capability means that they are immediately available to answer any queries and can work effectively regardless of where they are located. To provide access to these services councillors use a remote access service (RAS) dial-up connection. Increasingly, the RAS dial-up was causing the councillors problems. The connection was too slow and sometimes it failed completely. In order for them to work effectively and meet the Council's e-government vision to have access to information whenever it was required, Oldfield needed to make some changes.

Question

1 What might the council do in order to solve its problems for councillors, customers and other stakeholders?

Case study 14.3	The texting initiative

Texting some city council departments is easy. People text about litter, vandalism, drugs issues or rent arrears. In conjunction with a network provider, councils have launched high-profile text-based services, and people are invited to send text messages to one central number. Keywords such as vandalism are used to help deliver a message quickly to the relevant department. If the keyword appears in the text, it is automatically routed to the right department. Call centres intercept any texts without keywords and send them onto the relevant area.

The texting initiative gives voice to people living in more deprived areas – and councils are hoping to reach parts of the community who do not use other means to communicate with them. Many councils see SMS as a way of engaging with young people who traditionally pay little attention to their local authorities. One borough council set up a text database of young people so that it could inform them of services and consult with them. This borough council identified that it was not good at communicating with people who are hard to reach and felt that this was a positive step forward.

Questions

1 What problems do you see with using texting as a means of communicating with local authority customers?
2 Can you think of a number of customer-satisfying initiatives that could follow as the result of introducing these texting facilities?

Case study 14.4   A question of strategy

The city of Sidchester is in the North East of England and has begun to diversify away from its historically based main industry. It is trying to renew by creating a digital economy that will attract inward investment, and also generate high-skill job opportunities in what is essentially a low-skill city. It has acknowledged that the key to diversification is the need to improve and better coordinate services that the city offers to its residents and, in so doing, to stimulate inward investment based on a digital economy.

Sidchester is a comparatively poor city and only about 30% of its households have internet access. The city does not believe it can generate an e-government strategy on the current ability of its citizens to use web self-service without massive investment in computing hardware and IT training for its citizens. However, it does believe that something has to be done to improve service delivery as well as how citizens perceive the city's local government.

The city's citizen satisfaction surveys show discontent regarding most city services and that citizens have little interest in web self-service. In a recent survey, citizens were asked, 'Which channels would you find most convenient to make enquiries?' The results are that 42% of respondents indicated the phone, 53% stated face-to-face interaction, and only 5% said that the Web or e-mail would be most convenient.

Questions

1 How might Sidchester approach these problems?
2 What role would there be for marketing?

| Case study 14.5 | Designing electronic newsletters |

Sidchester NHS Trust is keen to make use of new technology that has been installed which enables it to communicate with its various stakeholders. The Trust believes that it can create greater value for its stakeholders if it uses e-marketing techniques to communicate with them. It has recently reorganised its non-medical departments and set up a unit to deal with corporate communications. There is a corporate communications officer and two part-time clerical assistants in the unit who make up one full-time clerical assistant in terms of hours. A member of the IT department has been seconded temporarily to the unit to help set up a database and generally help to establish a working system.

The corporate communications officer has been tasked with establishing a system that will facilitate e-marketing and e-communication on all matters of interest to stakeholders.

Questions

1 Analyse the situation and recommend in detail the steps that need to be taken in order to set up the envisaged system. Pay particular attention to how stakeholder segments should be identified and labelled, and the kind of information that should be held on stakeholders in the database.

2 Suggest topics and other information that might be included in newsletters that are directed towards identified audience segments.

| References |

Boyer, K. K., Hallowell, R. and Roth, A. V. (2002), 'E-services: operating strategy – a case study and method for analyzing operational benefits', *Journal of Operations Management*, Vol. 20, pp. 175–199.

Buckley, J. (2003), 'E-service quality and the public sector', *Managing Service Quality*, Vol. 13, Issue 6, pp. 453–462.

Doyle, P. (2000), *Value-Based Marketing: Marketing Strategies for Corporate Growth and Shareholder Value*, Chichester: John Wiley.

Kaylor, C., Deshazo, R. and Van Eck, D. (2001), 'Gauging e-government: A report on implementing services among American cities', *Government Information Quarterly*, Vol. 18, pp. 293–307.

Parasuraman, A. (2002), 'Technology Readiness and e-Service Quality: Insights for Effective ECommerce', E-Commerce Seminar Series, North Carolina State University, 17 April.

Further reading

Arnott, D. C. and Bridgewater, S. (2002), 'Internet, interaction and implications for marketing', *Marketing Intelligence & Planning*, Vol. 20, No. 2, pp. 86–95.

Dutta, S. and Segev, A. (1999), 'Business transformation on the Internet', *European Management Journal*, Vol. 17, No. 5, pp. 466–476.

Joseph, W. B., Cook, R. W. and Rajshekhar (Raj), G. J. (2001), 'Marketing on the Web: How Executives Feel, What Businesses Do', *Business Horizons*, Vol. 44, No. 4, pp. 32–41.

Index

Page references in *italics* denotes a diagram

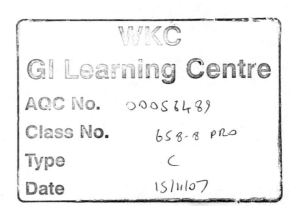